9/23

D1636620

SATELLiTE BOY

ALSO BY ANDREW AMELINCKX

*Exquisite Wickedness: Two Murders and the
Making of Poe's "The Tell-Tale Heart"*

Hudson Valley Murder & Mayhem

Gilded Age Murder & Mayhem in the Berkshires

SATELLITE BOY

The International Manhunt for a
Master Thief That Launched the
Modern Communication Age

ANDREW AMELINCKX

COUNTERPOINT ★ BERKELEY

This is a work of nonfiction. However, some names and identifying details of individuals have been changed to protect their privacy, correspondence has been shortened for clarity, and dialogue has been reconstructed from memory.

Copyright © 2023 by Andrew Amelinckx

All rights reserved under domestic and international copyright. Outside of fair use (such as quoting within a book review), no part of this publication may be reproduced, stored in a retrieval system, or transmitted in any form or by any means, electronic, mechanical, photocopying, recording, or otherwise, without the written permission of the publisher. For permissions, please contact the publisher.

First Counterpoint edition: 2023

Library of Congress Cataloging-in-Publication Data
Names: Amelinckx, Andrew K., author.
Title: Satellite boy : the international manhunt for a master thief that launched the
    modern communication age / Andrew Amelinckx.
Description: First Counterpoint edition. | Berkeley : Counterpoint, 2023. | Includes
    bibliographical references.
Identifiers: LCCN 2022039189 | ISBN 9781640094802 (hardcover) | ISBN
    9781640094819 (ebook)
Subjects: LCSH: Lemay, Georges, 1925-2006. | Bank robberies—Québec
    (Province)—History—20th century. | Artificial satellites. | Electronics in criminal
    investigation.
Classification: LCC HV6665.C22 B36 2023 | DDC 364.15/520971427—dc23/
    eng/20221024
LC record available at https://lccn.loc.gov/2022039189

Jacket design by Dana Li
Book design by Laura Berry

COUNTERPOINT
2560 Ninth Street, Suite 318
Berkeley, CA 94710

www.counterpointpress.com

Printed in the United States of America

10 9 8 7 6 5 4 3 2 1

This book is dedicated to my mother, who instilled in me a love for the beauty of language, and my father, whose deep knowledge of history inspired my passion for the past. They are both gone but continue to guide me as I make my way through life.

The only way of discovering the limits of the possible is to venture a little way past them into the impossible.

—ARTHUR C. CLARKE, *Profiles of the Future*

Contents

Part 3: Nowhere to Hide in the Global Village

(Spring 1965–Summer 1967)

Part 4: A Changing Landscape

(Fall 1966–1984)

SATELLiTE BOY

A Spirited and Turbulent Era

ARTHUR M. SCHLESINGER JR., THE HISTORIAN, FRIEND, AND advisor to President John F. Kennedy, predicted in January 1960 that the coming decade would be "spirited, articulate, inventive, incoherent, turbulent, with energy shooting off wildly in all directions." He was right.

The 1960s saw the growth of the Civil Rights and Anti-War Movements, Women's Liberation, and environmentalism, among many other sea changes. Culturally, the perceived staidness of the previous decade was replaced by an explosion of counterculture art critical of the status quo. The Beatles, Motown, and Bob Dylan; *To Kill a Mockingbird* and Malcom X and Alex Haley's *The Autobiography of Malcolm X*; James Bond films and *Breakfast at Tiffany's*; Andy Warhol's vision of pop art and its antithesis, minimalism, all burst onto the scene as both harbingers and catalysts for what was unfolding. The societal rifts that had been building for years finally ruptured into flames and bloodshed by decade's end.

This turbulent time also set the stage for an ingenious bank heist that dovetailed with the development of the world's first commercial communication satellite. At first glance, advancements in satellite technology—a largely forgotten aspect of the Space Race, which tends to favor marquee achievements like the Apollo 11 moon landing—might seem unre-markable. Yet the fundamental shift in how we communicate that was facilitated by those satellites would come to alter the course of history and redefine the very notion of what it means to be human to a much greater degree than a boot print on the surface of the moon ever could. In many ways, the story of the jubilant and volatile mid-century period that Schlesinger described is the story of advancements in communications. The moon landing is a prime example, but many of the iconic events of the era are memorable precisely because so many people witnessed them from the comfort of their own homes. Two radically different yet equally visionary men best exemplify this new era: master thief Georges Lemay and electrical engineer Dr. Harold Rosen. Though they never met, their energies crossed paths, came together, and gave rise to the modern com-munication age, forever changing our world.

To understand how the vastly different lives of these two strangers created the now-familiar world of instantaneous connectivity, weather re-ports, and even live televised sports, it's helpful to understand a little bit about how satellites work.

Communication satellites are launched into space via powerful rock-ets. When they reach their destination, they detach from the launch vehicle at a fast enough speed to stay in orbit and resist Earth's gravity. Once in place, ground stations beam up information, such as television broadcasts and phone calls, that has been converted from the original for-mat into electromagnetic waves. The satellite then relays that information to another ground station elsewhere on the globe, where it's converted back into the original data format and then sent on to its final destination through transmission lines such as telephone wires or cables. Without communication satellites, it becomes extremely hard to get electronic in-formation from point A to point B over long distances since radio waves and microwaves that are used to transmit electronic information can be blocked by objects like mountain ranges or tall buildings.

Beginning with the U.S. Army Signal Corps's Project SCORE, an experimental communication satellite launched in 1958, the push to de-velop practical systems accelerated. The issues SCORE suffered from included a miniscule life span measured in weeks, and limited real-world applications. Like several other satellites that came after it, SCORE operated in a low-Earth orbit. That meant ground stations had to constantly track it as it traveled across the sky, and SCORE would go dark when no longer in direct line of sight with its earthbound controllers. What was needed was a satellite that was in sync with the Earth's rotation by having a high enough altitude directly above the equator. Known as geostationary orbit, the idea was pure science fiction in the late 1950s.

But the original thinking and unbending will of a bold young Hughes Aircraft Company engineer named Harold Rosen, along with his small team, turned science fiction into fact when they created the world's first geostationary commercial communication satellite. Like all artificial satellites, Early Bird, as it was dubbed, orbited the Earth, but, crucially, it did so at a speed that matched the planet's rotation and at a high orbit above the equator. That meant that when viewed from the ground, Early Bird appeared fixed in the sky, granting it an important advantage over its predecessors. A stationary platform allowed for uninterrupted communication with ground stations.

Before Early Bird, there was no such thing as twenty-four-hour live global broadcasts. Instead, filmed news stories had to be sent by plane to the destination country. It could be days before a television audience could view important international news events. There were also no simulcasts of international sporting events. If you didn't live in the country where a match took place, you were out of luck. In 1966 that changed when Early Bird broadcast the World Cup, hosted by England that year, to audiences in the United States and Mexico, marking the first time in history when soccer fans separated by an ocean could watch the championship game live.

But Early Bird's importance went far beyond entertainment. The satellite made it possible to connect people in a more intimate way through its telephonic capabilities. Previously, if you wanted to make an international call, you would have to schedule it weeks in advance. Beginning in the late 1920s, international calls were handled via radio signals, which were spotty and limited. By the early 1960s, calls were routed through submarine cables that were only marginally better than radio. The fourth transatlantic telephone cable, which began operating in 1965, TAT-4, allowed for only 128 calls at a time and cost $50 million. When it went online, Early Bird could handle nearly 250 calls at once, close to the capacity of all the transatlantic cables then in use (317 phone calls), and it cost about $6 million to build and launch.

The communications possibilities ignited a Space Race between rival satellite manufacturers like Hughes Aircraft and AT&T, as well as between the West and the Soviets, that pushed the technology forward at breakneck speed. From 1958 to 1965, communication satellites matured from small experimental devices that fizzled out after a few weeks and had meager practical applications to high-flying machines laden with cutting-edge technology. It was like going from steam-powered locomotives to bullet trains in the span of a decade rather than the 150 years it actually took.

Georges Lemay, a French Canadian playboy and master thief responsible for a daring bank burglary in Montreal in 1961, was the first person to understand just what Early Bird's technology meant on a personal level.

Lemay, too, was a product of his time. He was always well dressed in mod suits with razor-thin ties. With his beautiful partner, a chanteuse named Lise Lemieux, by his side, he embodied the ultra-cool aesthetic of the swinging sixties. Like the jazz musicians he was so fond of, he delighted in using improvisation to push boundaries. Lemay chased the thrill of pulling off a brilliant and boldly executed bank heist—all the better if it included winging it when circumstances dictated a revision to his original plans.

Akin to the darkness that underpinned the era, violence seemed to follow Lemay.

Whether it was state-sanctioned brutality unleashed on peaceful civil rights and anti–Vietnam War protestors, underground radical groups using bombs to push agendas, the general rise in violent crime, or the 1969 Rolling Stones concert at Altamont that ended in bloodshed and death, the decade that has become synonymous with peace and love was rife with savagery. In Lemay's case, there were allegations he had a hand in the mysterious disappearance of his first wife in 1952 and the murders of two of his alleged associates two decades apart. While there was no definitive proof of Lemay's involvement in these crimes, the police certainly believed he was not above using brutality when it suited his needs.

Following the 1961 heist, Lemay went on the run. He might as well have fallen off the face of the planet, though in reality he was hiding out in plain sight in south Florida. His only disguise was an alias. No matter what the police tried—rewards, wanted posters, an international dragnet—nothing seemed to work. Lemay felt invincible as months stretched into years. Yet, just weeks after Early Bird's launch in the spring of 1965, he found himself behind bars.

Early Bird's role in his apprehension—the first such instance in history—made international headlines and helped boost the satellite's prestige, proving its ability to reach a massive global audience by transmitting television programs, telephone calls, and fax messages faster, farther, and more cheaply than ever before. Early Bird and its progeny also made it harder for anyone, whether fugitive or not, to remain anonymous in an increasingly interconnected world. It's the world we live in today, and it all started because of a Canadian bank robber and a Louisiana-born engineer.

Lemay may have been the first fugitive apprehended with the help of a communication satellite, but he wouldn't be the last. In the coming decades, advancements in this kind of technology would become an indispensable tool for law enforcement. Fugitives and criminals of all stripes also make good TV, as evidenced by the popularity of shows such as *Snapped*, *Dateline*, and *48 Hours*, which often rely on communication satellite technology to broadcast into millions of homes depending on how viewers receive their programming.

From our vantage point well into the twenty-first century, the 1960s can seem like a distant and primitive time. So much of what constitutes our modern lives was either nonexistent or in its infancy then, but many of the long-standing tensions that surfaced during those heady days have a direct resonance today. Lemay and Rosen's story encapsulates the spirit of the era as well as it does precisely because it shows how the confluence of technology and the audacious ambition that has defined so much of the decade created the very concept of the global village we inhabit. What it means to be a modern human is indistinguishable from our ability to instantly communicate with each other across the globe, our means to stay informed and watch as historic events unfold live anywhere on the planet, and our willingness to sacrifice the anonymity that such abilities require.

Though no longer in use, Early Bird remains parked in orbit above our heads, a reminder that no matter how much things may have changed on Earth in the years since its launch, the past continues to inform our present.

PART 1

The Master Thief
and the Visionary

(Fall 1957–Summer 1961)

*Dr. Harold Rosen's pursuit of a geostationary
communication satellite helped change the world.
Photo courtesy of Deborah Castleman.*

The Bank Robbery Capital of North America

SPRING 1961

AN ELECTRIC CURRENT RAN THROUGH NORTH AMERICA IN THE spring of 1961. It was a time when anything seemed possible, whether it was launching a communications revolution or pulling off the perfect crime.

And while the decade at that point was still just pure potential, it would soon build toward a crescendo that fundamentally altered society. Two driven men, one an electrical engineer, the other a bank burglar, tapped into this energy, and their endeavors would lead them toward a monumental convergence.

By the spring of 1961, the Kennedy administration was only a few months old. Eisenhower's moment had passed, and the sparkling era of Camelot was in fashion. The age of gray-flannel-suit conformity was ripping at the seams, giving way to a rising chorus of voices too long repressed.

In May, the Freedom Rides in the South, launched by student activists from the Congress of Racial Equality, began to protest segregated interstate bussing. In California, the student movement emerged at the University of California, Berkeley, where students and teachers rallied against the federal House Un-American Activities Committee that had come to the city to rout out alleged communist infiltrators. At the same time, across the country, second-wave feminism, blossoming from the civil rights and burgeoning anti-nuke and peace movements, made inroads against entrenched gender discrimination.

In New York City's Greenwich Village, where the likes of Bob Dylan and Lenny Bruce performed, a rising tide of politically charged and socially aware music and comedy bubbled up into the consciousness of America's youth.

Scientific breakthroughs also acted as catalysts to change society. The Food and Drug Administration approved the first oral contraceptive, colloquially known as "the pill," setting off the sexual revolution.

On May 25, Kennedy gave his "Moon Shot" speech to Congress, challenging the nation to send a man to the moon before the decade was out. The Soviets' surprise launch of the first artificial satellite, Sputnik 1, in October 1957, started the Space Race. Kennedy's speech supercharged it. A month before Kennedy's speech, the Soviet Union upped the ante when Yuri Gagarin became the first man to travel in space with his 108-minute orbit around the Earth.

Less than a month after Gagarin's feat, the United States launched *Freedom 7*, rocketing the first American to travel to space, Alan Shepard, toward his fifteen-minute suborbital flight.

The emerging aerospace industry understood that Kennedy's focus on space would be a new opportunity that went beyond manned space exploration. This was the chance to take international communications to the next level, if these companies could get past entrenched corporate mindsets and layers of bureaucracy that often strangled creative thinking.

At the Hughes Aircraft Company in Culver City, California, a dynamic thirty-five-year-old engineer named Harold Rosen raged against such a system frustrating his dream of creating the first geosynchronous satellite, a lightweight solar-powered device that would revolutionize the way the world communicated. But like billionaire Howard Hughes, the controversial Hollywood director, inventor, and recluse who started the company and was eventually forced out, Rosen discovered the company's conservative management wasn't so easily persuaded to take big chances. Rosen wasn't going to give up. He, like so many others during this unparalleled era of change, was swept up in the heady push to achieve the seemingly impossible.

Things were also changing to the north. Quebec—especially its largest city, Montreal—was heaving aside a past steeped in ossified traditionalism for an outward-looking future that embraced change.

In June 1960, Jean Lesage was elected premier of Quebec when his Quebec Liberal Party took a majority in the legislative assembly. Lesage oversaw the first progressive government in sixteen years, a shift echoed in his election slogan: "C'est le temps que ça change" ("It's time to change"). Lesage ushered in a sweeping new social and political ideology that would become known as the Quiet Revolution—Révolution Tranquille—which scraped away the remaining secular and political power of the Roman Catholic Church and ended the "Grande Noirceur" (Great Darkness) of Quebec premier Maurice Duplessis's tenure, an era marked by social and economic conservatism and isolationism. Lesage's policies reshaped the province and its largest city, especially regarding health care, social services, and cultural affairs.

In the spring of 1961, Georges Lemay, a dapper thirty-six-year-old French Canadian, spent his days holed up in his cottage on a private island on a river in the Laurentian Mountains north of Montreal, devising his greatest feat yet: the perfect bank burglary.

Emerging in a crowded field encompassing every kind of Montreal criminal, from competing mobs to well-organized groups of bank robbers, Lemay clawed his way to the top of the heap. Maybe *claw* wasn't the right word. Lemay was from an upper-middle-class family and had never wanted for anything.

Joseph Louis Georges Etienne Lemay was born in Shawinigan, Quebec, a hundred miles north of Montreal, on January 25, 1925, to Joseph Oscar Lemay and Marie-Lucie Demers, the only boy of their five children. The Lemays were an old and established family originating in the Anjou region of France but had been in Quebec since the seventeenth century. When Georges was a toddler, his father died, leaving him the only male in a family of women who doted on him. He was well educated and at one point even considered going into the priesthood. Instead, his extravagant tastes and his thirst for thrills, whether on a speedboat or in a sports car, scuba diving or flying planes, led him to crime to help finance the lavish lifestyle that was beyond his family's means.

He worked for his mother's real estate company, Immeubles Demers, in Montreal, and the legitimate side of his business pursuits was doing well. The city was transforming. Montreal's metropolitan population was soaring, adding almost a million residents between 1941 and 1961. Construction projects surged in both the public and private sectors. The city's metro system was being planned, city streets were being renovated, and new skyscrapers were rising downtown. Dorchester Boulevard West, as it was then known, quickly became the financial center not just of the city, but of the entire country. All of Canada's major banks and insurance companies had a presence there, with three massive bank buildings—the Canadian Bank of Commerce Building, CIL House, and the Royal Bank Tower—in the midst of construction.

At the same time that Montreal was experiencing a surge in growth and prosperity, the city was also becoming the epicenter for Canada's underworld. The city's new concentration of wealth was too tempting a prize for Lemay and a host of other criminals to pass up. Besides the thriving international heroin trade that involved the Italian Mafia and a local Irish gang, the city had recently earned the disreputable moniker of the bank robbery capital of North America. In 1959 alone, there had been six hundred armed robberies, many of those involving banks and savings and loans. As Montreal entered a new decade, the crime statistics were only going up. It was estimated that one out of every fifteen chartered banks in the city was robbed a year. The various strong-arm men, desperate drug addicts, wild boys, and well-organized professionals preyed on Montreal banks that leaked like sieves thanks to antiquated security systems—a lack of cameras, enfeebled guards—and a lot of cash on hand at the counters. Then there was the added benefit of provincial and national laws that were as antiquated as the bank security systems. A bank robber was likely to get a five- to seven-year prison sentence if caught in Quebec, less than half of what they would typically end up with just across the border in the United States.

Among the many Montreal criminals at work in the late 1950s and early '60s, there was Lawrence Day, "The Gentleman Robber," who'd pulled off a series of precisely planned bank robberies before finally getting caught in 1960 and being sentenced to twenty-five years in prison.

In May of 1960, the fifteen-man-strong Red Hood Gang was busted by the nemesis of the city's underworld, Joe Bédard, the head of the Montreal Police holdup squad. After forty-five robberies in four years, the gang's reign was abruptly ended by a shootout with Bédard and his team. Bédard learned of the gang's plan to rob a bank in north-central Montreal, and he and his men were waiting outside when the robbers emerged from the bank.

Lemay looked down on strong-arm bank robbers. The risk was great and the payoff paltry. He preferred beautifully planned and executed bank burglaries where the scores were high and the risk minimal. He'd cut his teeth as a safecracker working with various Montreal underworld denizens before venturing out on his own, according to police. He was an artist, not a thug, who was enraptured by the planning and precise execution of his burglaries. Even so, Lemay was not squeamish about violence.

In 1955, Lemay was arrested for trying to choke a police officer over a traffic ticket. Two years later, during an investigation into the July 2, 1957, disappearance of his friend Larry Petrov, a thirty-six-year-old Romanian-born welder, drug trafficker, and robber, police arrested Lemay for possessing two unregistered pistols. He was also the prime suspect in Petrov's disappearance, but the Montreal Police couldn't prove it.

Investigators also believed Lemay was behind the January 1957 burglary of the Outremont branch of the Bank of Montreal. The branch, in a wealthy suburb north of Montreal,[1] had netted the thieves somewhere between two and five million dollars[2] in cash and securities (between twenty and fifty-one million dollars today), making it one of the biggest bank

---

1. At the time, Outremont was a separate city, but since 2002, it has been a borough of Montreal.
2. All monetary references are in U.S. dollars unless otherwise noted. All monetary references are in the original amount unless otherwise noted.

heists (if not *the* biggest) in North America up to that time. The thieves targeted the bank specifically because members of the underworld banked there, as did shady stockbrokers and other operators who straddled the line between the straight world and criminality. The victims' reticence about what they had stored in the 132 looted safe-deposit boxes kept the police from determining an accurate figure for the losses.

Petrov had been in on the score but attempted to cash in some of the stolen bonds too soon. He paid with his life. Petrov was also facing drug charges. There was talk he was going to flip on his accomplices in the bank job to get a pass in the narcotics case.

On July 25, 1957, two teenage girls boating on Lake Ouareau, nearly a hundred miles north of Montreal, discovered a leg wearing a dress shoe and sock floating in the water. It was the only part of Petrov ever found. A thorough search of the lake by police divers turned up no other evidence. The medical examiner determined someone had taken the leg off while Petrov was still alive and surmised that the body part had been deposited in the lake a few weeks after the killing, perhaps dropped in the water from a low-flying plane with the intention of it being found. The medical examiner believed it was a warning to anyone else who might be thinking of turning state's evidence.

The police interrogated Lemay about Petrov's disappearance to no avail. He pleaded guilty to the gun charges, was fined twenty-five dollars, and was given time served for the eight days he'd sat in jail.

The Petrov murder went into the cold case pile, as had another investigation involving Lemay, five years earlier and nearly two thousand miles south.

Lemay's wife, Huguette Daoust, a blond-haired twenty-one-year-old beauty queen, went missing in January 1952 while the couple was honeymooning in the Florida Keys. Police and local citizens conducted a massive weeks-long search near Marathon in the Florida Keys, where she was last seen. Searchers, including Lemay, went on foot, by boat, and in small private planes that flew low over the mangrove-choked waterways looking for any signs of her. At the beginning, the police worked on the assumption that Huguette had either fallen into the fast-moving water and drowned or that she had been abducted. But soon their suspicions turned toward Lemay. While scant evidence connected him to the disappearance, Lemay found himself being interrogated by the lead investigator, Deputy Sheriff James Otto Barker. Barker's pressure, instead of breaking Lemay, sent him fleeing back across the border to Canada. Barker's hunch that Lemay knew more than he was saying about what happened to Huguette wasn't enough to detain Lemay.

A Key West grand jury looked at the case that March. "All we lack is a confession and a body to prove a crime was committed," Barker told the grand jury after presenting his evidence. While the grand jurors found that "Mrs. Lemay could be dead, and if dead, she died as a result of an act of violence," they wanted to hear from Lemay in person; however, Lancelot Lester, the state's attorney, wasn't willing to give Lemay immunity from prosecution for whatever the witness revealed during his testimony. It was the only way Lemay would appear for the proceedings. This impasse helped derail the flimsy case. The Florida authorities made a big show in the press about Lemay's unwillingness to tell his side of the story to the grand jury. Lemay responded that he had been in Montreal since leaving Miami, he wasn't hiding, and under advice from his lawyers, he wouldn't be going to Florida or making any other public statements. He didn't appear before the grand jury, and with that, a judge released the eighteen men from jury service on April 18, 1952—less than a month after the proceedings began. The U.S. and Canadian newspapers quoted Lester as saying they would "simply have to seek new and more conclusive evidence." They never did. When Barker was shot and killed by his son on Christmas Day during a domestic dispute, the case died with him.

In the midst of all this, Lemay wrote a book, *Je Suis Coupable* (*I Am Guilty*), cowritten with the Montreal journalist André Lecompte and published in Canada in both French and English, in which he excoriated Barker and the other investigators. The title, Lemay said, meant that he was guilty of losing his wife's love by his shabby behavior toward her. He claimed he had evidence his wife was alive and had simply run off. He never provided any such evidence, but he did file for divorce.

Lemay had been lucky. His dealings with the law had been minimal considering his line of work, but then he was an adherent to the old adage, "Luck is what happens when preparation meets opportunity." Lemay might add money into that mix as well.

Police suspected him of being involved in several bank burglaries in the late 1950s, though they never charged him. The one he was working on in the spring of 1961 would be his greatest for its boldness and perfect execution.

Montreal's waterworks dated from the early 1800s. The city was honeycombed with old iron pipes once used to deliver water straight from the Saint Lawrence River. Lemay learned that one such conduit, reconfigured for modern water, gas, and heating lines, connected to the Bank of Nova Scotia branch at 453 Saint-Catherine Street West. More important, it passed directly under the bank's vault. Lemay's plan involved slipping undetected through the tunnel from a building at 1408 Saint-Alexandre Street that adjoined the bank's north side and then punching a hole into the vault floor, where hundreds of safe-deposit boxes, many owned by the city's diamond dealers and by fellow criminals, waited to be looted.

From there it was a matter of getting a decent team together and rounding up all the equipment—drills, dynamite, blasting caps, a gas generator, and black coveralls of the type used by Montreal city workers. He spared no expense and liked to take his time with his bank heists. The planning was part of the fun.

His audacious thinking reflected the spirit of his times. The same unstoppable energy that animated the race into outer space and the creation of the new technologies needed to achieve this goal also pushed Lemay to bolder and more brilliant break-ins. He'd plugged into the zeitgeist.

For Lemay, that meant pulling off the greatest heist of his life. He spent the spring of 1961 putting his team together. He chose Roland Primeau as his second-in-command. Lemay had worked with him on various capers over the previous seven years. Lemay trusted him implicitly. Primeau, at thirty-five, had a lengthy police record—most recently being arrested for forging checks stolen by an accomplice working in the office of the Montreal Light, Heat and Power Company, totaling close to seventy-five thousand dollars. He was out on bail but happy to participate in what looked to be a big score. Primeau was a big man with big appetites that his front as a car salesman was unable to satisfy. Although he was several inches taller than Lemay, they shared some physical characteristics: large, powerful chests and dark hair, and both were getting jowly from lives of excess.

André and Yvon Lemieux were also a natural fit for the team. André, twenty-seven and just out of prison for selling stolen cars, was smart and energetic. His younger brother, Yvon, nineteen and the youngest of the crew, was also eager to get in on such a huge and adventurous heist. The Lemieux brothers, although eight years apart in age, could nearly have passed for twins. Both had hooded eyes, Roman noses, thin faces, full lips, and wavy hair. André wore his hair shorter than his younger brother, who was hipper and had a longer, greased-back hairstyle. The pair liked to dress flashy, with razor-thin ties and modish suits. Lemay was dating their sister, Lise Lemieux, a beautiful singer with dramatically arched eyebrows and pouty lips. Like Huguette, his former wife, Lise was petite and thin, standing five foot two and weighing one hundred pounds. She wore her long raven hair styled in a variety of ways but most often just kept it in a ponytail. Lemay spent lots of time with the Lemieux family, which was headed by the patriarch, Rosaire. Although Rosaire was in his sixties, he was still in the burglary game, according to police.

The final member of Lemay's crew was Jacques Lajoie, a burly man with prematurely graying hair and the oldest of the crew at thirty-nine. Lemay didn't know him, but André Lemieux had vouched for Lajoie. The pair met in February 1961 when they were both serving time in Bordeaux Prison, Montreal's massive jail featuring six wings that look like a broken wagon wheel. Lajoie was in for a forgery charge, one of many over the years. His criminal career stretched back to 1938, when he robbed a farmer for whom he'd been working, taking the man's car, horse, and even his dog. After serving three years for a robbery in Baie-Saint-Paul, a small city on the shore of the Saint Lawrence River sixty miles northeast of Quebec City, Lajoie joined the Canadian army during the height of World War II. He fought in the European campaign and stormed the beach at Normandy. Wounded three times during his army stint, he was honorably discharged and returned to his life as a small-time thief and forger.

The Bank of Nova Scotia job was going to be the biggest caper of his life.

At the beginning of June, Lemay gathered his team at the home of Primeau in Chomedey, a suburb west of Montreal, to test out the various equipment. André turned on the generator, grabbed a high-powered circular saw, and began cutting into the concrete basement floor. It dug into the hard surface as if it were butter, and Lemay, excited, patted André on the back.

"That's perfect. Great job, André," he told his friend, who continued to slash the saw across the floor.[3] Lemay grabbed another saw and hacked off a piece of the railing from the basement staircase. The men's laughter could barely be heard above the machines' roar.

Once his sense of elation subsided and the room was again quiet, Lemay turned to André. "Make sure nothing's missing," he said, his smile gone. André knew Lemay wanted all their gear in order, their tools in pristine working condition, everything perfect.

Primeau's brother-in-law, Yvon Bélanger, who lived at the house, watched the men's antics. Lemay had gotten him to purchase two large canvas bags, a drill, and coveralls earlier that day but hadn't told him what they were for. Bélanger knew better than to ask too many questions. Before the crew left, Primeau handed Bélanger a bag of cement and told him to repair the gash in the floor. Playtime was over. That afternoon they drove over to the bank to see what they were going to be up against.

---

3. All dialogue has been translated from the original language into English by the author unless otherwise noted.

2

Go Time

SUMMER 1961

ON THE EVENING OF FRIDAY, JUNE 23, THE TEAM ASSEMBLED at the Lemieux family home in Montreal's Sault-au-Récollet neighborhood, eight miles to the northwest of the Bank of Nova Scotia. The heist was planned for that night.

André hauled in all the equipment the team had stored at Primeau's house in Chomedey. The large pile of tools would have impressed any contractor. There were drills, sledgehammers, a generator, work lamps, a heavy-duty circular saw, and even a hydraulic jack.

The men quietly slipped into their coveralls and mentally prepared for the job ahead. Lemay ordered a disappointed Yvon to stay home. They wouldn't need him. Lemay decided two lookouts on the street, Primeau and himself, were enough for the job.

In two cars, the team drove east to the city's business district. Lemay told his men not to look at the bank as they passed. Primeau was the only team member allowed to scan the bank. The bank was dark, and the street was empty. It was a go! The cars stopped in front of 1408 Saint-Alexandre Street. After using a stolen key to unlock the entrance, André and Lajoie hauled the equipment inside.

"Go make sure there's no one in the building," André told Lajoie. Lajoie went to the second and third floors of the small office building. Everything was absolutely quiet.

When Lajoie came back down to the foyer, André was using a screwdriver to pry up a rusted iron hatch. Underneath was a gaping hole, an old, unused well that led to a tunnel. André quickly jumped inside. The hatch slammed shut, like "the mouth of a snake," Lajoie thought. He lifted the hatch, dragged it away from the tunnel entrance, and began handing the tools, power cords for the lights and other equipment, a generator, the heavy-duty jack, and other various supplies to André, who then carried the equipment farther into the tunnel.

While André worked below, Lajoie stayed in the lobby. Lemay and Primeau walked to the next block to act as lookouts. If anyone came snooping around, the pair would pass by Lajoie and light a cigarette to signal trouble. Lajoie would then yank on one end of a cord that André had taken with him into the tunnel. André would then stop working and keep quiet until the coast was clear.

Down below in the dark, André hauled the equipment through the dank tunnel. It was hard work. He had to crawl on hands and knees for some fourteen feet while avoiding various pipes.

André worked alone in an inky blackness broken only by the spotlight illuminating the ceiling where he was drilling and inserting blasting caps, which had an explosive charge but were much quieter than sticks of dynamite. André set several off. Unfortunately, they were too weak to do much damage. As his eyes adjusted to the gloom of the tight quarters, a creeping suspicion slowly overtook him. In his haste, he hadn't gone far enough through the tunnel. He wasn't actually below the vault room.

André stopped drilling and pushed deeper into the darkness. The tunnel narrowed to a diameter of only two feet, little more than shoulder width. He continued crawling forward and finally made it into the bank's sprinkler control room, located under the vault. The room was extremely tall and narrow, ten feet high but only five feet wide, and at three feet long, the space was just as claustrophobic as the tunnel had been.

André crawled back to where he'd left the equipment and after a slow and arduous journey back and forth, sometimes pushing, sometimes pulling the various pieces of heavy equipment, he was ready to begin again.

Lemay had ordered him to bring the high-powered hydraulic jack into the tunnel with the idea that they could push through the ceiling and into the vault with it.

"It can lift a load of more than fifty tons," Lemay had bragged. "With that, we can lift the entire bank."

The reality was a bit different. André situated the jack and began cranking it, but instead of breaking through the ceiling into the vault, the jack simply sank into the floor. André soon discovered that the ceiling was reinforced with a trellis of steel, while the floor was made of a less durable material. When André later explained what happened with the jack to Lajoie, the older man laughed to himself and thought the team could have used the services of a materials resistance engineer. He didn't say so out loud.

With both the blasting caps and hydraulic jack André had planned to use now useless, he switched to the electric saw and began to cut into the concrete ceiling. It was hard going, as he had to stretch his entire body upward and hold the heavy saw in place.

As the hours dragged on, Primeau and Lemay continued pacing up and down Saint-Alexandre Street, which remained deserted. This was the business district and with no nightlife to speak of, there were few pedestrians to worry about. It was still dark out, but Friday night was quickly giving way to Saturday morning.

Lajoie grew bored standing in the building's foyer with nothing to do. Finally, André popped his head up out of the hole. His face was smeared with dirt and grime. Sweat and blood had soaked through his coveralls. He'd rubbed his shoulders raw from the pressure of trying to saw into the ceiling.

"Christ, it isn't working," he said, sounding exhausted. He crawled out and the two men left the building to find Lemay and Primeau.

They found the pair at the corner of Burnside Place and Stanley Street. Lemay was frustrated but kept it together. They still had time.

"We'll have to try something else," he told the men. They left the tools in the tunnel and headed back to the Lemieux house to regroup. There, Lemay and Primeau discussed what to do. They had dynamite back at Lemay's cabin. Lemay decided to go get it.

While the others stayed at the Lemieux family home to rest, Lemay drove north to his chalet. Once back in the Laurentians, Lemay decided that he should shorten the sticks of dynamite. He was afraid if the explosions were too big, they'd draw unwanted attention to their endeavors, so he turned his kitchen into a makeshift explosives lab as he carefully cut the sticks of dynamite into shorter lengths.

The clock was ticking. It was now Saturday morning, and the bank opened in less than forty-eight hours. Even so, he couldn't rush. One misstep while shortening the sticks of dynamite and he'd be dead, or at least seriously injured. Finally, he finished and loaded the sticks into his car.

He also rigged up a homemade detonator that he believed would allow André to ignite the explosives from a safe distance. At one end of a seesaw-like wooden plank, he attached a small can of turpentine. The idea was that the turpentine would slowly run down to an electrical contact at the other end, where he'd nailed two tomato can lids. The device could be plugged into the wall. Once the turpentine reached the other end of the wood, it would create a current that detonated the explosives via the blasting caps' wires, which were connected to the can lids.

Lemay returned to Montreal with the device but was not willing to go back to the job until darkness fell, believing it was too risky during the day.

The heist resumed on Saturday night. André went down into the tunnel and drilled out a hole, inserted the shortened stick of dynamite, and hooked it up to Lemay's device. He set it off and hurried back up to where Lajoie was stationed in the foyer.

"Did you hear anything?" André asked.

"Nothing. Not the slightest shock," Lajoie answered.

They waited a full ten minutes before André reentered the tunnel.

"It takes guts to go back down there," thought Lajoie, watching André slip back down into the darkness. "I wouldn't do it."

André stayed down for several more hours before again poking his head out.

"It's not working," he admitted. "It's bad."

Lemay's device had crapped out. André returned to the circular saw to get through the ceiling, but he made very little headway. Nothing seemed to be working right. Their planning, time, expenses, and labor was all for nothing. They now didn't have enough time to get in and out before the bank opened on Monday.

The two men, feeling defeated, rendezvoused with Lemay and Primeau, who were walking up and down the street continuing to act as lookouts.

When Lemay saw them coming, he was confused and angry. He asked them what the hell was going on. They mumbled their apologies for the disastrous failure. All his planning as well as the money spent on equipment and the endless hours preparing for this one moment now seemed wasted.

"This weekend's a big zero, a fiasco," Lemay shouted. "A total disaster."

Lemay told them to leave everything in the tunnel. They got into their cars and headed back to the Lemieuxs' house.

Once Lemay calmed down, he and Primeau discussed a new plan—go big. As in bigger explosives, and in order to do that, they needed to drill deeper holes to hold the dynamite in place. They would need specialized drill bits, along with several other items Lemay decided would make this job easier. Lemay also felt they needed a better way to communicate and a base of operations that gave a commanding view of the bank and street.

The coming weekend was a better time to pull off the heist, anyway. It would be Dominion Day weekend, a national holiday, so the city's business district would be virtually deserted, even during the day.

But his first concern was whether André's work under the vault might be noticeable to any bank employees who walked into the vault. If the blasting and drilling had damaged the vault floor, they'd be sunk.

On Monday evening, Lemay told the others that he'd sent someone to the bank, who reported back that nothing appeared to be wrong inside the vault and that no one was any the wiser. Lemay didn't say who it was, only that "we're miraculous. Nothing has been disturbed or broken."

Lemay knew they had only one more shot at pulling off this burglary and redoubled his efforts to guarantee this second attempt wouldn't fail. On the morning of June 27, he drove Lajoie into Montreal, to the home of Lemay's mother, and took him into his bedroom. He pulled down a tasteful iron-gray suit from the closet and held it up in front of the other man. "Put this on," he instructed. While Lajoie tried on the suit pants, which were tight but fit well enough, Lemay found a white dress shirt, a tie, and a pair of dress shoes and gave them to Lajoie. As Lajoie dressed, Lemay explained that his gray hair made him look distinguished. He wanted Lajoie to pose as a businessman and rent an office space they would use as the nerve center during the upcoming revamped operation.

"I can't send any of the other guys," Lemay explained. "They look like a gang of thieves."

Lemay told Lajoie he was going to portray an advertising man who was starting his own agency working with department stores.

Later in the day, André pulled up to the house in a late-model Cadillac he'd boosted and drove Lajoie to the office downtown.

Lajoie was a bit nervous as he approached the building owner, introducing himself as J. P. Villeneuve. He became even more nervous when the man seemed unenthusiastic about leasing the office to "Mr. Villeneuve, advertising man."

Backing down wasn't an option. Lajoie knew Lemay would likely toss him aside, or worse, if he failed at this important job. If only the owner would rent him the office, he promised to do repairs in the space, fix the floor, and replace the wiring. He also insisted on a west-facing view as he needed lots of daylight for his line of work. The owner finally agreed and Lajoie signed the five-year lease at a cost of sixty-five dollars a month.

The second-floor office at 1407 Saint-Alexandre Street, which faced the Bank of Nova Scotia at the corner of Saint-Alexandre and Saint-Catherine Streets, was the perfect spot to see anyone's movements along either street. Visibility would be important since they were planning on using larger sticks of dynamite this time around. Lajoie, with a sense of relief, met back up with André and headed back to Lemay's mother's house to give him the good news.

That night, Lemay and Primeau drove across the border and headed more than three hundred miles south to New York City. They had to sing at the top of their lungs to keep from falling asleep en route.

In Manhattan, they picked up a set of walkie-talkies. The devices had come into their own during World War II but were still mostly used only by the military and police. They were hard to come by for civilians, but Lemay had gotten a lead on a pair made by the British electronics company Redifon.

Lemay and Primeau arrived back in Montreal on June 28, running on little more than adrenaline and coffee, and met up with the rest of the gang. Primeau told the others about it. "I had a great time," he said.

Next, they traveled to Lemay's island chalet to test the walkie-talkies. They worked perfectly within a mile range. Lemay then decided they needed some place to hide in the office in case anyone discovered them. The bare space had nothing that would serve those purposes, so Lemay asked Primeau to look into buying a cheap wardrobe. The Lemieux brothers recalled something at their parents' house that might work. After taking a look, Lemay agreed it would suffice. The brothers offered their mother one hundred dollars for the wardrobe, to be paid once the job was over. They also grabbed an old stepladder from the house so André could get closer to the ceiling with the saw.

On Friday, June 30, the day the gang planned to return to their endeavors below the Bank of Nova Scotia, they made a final shopping run at J. Pascal's, a hardware store chain in Montreal. They picked up mineral wool, a type of insulation made from molten glass, to dampen the sound of their work, and foam rubber for André's shoulders, which were still raw and bruised from rubbing against the concrete ceiling as he worked. They also collected the rest of the dynamite and detonators. Lemay refined his homemade device for remotely detonating the explosives. The gang moved the empty wardrobe into the rented office and put up bamboo blinds in the windows, banging the nails in with a bottle. With all the equipment they'd gotten for the job, they hadn't brought a hammer.

The wardrobe would make a good hiding place in case anyone came snooping, but both Lemay and Primeau were too heavy for the flimsy wood bottom, so they flipped it upside down. What had been the top seemed sturdy enough to hold their combined weight, if need be.

That night, the team went back to finish the job.

3

Dominion Day Weekend

SUMMER 1961

THE MEN DROVE SLOWLY THROUGH THE STREETS OF DOWN-town Montreal on the night of Friday, June 30, heading toward Saint-Catherine Street West. In their matching coveralls, they looked like a convoy of city workers on their way to some late-night construction job. Jacques Lajoie drove one car with André Lemieux, and Lemay drove another vehicle with the rest of the crew. They parked near the office building at 1407 Saint-Alexandre Street, across from the north side of the bank, where they had rented the office space to use as a command post.

The neighborhood during the day was abuzz with the city's business pursuits, but it was deserted on weekends and especially so this Friday, the start of the long Dominion Day weekend. The holiday, which was beginning to be informally known by the simpler *Canada Day* (a title made official in 1982), marked the founding of Canada's federal union on July 1, 1867, when Nova Scotia, New Brunswick, and the province of Canada (made up of Quebec and Ontario) joined to form the Dominion of Canada, the first semiautonomous country within the British empire.

The neighborhood's office workers were long gone, off to celebrate the nation's ninety-fourth birthday in livelier parts of the city or at home with family and friends. While it was a three-day weekend for most because Dominion Day fell on a Saturday, the bank's employees wouldn't be getting an extra day off. It would be business as usual come Monday morning. It also meant Lemay and his gang would have to get in and out of the vault in an unmovable timetable that would end in prison if they failed.

Lajoie and André lugged supplies, including dynamite, into the office building next to the bank. They added the new equipment to the pile of tools they had left in the tunnel the previous weekend during their botched first attempt. Lemay had given the two men strict orders for the heist: wear gloves at all times and do not smoke.

While André and Lajoie hauled in the equipment, Lemay, Primeau, and Yvon headed across the street to set up the command post at the office.

André, followed by Lajoie, entered the tunnel through a hatch that covered a square-shaped hole in the foyer. As in the previous attempt, André dragged the various tools through the tunnel but this time insisted Lajoie help him. André once again found himself in the awkward confines of the sprinkler room. The space was so narrow he couldn't even stretch his arms out all the way while working. But that was a minor inconvenience compared to the task at hand.

An eighteen-inch-thick slab of steel-reinforced concrete separated him from the goal. Once the equipment was in, they fired up the generator. André strapped thick foam-rubber pieces onto his shoulders to protect himself from the jagged edges of concrete as he worked. He slipped on swimming goggles to keep the dust and debris out of his eyes and pulled on an old cap embroidered with cartoonish-looking carrots. Lajoie stretched out the thick rolls of mineral wool around the space to help baffle the sound.

To reach the ceiling, André stood on an old stepladder with slightly uneven legs they had brought from his parents' house. He turned on the high-powered electric saw attached to the generator and went to work. Soon the cramped space was choked with dust. The ear-splitting whine of the saw overpowered all.

Lajoie waited with a walkie-talkie at the entrance of the tunnel, where it connected to the bank's sprinkler room. The tunnel was dark, and water oozed down its interior. It was overbearingly hot and smelled of mildew and must, now mixed with the scent of concrete dust. Lajoie was nervous. He was a career forger, not a bank robber, and this was all very new to him. His job was to relay instructions between Lemay and Yvon, who were in the rented office acting as lookouts, and André, who was hammering away at the ceiling in the sprinkler room. Primeau floated back and forth between the two buildings but spent the bulk of his time in the command center.

Lajoie was also in charge of the homemade detonator used to blow the dynamite. Lemay's reconfigured device comprised two wooden boards with tin disks attached to each end and a tangle of extension wire. Lajoie plugged it into a wall socket in the sprinkler room. The device delivered a jolt of 120 volts of electricity, enough to set the dynamite off. Lajoie tested it by putting the two wires under his chin. He got a good shock. It was going to work this time. This detonator was a simpler device than the first one Lemay had rigged up but much more effective.

André carved a ragged rectangular cavity into the ceiling with the power saw. It was slow going, his progress measured in fractions of an inch. They had a tight deadline, less than forty-eight hours, since Lemay didn't want to work during the day for fear of being discovered. The bank would reopen at 7:00 a.m., Monday, July 3. To speed up the process, André drilled into the concrete and stuffed dynamite into the borehole. He slid the blasting cap into the dynamite and attached the lead wire from the cap to the firing wire connected to the homemade detonator. André scurried farther into the tunnel near Lajoie to take cover and told him to blow the dynamite.

There was a roar and a flash. A thick cloud of dust and smoke rushed into the tunnel where the men crouched down. An overpowering and strangely sweet smell given off by the explosive lingered in the thick air. Their ears rang from the noise. André went back to see how deep the dynamite had cut into the steel and concrete. The hole wasn't much deeper than it had been. André went back to the saw for a few more precious inches.

As André continued alternating between sawing and blasting, he became paranoid that the explosions could be heard outside. He decided he'd go have a listen the next time Lajoie set one off. He had Lajoie radio Yvon via walkie-talkie to find out whether the street was empty. When Yvon answered that it was deserted, André crawled back through the tunnel into the adjoining building and stuck his head outside to listen. When Lajoie set off the dynamite, André heard nothing. He returned to the tunnel with an obvious sense of relief.

The sound may not have traveled to Saint-Alexandre Street, but inside the bank was a different story. The blasts echoed through its dark corridors.

Above the two thieves in the tunnel, a seventy-nine-year-old janitor and night watchman named George Rockett was slowly going about his work cleaning up the cavernous, block-long St. James Building that housed the bank. He was on the other side of the building when he heard an explosion around 1:00 a.m. It sounded like it came from outside. He ignored the noise and went back to cleaning. A few minutes later there was another explosion. It could have come from the side of the building where the bank was located, but he'd already cleaned up over there and wasn't about to go back. He kept working. His assistant heard nothing.

Later that night, Lajoie's walkie-talkie jumped to life and Yvon's crackly voice came through with a sense of urgency. A cop walking his beat was on Saint-Alexandre Street, near the bank. Lajoie was told to hold off on using any more dynamite, but it was too late. Another explosion rocked the claustrophobic space where Lajoie crouched. He held his breath. There was silence from the other end of the walkie-talkie. Every second of dead air was excruciating. Then, Yvon, with a laugh, reported that the cop had heard nothing and was leaving the area. Lajoie let out his breath. They were safe.

The dynamite made more headway than the saws and drills alone and soon André had depleted their stock of explosives. He once again left the bank through the tunnel and ran across the street to the command post to speak with Lemay about the dynamite issue. Yvon radioed Lajoie to tell him to come back to the command post. Once the team had gathered,

Lemay ordered everyone back to the Lemieuxs' home. It was past dawn, and they were all tired, especially André, who'd done the bulk of the night's work.

Back at the house, the crew discussed their next steps. André felt bigger sticks of dynamite were needed. Lemay agreed and decided he and Primeau would make the two-hour round-trip drive to his cabin in the Laurentian Mountains that evening to get the rest of the explosives. Lemay hadn't slept, but if they hoped to finish the job before the bank reopened on Monday morning, he had no choice. They needed more dynamite. While Lemay and Primeau headed north, the Lemieux brothers and Lajoie took the opportunity to get some sleep.

It was now officially Dominion Day, and while they fitfully napped, the rest of Montreal was waking up and preparing for the day's festivities. Across the city there were children's carnivals, band concerts, and fireworks. At noon, there was to be an artillery salute by members of the Canadian army from the chalet at the top of Mount Royal, the small mountain that overlooks downtown Montreal to the west and gave the city its name. It was the perfect spot to see the changing face of downtown, where so many skyscrapers were under construction.

The city government had taken great pains to make Montreal sparkle for the holiday. At the Places d'Armes—a square that features a statue of Paul de Chomedey de Maisonneuve, the French military officer who founded the city in 1642—city workers had hustled to get the rows of trees and shrubbery, flowers and ornamental grasses, along with new lighting, in place before the big weekend. It was going to be a perfect Dominion Day.

Lemay and Primeau returned later than expected, delayed by holiday traffic, and Lemay went to bed. He didn't think it was safe for them to work during the day, so they had time to get in a little rest before getting back to work. The delay presented Primeau with a handy alibi. He left the house for a few hours to attend the funeral of his wife's grandfather—missing it would draw unwanted attention. His family was waiting impatiently for him at home. He arrived late, at 8:30 a.m. While he quickly changed into a suit, his wife scolded him for his tardiness. They missed their chance to go to the funeral home prior to the church service. Primeau brushed off her questions about where he'd been all night, and in light of the somber occasion, she didn't push the issue.

After a few hours of sleep, everyone got up and ate breakfast. They sat around chatting, trying to kill time. It was a beautiful day, sunny and seventy-five degrees, but the men stayed inside waiting for the sun to go down.

Lise, who was starting to make her name as a singer of popular jazz-inflected tunes, hung out with them that day. She was well aware of their plans but didn't participate in the actual heist.

When it was time to get back to work, Lemay, Primeau, and Yvon drove over with the dynamite in their trunk. Lajoie followed with André in a second car. Back on Saint-Alexandre Street it was a repeat of the night before, except George Rockett wouldn't be on duty. It was one less thing to worry about.

The city police were also busy that weekend, chasing after other, more conspicuous criminals. Detectives were looking for a man in his twenties who had abducted a seven-year-old girl that afternoon while she played near her home. He'd returned her four hours later. There were also two armed holdups that night. In the first, less than a mile to the east of the bank where Lemay and his crew were busy breaking in, two men armed with revolvers held up a delivery man and robbed him of $150. An hour later, a few blocks north, a pharmacy was robbed at gunpoint.

The week leading up to the holiday had been a bloody one that stretched the city's police department thin. There had been shootings, beatings, even a bombing, all related to a Mafia turf war that was brewing.

The violence climaxed on June 29 with a bomb at the home of Leo Scanzano, a nightclub owner with mob ties. Detective-Sergeant Leo Plouffe, the Montreal Police forensics and explosives expert, was injured while trying to disarm the bomb. The explosion sent him flying and singed his face and body. Plouffe, on whom the department relied heavily for crime-scene analysis, was temporarily out of commission.

Back on Saint-Catherine Street, André and Lajoie returned to their assignments underneath the bank vault. They again crawled through the tunnel on hands and knees, carefully hauling the dynamite. Once André had drilled out a new hole and stuffed the bigger stick inside, he crawled back through the tunnel and waited in the street while Lajoie triggered the explosion. "I couldn't hear anything," he happily told Lajoie, once back inside the tunnel. They were finally going to make some real headway against the steel and concrete. Out on the street, the explosions couldn't be heard, but inside the tunnel was another matter once they got back to dynamiting the concrete. Lajoie's ears rang from the sounds that reverberated through the sprinkler room and tunnel, which was now even hazier and smelled more strongly of exploded dynamite than the evening before. It was going to be a long night.

Hours passed and the hole grew deeper. The sweat poured out of André as he worked. His arms were rubbery with the effort of sawing and drilling through concrete and steel. They were so close. Then the saw broke through the final inches, and André could see into the vault above. He worked with renewed energy, knowing they'd soon be rich. He expanded the hole. It was now about five inches wide. André couldn't wait any longer. He ran to tell Lajoie.

"I got it!" he shouted with triumph. "Call the other side and tell Yvon to let Georges know he should get ready. I'm going to put in one more charge to make the hole bigger."

Across the street, Primeau, tired and dirty from helping André, lounged in the rented office. The air was thick with cigarette smoke. They waited impatiently for news from inside the bank building. Lemay pushed the bamboo blinds aside with one hand as he scanned the empty street below.

Suddenly, Yvon's walkie-talkie squawked and Primeau's tinny voice came through, puncturing the silence. "André has made it through the floor," Lajoie excitedly reported.

Lemay snatched the walkie-talkie from Yvon's hand. "Tell him not to go in. I want to be first."

There was a long pause before Lajoie answered Lemay. They would have to wait a bit longer, until André chipped away more of the floor to widen the entrance. Where André was long and lean, Lemay was heavier with a barrel chest, and he had upward of fifty pounds on André. After André widened the hole, Lajoie got back on the line and told Lemay it was time.

Lemay was ready for his big moment. Dressed like the other men in black coveralls, he bounded out of the office building and across the street to 1408 like a conquering hero. Lajoie was there waiting for him. He opened the door and removed the well's cover. Lemay smoothly hopped into the waiting hole. He crawled through the tunnel and into the sprinkler room, Primeau and Lajoie following close behind.

Yvon stayed at the command center, monitoring the street. Lajoie headed toward the sprinkler room, but Primeau stopped him, telling him to bring them some water and then to wait at the entrance of the tunnel with his walkie-talkie. It was obvious Lajoie would not get to experience the thrill of opening any of the safe-deposit boxes or even seeing the vault, that grail they had worked so hard to reach. While the rest of the crew, besides Yvon, who was just a teenager, looted the vault, Lajoie sat stewing at the indignity of waiting at the bottom of a well.

Lajoie first met Lemay at the end of April 1961. André Lemieux brought him to Lemay's cottage on Ile Lachaine, a small island accessible only by a wooden bridge, near Mont-Rolland. As Lemieux and Lajoie drove up to the secluded, heavily wooded property, Lemay came out to meet them. He'd heard about Lajoie's forgery skills and took the time to compliment his guest.

"You pass counterfeit checks," Lemay said. "You have a beautiful signature."

The remark pleased Lajoie. It seemed he, too, would fall under the sway of the Seigneur du Nord (Lord of the North), as the Lemieux brothers sometimes referred to their new leader. Lemay, while on the shorter side at five foot eight, was powerfully built. He had piercing steel-blue eyes and an air of authority, entitlement, and dynamic charisma that effortlessly drew people into his orbit. Lajoie was no less susceptible to Lemay's charms than the Lemieux family had been.

A week after their first meeting, Lemay invited Lajoie to stay at his cottage in the Laurentians. Lajoie was soon running errands, cleaning the house, and doing whatever other menial tasks Lemay could think up, including sitting by the phone installed next to the pool and taking down notes when anyone called—a somewhat humiliating experience for Lajoie, who was a few years older than Lemay. Lemay didn't even pay Lajoie for all the work he was doing. Lajoie bounced between the chalet and André's house, since his friend would at least feed him when he stayed there.

Lemay wasn't particularly fond of Lajoie; he nicknamed him Bonhomme, after the rotund snow-white mascot of the Carnaval de Quebec, a winter celebration in Quebec City. Lajoie had an ingratiating manner and seemed slippery, but over the course of the next few weeks, Lajoie proved willing to do whatever Lemay asked of him, which made up for his shortcomings in Lemay's mind. Lemay told the others not to share their plans with the new man, but he could see that Lajoie had some vague idea that something big was brewing. He'd caught Lajoie eavesdropping when he and André were discussing what equipment they would need for the burglary.

In early May, Lajoie approached Lemay to ask him about a new portable generator he'd noticed at the cottage. Lemay figured it was time to let him in on the plan. He instructed André to take Lajoie aside and offer him ten thousand dollars for his help in pulling off the bank burglary. Lajoie jumped at the chance. Now, the longer Lajoie sat in the darkness of the dirty little tunnel, the more he questioned his allegiance to his new boss, who was turning out to be like every other boss he'd ever had—taking advantage, belittling him, giving him scraps.

Lemay pulled himself up through the hole in the vault's concrete floor and paused to savor this moment as he stood in the austere room. He took his time, knowing there was no alarm to worry about—the bank had been too cheap to install one—and let his eyes hover over the four hundred safe-deposit boxes that lined the space. He walked over to the first box. He was prepared to pick the locks, but thankfully these all had protruding hinges. All he needed was a crowbar. He called to Primeau in the sprinkler room below and told him to pass him the tool.

André scampered up into the vault from below to help collect the loot. Primeau was too big to fit through the opening, so he remained in the sprinkler room, holding a massive army-issue duffle bag open beneath the hole. Lemay pried open the boxes, one by one, and dumped the contents—cash, bonds, stock certificates, and jewelry—onto the floor. André collected the valuables and tossed them through the hole into the waiting duffle bag. Lajoie, from where he sat, could hear the beautiful sound of what he imagined were coins (gold?) raining into the bag.

Lemay mentioned to André that there were a few of the boxes whose contents greatly interested him. He never said how he knew what was inside them. By five in the morning, Lemay had gone through several hundred boxes.

"We need to go. Haven't you opened enough?" Primeau shouted up at him.

"Just fifteen more," answered Lemay.

A few minutes later: "Ten more."

More time passed and Primeau again tried to hurry Lemay.

"Just a few more," Lemay replied, like a petulant child unwilling to leave the playground. Finally, after he'd looted 377 of the 400 safe-deposit boxes, he was ready to go.

They left a pair of women's panties Lemay had found among the valuables in one of the boxes, but not much else.

Lajoie was still sitting at the end of the tunnel. He'd waited for hours. Primeau crawled toward him through the tunnel, followed by Lemay, who was dragging the duffle bag, which was stuffed to overflowing. André was last. They went up through the well and into the foyer. Lemay stuck his head out of the building's front door and peered around. The street was empty. He made a beeline for the cars, with André and Primeau close behind. Lajoie remained alone in the foyer to close the well's hatch. Once done, Lajoie's orders were to run across the street to the office, tell Yvon it was time to go, collect anything that might incriminate them, put the walkie-talkies into a suitcase, and wait for Primeau to pick him and Yvon up.

Yvon went downstairs while Lajoie cleaned up. Suddenly, someone came into the building and up the stairs toward the office. Lajoie, thinking fast, stepped into the hall and began sweeping. The man passed by him without speaking but glanced in Lajoie's direction as he headed toward the office next door. When the man went inside, Lajoie took a final look around the command center, turned off the light, and left. He left the armoire, chair, and bamboo shades behind. Lajoie flew down the stairs, exited the building, and took a left onto Saint-Alexandre Street. He scanned the road as he hurried toward Saint-Catherine Street. Primeau pulled up south of Saint-Catherine. Lajoie ran over and got in. The car sped off to rendezvous with the others at Lemay's mother's house on Mansfield Street, less than a mile south of the bank. The men drove through the quiet Montreal streets. The sun was already high, but it was Sunday morning and there were very few people on the roadway as they headed south to the luxurious downtown apartment of Marie-Lucie Lemay. It was going to be another beautiful day.

André and Lemay arrived at his mother's house a few minutes before the rest of the crew. Lemay hauled the bulging duffle bag inside, its heft a sign that he'd chosen the right bank to hit. Just as in the 1957 burglary of the Outremont branch of the Bank of Montreal, he'd picked this bank because other members of the underworld used it. Located only a few blocks away from the diamond district, it was also where many of the city's diamond traders did their banking.

The adrenaline high was wearing off and Lemay felt disappointed at how easy the heist had turned out to be, but at least he had a fortune with which to boost his spirits. For Lemay, the rush he got from pulling off a bank job nearly equaled the monetary rewards. It was time to split up the profits and think about the next big adventure.

4

Here's Your Lunch

WHEN LAJOIE, PRIMEAU, AND YVON ARRIVED AT MARIE-LUCIE Lemay's plush downtown apartment on the morning of July 2, they were dirty and exhausted, but elated, and were hoping to celebrate their victory. Instead, they found Georges Lemay all business.

Even though they left all their tools, including blasting caps, in the tunnel, Lemay believed everyone had worn gloves. He wasn't worried the police could tie any of the items to himself or his men. They were golden. Lemay had banned André and Lajoie from smoking during the heist.

There were several reasons Lemay didn't want them to smoke, the most obvious being that they were working with explosives, but, more importantly to Lemay, to light a cigarette, the men would have to remove their gloves, introducing the possibility of fingerprints.

Everyone except Lemay sacked out for a few hours. When they rendezvoused at Lemay's chalet later that day to split up the proceeds, everybody was still tired and dirty except for Lemay, who had showered and changed and was back to his usual dapper self.

The heist's total came to nearly $2 million (about $19.2 million today)—only Lemay knew the exact figure. He doled out the loot, taking the lion's share for himself. He gave $65,000 in cash to André for all his hard work. Primeau also got a large piece of the score. Yvon received little more than pocket change, a measly $100.

Lemay, with a big grin, handed Lajoie a brown paper bag.

"Here's your lunch," he said.

Lajoie opened the bag and looked in. It was stuffed with money. Lajoie figured he'd count it later, since Lemay had asked him to run an errand. He needed some prescriptions picked up from the pharmacy. Lajoie drove off while the others hung out at the chalet. His bag of cash was sitting on the kitchen table, the top folded over.

When he returned, Lemay was gone, and it looked as if someone had opened Lajoie's bag of cash. He couldn't tell if anything was missing.

Lajoie and André left the chalet and stopped at André's apartment in Saint-Sauveur, five miles to the south. André wanted to wash up before giving Lajoie a ride to his place.

When André got home, he found his twenty-four-year-old cousin, André Dagenais, and Dagenais's wife hanging out at the house.

André was covered head to toe in dust and grime and was exhausted but jubilant. He was running on an adrenaline high that made him talkative. Lajoie was also filthy. They were both dressed in coveralls and looked like city workers who'd spent days inside a sewer.

André began bragging to his longshoreman cousin about the heist, which he called "a big coup." He promised to tell him more and show him something after he cleaned up.

André went into his bedroom, opened one of his dresser drawers, removed some linens, neatly stacked his cash inside, and covered it. He stripped off his filthy coveralls, took a hot bath, and got dressed. André went into the kitchen and ate. Afterward, he brought Dagenais and his wife into the bedroom and pulled open the drawer to show them the fat stack of cash held together by rubber bands.

"There's sixty-five thousand dollars there," André bragged. "Do you want to count it?"

While Dagenais's twenty-two-year-old wife sat on André's bed counting the money, he described how hard it had been to break through the reinforced concrete and how he had finally made it into the vault.

The woman grew bored with counting after hitting the forty-eight-thousand-dollar mark. André wrapped most of the cash in tinfoil and stuffed it into a large thermos that he then covered in a pillowcase.

Dagenais agreed to put the money in his trunk and drive into Montreal as an extra precaution in case André was pulled over. He followed closely behind in his own car. Once there, André took the money and left.

His cousin wanted a piece of what André had. He would get his chance a few months later.

It wasn't until Lajoie returned to his rented cottage that he finally counted his money. He dumped it out and tallied it up. Lemay had paid him in old, dirty notes in denominations of ones, fives, and tens. It took a while to count.

Lajoie's pulse began to race as he neared the end of the pile of money. It was short. Really short. He counted it all again. His cut was supposed to be $10,000, but the bag contained only $7,300. It was nearly $3,000 short.

He didn't know whether Lemay had screwed him or if one of the others had swiped the money later while the bag sat on the table and he was out running errands. Lajoie was angry that one of the gang had ripped him off but decided not to complain. Maybe down the line he'd be able to get his revenge. In the meantime, he had some other things lined up, including setting up a burglary crew with yet another Lemieux brother, the teenage Richard. There were plenty of empty weekend homes to loot in the Laurentian Mountains, and he could always return to forgery, his bread and butter.

* * *

Yvon Bélanger, Primeau's twenty-one-year-old brother-in-law, who'd witnessed the equipment tests in the basement of Primeau's house—where he and his family were living rent-free—and run errands for the gang in the weeks before the heist, suspected they were behind the Bank of Nova Scotia burglary.

When Primeau asked him to open two safe-deposit boxes at different banks, his suspicions grew. Primeau told him they were for his automobile business and house, but Bélanger didn't believe it. The two large envelopes Primeau gave him to put in the boxes were hefty and piqued Bélanger's interest, but with his hulking brother-in-law close by, he didn't dare look inside. He would have to figure out where his brother-in-law kept the keys and bank information before he could satisfy his curiosity. Bélanger was sick of living off his handouts and hoped he could siphon off a little something for himself. The newspapers reported that somewhere close to four million dollars had been taken, a fortune for sure. Bélanger bided his time, looking for a chance to get his hands on whatever was in those boxes.

A few days after the heist, Lemay and Primeau flew to New York, where they hooked up with one of Lemay's underworld contacts and paid 10 percent of the face value for one hundred thousand dollars' worth of Cuban pesos. Lemay figured they could get a huge return on the money they'd just gotten from the burglary by reselling the pesos at a higher rate in Cuba for U.S. dollars.

The black market in pesos was a burgeoning business following Fidel Castro's victorious Cuban Revolution in January 1959, as fleeing Cubans siphoned off vast amounts of cash. In 1960, Castro nationalized the entire banking sector, including the U.S. banks in Cuba (the Bank of Nova Scotia was one of two Canadian institutions that cut a deal with Castro to sell off its assets to Cuba's central bank).

Ernesto "Che" Guevara, an Argentinian revolutionary who was a tough fighter with a keen intellect but knew next to nothing about finance and banking, was in charge of the country's central bank. By March 1961 the value of the peso had plunged, and inflation jumped by nearly 13 percent.

With their haul of pesos, Lemay and Primeau planned to fly to Cuba via Mexico after first stopping in Las Vegas, one of Lemay's favorite cities. There were no direct flights from New York City to Havana due to escalating tensions between the two countries. Skittish U.S. airlines had been scuttling flights to Cuba.

In January 1961, the U.S. broke off diplomatic ties. In May, Castro declared Cuba a socialist country and abolished elections. The pressure was building toward a potentially cataclysmic crescendo the following year with the Cuban Missile Crisis in October 1962.

In Las Vegas, Primeau waited on his passport to arrive from Canada. He'd never had one before, and they had left Montreal before it had arrived in the mail. At the time, Canadians didn't need a passport to travel to the United States but they did for Mexico and Cuba. Primeau's wife forwarded the document to Las Vegas once it arrived from Ottawa. Meanwhile, the two friends lived it up in Sin City and Lemay paid for it all.

When they landed in Havana on July 17, 1961, the two men quickly made their way through the airport. They were wearing large money belts stuffed full of Cuban pesos hidden under their shirts. The airport was crowded with Cubans trying to leave the country who stood packed together near a large colorful banner that read, THOSE WHO ARE NOT WILLING TO BE SOLDIERS OF THEIR COUNTRY IN THIS EXCEPTIONAL MOMENT OF OUR HISTORY, LET THEM GO! —FIDEL.

Lemay and Primeau were playing a very dangerous game, especially being foreigners visiting the new socialist state only three months after the failed U.S.-backed Bay of Pigs Invasion. They had a little more clout as Canadians but risked arrest or worse since what they were doing was highly illegal. It was an especially touchy subject with Castro, who obsessively worried over Cuba's precarious financial situation. He blamed "counterrevolutionaries" who were "in possession of great sums of national currency" for the country's problems.

Lemay had been to Cuba back in 1953, when Fulgencio Batista still ruled the country and the Mob ruled Havana's nightlife (with appropriate payoffs to Batista). You could get anything you wanted if you had the money, and the choices seemed endless. Cuba was a paradise for tourists, but not so much for the rural workers who subsisted on seasonal sugarcane harvesting overseen by American companies that treated their plantations like personal kingdoms.

Havana in July 1961 was in the midst of radical change. The roof of the Hotel Nacional de Cuba, a grand Spanish-meets-art-deco-style hotel, had become a watchtower with machine gun emplacements and soldiers with field glasses scanning the nearby Malecón, the broad esplanade hugging Havana Bay. At night, the secret police were out in force, and there was a pervasive feeling of being watched. But there was also a sense of enthusiastic change and a lot of new construction as Castro's government threw its weight into building housing, schools, hospitals, and recreation centers. Castro had opened the yacht club, tennis club, and country club, once the playground of the wealthy elite, to the public.

Havana remained a cosmopolitan city, although it was now radical politicians and wide-eyed student revolutionaries, rather than movie stars and mobsters, who roamed the streets.

A few casinos remained open (Castro would shutter them that fall), and the nightlife still was hot at spots like the Tropicana (even though the mobsters who had controlled them were now gone and the shows had a political bent).

Lemay and Primeau stayed at what had been the Habana Hilton, built in 1958 with great fanfare from the Batista government. At twenty-five stories, the International Style resort was the tallest hotel in Latin America at the time, boasting more than six hundred rooms; six restaurants and bars, including the Polynesian-themed Trader Vic's; an immense pool lined with colorful cabanas; a casino; and murals by famous Cuban artists.

By the summer of 1961, Castro had nationalized the massive resort and renamed it the Hotel Habana Libre. It served as Castro's headquarters for three months in 1959. The hotel opened its doors to working-class Cubans, who got a chance to experience what only the wealthy and well-known had previously been able to afford—except that with the quickly dwindling supplies of basic necessities Cuba was experiencing, the food and beverage service wasn't what it had been before the revolution. At least the casino was still open.

Lemay and Primeau stayed in Cuba for eight days without any problems and made a good profit selling the smuggled pesos they had purchased for 10 percent of their face value in New York. In Cuba, the pair received U.S. dollars for the pesos, which were trading at close to 30 percent of their face value on the black market. This meant Lemay and Primeau were able to double their profit.

On Saturday, August 5, 1961, just a few weeks after they left, all ship and plane travel in and out of Cuba abruptly halted. The next day, Castro announced that the country was getting a new currency. He said they were forced to change the currency because of the "hundreds of millions of pesos" illegally taken out of the country and to "prevent employment of counterrevolutionary resources abroad for acts against the revolutionary government." The United States, Castro said, was involved in the black-market trade in pesos to destabilize Cuba's currency.

The money taken out of Cuba by refugees would become worthless in a matter of hours. Inside Cuba, all old pesos had to be traded in for new ones by the next day, and people could exchange only two hundred pesos' worth per family, with the rest of their money going into a special bank account from which they could only withdraw one hundred pesos a month. Anyone who deposited more than ten thousand pesos had the money confiscated by the government for "hoarding" in violation of a law put in place that May.

The news greatly disappointed Lemay. The venture was lucrative. Primeau made ten thousand dollars in Cuba, the equivalent of more than ninety-six thousand dollars today. Lemay made even more, exponentially increasing his take from the Bank of Nova Scotia heist. He'd hoped to keep it going for a while longer, as it allowed him to both travel and make money, two of his favorite things.

5

A Psychic Cop Without a Crystal Ball

SUMMER–FALL 1961

ON THE MORNING OF MONDAY, JULY 3, AT 8:15, TWO BANK employees at the Bank of Nova Scotia in downtown Montreal entered the combinations required to unlock the massive vault door. It was a routine task, but when they swung the door open, they realized their day was going to be anything but routine.

A gaping hole filled the center of the concrete floor and nearly all of the four hundred safe-deposit boxes were empty—their metal doors hanging open, some completely torn off the hinges.

Ewen Sinclair, one of the two bank clerks, stared dumbfounded, trying to take it all in. Besides the jagged hole in the floor, there were papers strewn everywhere and a small light burning at the back of the space. It stank like gunpowder. He'd locked the vault on the evening of Friday, June 30, the last day the bank was open before the Dominion Day holiday. Neither man moved, and they didn't bother to enter. They turned and ran to tell everyone what they'd found.

The assistant branch manager, Clarence Bartlett, cut short his vacation. He arrived at the bank at 9:30 a.m. and went straight to the vault to deal with the literal and figurative mess. He thought he knew what to expect, but what he found shocked him. Paperwork was everywhere, including insurance policies, bonds, and stock certificates. He would have to collect it all, sort through it, and then make embarrassing phone calls to all the customers whose safe-deposit boxes had been looted. They wouldn't know for sure how much had been taken until Bartlett spoke to each of the safe-deposit box holders, but he guessed it would be a staggering amount based on what he knew of the bank's clientele.

Detective-Sergeant Plouffe, barely recovered from his bomb-dismantling mishap of a week earlier—his face and chest still scorched—arrived just before 11:00 a.m. to begin his investigation, with the police photographer Paul Pothier in tow. A fingerprint technician was already at work.

Plouffe was the forensic and explosives expert for the Montreal Police and his commanders needed his expertise. The heist was sure to make headlines, which meant mayor Jean Drapeau, the Executive Committee, and the city council would want quick results.

Detective-Inspector Joseph "Joe" Bédard, who headed up the Montreal Police's brand-new Criminal Investigation Bureau, ordered the department to maintain radio silence to ensure no nosy reporters caught wind of the crime and spread the news. This gave the police time to quietly round up many known bank burglars and other criminals in Montreal and grill them about the break-in.

It turned out to be a pointless endeavor, providing no clues as to who the perpetrators were.

Plouffe walked into the open vault. Besides the papers still scattered across the floor, there were a variety of tools—screwdrivers, chisels, pliers, and files—and a gaping rectangular hole about twelve inches by eighteen inches punched through the concrete floor. He crouched down to get a better look. There was still a work light on below, shining up into the vault. Looking down into the hole, he could make out a stool, a plywood panel, an extension cord, and more tools scattered on the ground.

Plouffe, a big man with a deep religious conviction who neither drank nor smoked, always seemed to be on call. He had made himself indispensable to the force. He quit his job as a chemist to become a cop in 1946 and pioneered forensic science in Montreal. He created their first mobile crime lab in 1958 and developed bomb-disposal techniques that were later implemented worldwide. The newspapers sometimes referred to him as Montreal's Sherlock Holmes.

Plouffe was the first French Canadian to go to the FBI National Academy in Quantico, Virginia, and he was on a first-name basis with the organization's top dog, J. Edgar Hoover, who had personally invited him to attend when he was still just a constable. Besides all this, he was affable, loved a good joke, and was well-liked, and always had been. He was also an amateur boxing champion and a crack shot who once machine-gunned a bank robber during a bloody standoff.

He wanted to figure out how the thieves had gotten into the bank, so he left the police photographer snapping shots of the vault and headed outside. Walking around the building's perimeter, he noticed that the bank abutted another building, 1408 Saint-Alexandre. He went over for a closer look. Inside the foyer, there was a large iron plate. He fetched a pair of pliers and prized open the metal covering. Underneath, there was a hole large enough for a person to get through. He went down and found himself in a passage leading in the direction of the vault. As he made his way through in the semi-darkness, Plouffe found gloves, a cap, electrical wires, high-powered spotlights, and various tools on the path, which narrowed to a point where he had to crawl on hands and knees to continue going forward.

Plouffe noticed several jagged holes in the passageway's ceiling he could tell had been made with explosives. The holes looked exploratory, as if the thief had been trying to determine exactly where to best place the explosives. Several unexploded blasting caps dotted the ceiling, the wires dangling down. Though the explosives were fairly safe under normal circumstances, if one went off in these close quarters, they could injure or kill someone. He crawled quickly on until he came to the entrance of another room, where he had space to stand. It was narrow, but tall, about ten feet high. Looking up, he could see the interior of the vault. "This is the path the intruders used," he thought. It was impressive. They had blasted, sawed, chiseled, and hammered their way through reinforced concrete that had a trellis of thick iron bars running through it. The bars they couldn't remove had been bent back toward the edges of the hole to allow the thieves to pass through into the vault. It looked as if they'd worked in several phases to break through the four-foot-thick floor.

He backtracked to see what else they'd left behind.

Plouffe eventually catalogued a huge array of expensive equipment the thieves had abandoned. There was a Black & Decker hammer drill, two different electric high-speed grinding wheels, and a homemade detonator for blowing dynamite, which the detective considered rudimentary but effective. Plouffe also found drill bits and various abrasive grinding disks, a massive eight-pound bronze hammer, an iron saw, a thirty-six-inch-long lever-type tool with a curved end, wrenches, chisels, bolt cutters, four pairs of gloves, and two sets of goggles. The unexploded blasting caps worried him. Plouffe carefully approached the low ceiling and slowly removed a dozen caps and laid them on the ground near his feet. A thirteenth was jammed into the cement and wouldn't come out. He was afraid it could blow if he continued trying to wriggle it out. He retrieved a tool to properly detonate it. Plouffe wasn't going to risk a repeat of the week before when the bomb he was defusing went off and sent him flying off a porch. At the hospital they'd pulled out slivers of glass from his shoulder.

After blowing the detonator, Plouffe left the tunnel but was soon called back in after a workman noticed a hole in the concrete under the vault that appeared to be plugged up with a piece of wood. Plouffe took one look and cleared the area. It was an unexploded stick of dynamite.

He worked slowly and carefully, and he eventually managed to remove it. When he left the tunnel this time, Plouffe was convinced of one thing: the thieves would have done whatever they needed to get to their prize. They certainly were tenacious.

*　*　*

By that afternoon, local crime reporters were onto the bank heist story. It soon filled the pages of the Montreal papers and made headlines across Canada. The Canadian Press, a news agency similar to the Associated Press in the United States, noted "similar robberies in the Montreal area in the last two years have resulted in losses totaling more than $3.5

million." It was just another reminder that the city was losing the battle against criminals who preyed on banks.

While Montreal held the dubious distinction as the bank heist capital of North America, Bédard had been a one-man bastion against bank robbers. He made more than two thousand arrests in his long career. In 1960 alone, the Holdup Squad had investigated 635 complaints, recovered about $330,000 in stolen loot, and closed out 442 cases.

In the summer of 1961, Bédard became the head of the Criminal Investigation Bureau in charge of special investigations with eight different squads under him. This meant he now spent most of his time behind a desk. But he still stayed close to the streets, drinking with his men in the dives where the "fringe element," as he called the denizens of the underworld who supplied him and his men with important tips, hung out. He insisted that his officers do the same to maintain connections with their informants and to let the criminal element know that the police were willing to get into the muck with them if that was what it took.

Bédard arrived at the bank and was greeted by Detective-Inspector Leslie Hobbs, who was in charge of the West Division Detective Unit. They toured the looted vault and examined the tools that Plouffe had discovered in the tunnel. Bédard could see that this was a carefully planned and well-executed operation. It wouldn't be easy to catch whoever was behind it.

Bédard had been a cop practically his whole life and had seen myriad changes in the business of apprehending criminals. Born in 1900 in Sherbrooke, a small city two hours east of Montreal, he joined the Royal Canadian Mounted Police (RCMP) at eighteen before making the move to the Montreal Police in 1923. A year later he was already making a name for himself both within the department and in the newspapers after he single-handedly captured three armed burglars during a store break-in.

By the early 1930s he had become a member of the force's elite holdup squad, which he would eventually head. Bédard was an old-school cop who relied on tried-and-true methods to do his job, including conducting coercive interrogations, using paid "stool pigeons," and trusting his hunches. The Montreal Police officers who worked with him thought he was a psychic, but it was his agile intellect and a wide network of informants, not hocus-pocus, that had made Bédard the scourge of the city's criminal class.

Bédard, whose mild-mannered appearance belied a deep understanding of the criminal mind and a penchant for gunplay, always seemed to know just when and where to look for the bank robbers and thieves he had become famous for putting behind bars or in the hospital, often both, and even, on occasion, the morgue. Roughing up suspects was commonplace. Many a judge heard the same story from the cops when a defendant appeared in court bruised and battered: "He tripped and fell down the stairs on his way here, your honor."

By the next day, July 4, United Press International (UPI) had picked up the story, and news of the bank break-in was making headlines across the United States and the rest of the globe. UPI quoted Hobbs as saying a million dollars was "a conservative estimate" of what had likely been stolen, but that they would have to wait on the bank to tally up the losses. He knew, but didn't say publicly, that getting the actual figure would depend on whether the victims were willing to divulge what they'd been storing in their safe-deposit boxes. Hobbs's detectives helped bank officials with the tedious task of contacting all 377 box holders.

The first real clue came a few days after the break-in, when the owner of an office building across the street from the bank contacted the Montreal Police with information about some tenants who'd signed a five-year lease but had apparently abandoned the premises. Officers searched the office, which was empty except for a wardrobe, a chair, and bamboo shades. They recovered two fingerprints, but they didn't match any in the police files of known criminals.

Bédard's old-school methods may have worked for him up to the summer of 1961, but as the days stretched into weeks, they weren't getting him any closer to solving the Bank of Nova Scotia heist. He was set to retire the next year, and he didn't want to leave with a case this big unsolved. This was also the first case for Bédard's brand-new Criminal Investigation Bureau, and it involved coordinating with Hobbs and his detectives at West Division and Bédard's bosses at the central headquarters. Hobbs was officially in charge of the investigation but was working in tandem with Bédard. He was a no-nonsense, by-the-book cop who had also risen through the ranks and was being groomed for a top spot in the department. Where Bédard preferred the street, Hobbs was an administrator through and through.

The Bank of Nova Scotia break-in was another black mark on the Montreal Police's tarnished reputation, suffering under the burden of a growing crime problem. By 1960, it had gotten so bad that the civic administration brought in outside help from two "counselors," André Gaubiac, the former director general of the municipal police in Paris, France, and Commander Andrew Way of Scotland Yard. A third outside consultant, J. Adrien Robert, the chief of the Hull, Quebec, police department, joined the other two in early 1961.

As Bédard, Hobbs, and the other officers worked the Dominion Day bank heist, they also had to deal with a shake-up of the entire police department. On July 5, the Executive Committee of the city council swore in Robert, who'd quickly gone from outside consultant to Montreal Police insider, as the new interim police chief. He immediately began implementing a sweeping "decentralization" plan that city hall had announced a few months earlier on the advice of the three police consultants. The move involved setting up twenty-one precincts around the city, with detectives assigned to each in order to improve efficiency and to put more cops on the street. Up to that point, the entire detective branch had worked out of central headquarters. They were starting with West Division, affecting forty-seven officers, mostly detectives, just as they were digging into the bank burglary.

There was grumbling among many of the 250 detectives on the force, who wondered what would happen to the seniority system, the unique specializations they'd taken on in the centralized force, and even the camaraderie of the "bullpen," where they shared information and discussed problems over a cup of coffee.

"What are we going to do while they're working out new routines for us?" grumbled a senior detective to a *Montreal Gazette* reporter. "Maybe the criminals will take a holiday until we get things worked out."

While the police were searching for clues back in Montreal, Lemay and Primeau were stringing out their Cuban peso scheme into a long holiday. Their leisurely return trip to Montreal included stops in Mexico, California, Las Vegas, and New York City.

Yvon Bélanger, Primeau's brother-in-law, took advantage of his relative's departure from Montreal to steal from him even as he and his family were living under Primeau's roof for free. The safe-deposit boxes Primeau had asked Bélanger to open for him became Bélanger's private piggy bank when he discovered the key and bank information at the house. At first, it was one hundred dollars here and two hundred dollars there that Bélanger "borrowed" to play barbotte, a Canadian dice game similar to craps, among other pursuits. He rolled one too many snake eyes and continued to go back to the till until he'd burned through five thousand dollars of Primeau's money.

Primeau finally discovered the theft after his return, and he and Lemay took Bélanger for a ride. They scared the hell out of him but nothing more. Their relationship suffered, and Primeau eventually threw his brother-in-law out of his house.

In November, Lemay set sail on his forty-two-foot yacht, *Anou*, with Primeau, Lise, and her brothers André and Yvon, for a holiday to celebrate the lucrative bank heist and Cuban peso deal. Lemay hadn't invited Lajoie. His absence from the boating holiday was stark evidence of how Lemay and the others felt about him. He was on his own.

Lemay had paid fifteen thousand dollars in cash for the yacht, which was valued at around forty thousand dollars. He loved to sail and was an expert yachtsman. The leisurely journey took them north from Montreal through the Chambly Canal connecting the Saint Lawrence River with the Richelieu River. They then sailed to Saint-Jean-sur-Richelieu, with its striking St. John the Evangelist Cathedral, visible from the river. They spent a few days sightseeing before sailing into Lake Champlain, then through the sixty-mile-long Champlain Canal that connects to the polluted but still stunning Hudson River.

Sailing past the Hudson Valley's historic villages and massive factories, they headed south to where the river widened to reveal the majestic

Hudson Highlands, a series of craggy mountains abutting the riverbank. They eventually reached New York City. From there it was open ocean until Atlantic City and the Intracoastal Waterway to Florida. They docked the *Anou* at Miami's City Yacht Basin, near downtown, on November 27, happy to have escaped the snow, wind, and freezing drizzle to the north.

They stayed for two days before deciding to relocate to the Ocean Ranch Hotel, a sprawling luxury complex that once had been a mansion, one of many in the posh Brickell neighborhood known as Millionaire's Row. In 1961, it was a resort overlooking Biscayne Bay with a massive pool where the hotel offered everything from calypso bands to water ballets to fashion shows while guests enjoyed tropical drinks under multicolored sun umbrellas.

Miami in the early 1960s was a city synonymous with glamorous fun in the sun—a neon-lit crossroads where snowbirds, the Mafia, anti-Castro refugees pouring in from Cuba, and the Rat Pack and other A-list celebrities converged.

Lemay paid sixty dollars a month in advance for docking privileges, rented a motel room across the bay in Miami Beach, and leased a new black Chevrolet for the crew to use while in town. For Lemay and his gang there were an endless number of activities to indulge in—shopping on Lincoln Road, dancing at various nightclubs, and seeing big-name performers at Miami Beach hot spots like the Fontainebleau and Eden Roc. Lemay loved jazz.

Mostly they just enjoyed relaxing in the sun at the Ocean Ranch Hotel, where they kept to themselves.

Back home, the police were putting the pieces together, and the gang's extended families were taking advantage of their absence to steal from them. Before they'd set sail, André Lemieux had invited his cousin André Dagenais and his wife to stay at his house in Saint-Sauveur while he was away. Dagenais seemed grateful and even saw his cousin and his friends off at the dock in Longueuil, a Montreal suburb where the *Anou* was moored. After the gang left for Miami, Dagenais went looking for Lemieux's money. Dagenais was convinced there was cash secreted away somewhere. He found $7,900 stuck behind the radiator. He and his wife

promptly went on a vacation in Matane, near the mouth of the Saint Lawrence River where it meets the Atlantic at the Gulf of Saint Lawrence.
They lived it up on their cousin's money, unbeknownst to Lemieux.

The gang's leisure time would soon be at its end. Primeau and the
Lemieux siblings flew back to Montreal in mid-December for the Christmas holidays, while Lemay stayed in Miami.

After Lise left, Lemay returned to the bachelor's life. He got in
contact with Lise Vaudry, a seventeen-year-old in Montreal he'd begun
pursuing a few months before the Dominion Day Heist. Lemay had sent
her postcards from Cuba, California, and Mexico while he was traveling
with Primeau. When he returned that September, he had given Vaudry
expensive jewelry and a mink stole. Now, he convinced her to meet him in
New York City for a rendezvous in January.

As the New Year approached, Lemay fell into a routine. He relaxed on
the deck of the *Anou* during the day and, like a kid, every time the ice cream
truck came around, he'd get a frozen treat. At night, he'd hit the nightclubs,
sometimes with another young brunette from Montreal he'd just met.

At least once, Lemay's behavior stood out even in the wild atmosphere
of Miami in the early 1960s. The groundskeeper for the Ocean Ranch
Hotel, Sam Nodel, a Cuban refugee, spotted Lemay on the deck of the
Anou scrubbing it down. He was wearing nothing but a pair of ladies' blue
panties. "Oddest thing I ever saw," Nodel would later remark.

Lemay wasn't worried about making a scene or being caught. He
knew the Montreal Police had gotten nowhere with uncovering who was
behind the Bank of Nova Scotia heist. Lemay and his gang had left no
evidence that could be traced back to him, and he believed none of his
crew would spill what they knew if by chance they were picked up by the
police. He was safe.

While Lemay sunned himself in Florida, confident that he'd gotten
away with the biggest heist of his career, across the country, a man he
would never meet was working tirelessly on a revolutionary piece of technology that would even the playing field between the cops in Montreal
and the master thief.

6

Getting Off the Ground

FALL 1957—WINTER 1959

LONG BEFORE GEORGES LEMAY HAD CONCEIVED OF HIS BANK burglary plans, Dr. Harold Rosen stood atop one of the buildings of the Hughes Aircraft Company's Culver City, California, plant watching Sputnik 1—the world's first artificial Earth satellite—slowly move across the sky. It was a clear fall night in October 1957, and Sputnik elicited equal parts fear and awe from the gathered group of engineers, as it did for most Americans at the time. To be beaten by the Soviets in the burgeoning Space Race was both frightening and embarrassing, but the Soviets' feat was also astounding.

The thirty-one-year-old Rosen ran his fingers through his wavy dark-red hair, his light green eyes staring out toward the horizon, watching the Russian-made satellite. The small craft, about the size of the planet Venus from his vantage point, arced upward, rising above the jagged mountains of the Los Angeles basin. The satellite didn't do much more than emit a beeping sound amateur radio enthusiasts could easily pick up. But Sputnik 1 was a battle cry—a loud, boastful Soviet bellow of superiority over the West.

Rosen imagined building a lightweight satellite that, when launched into a high orbit above the equator, would mimic the Earth's rotation and retain its relative position, like a spoke on a wheel. This geostationary satellite would provide twenty-four-hour global communications, something never before attempted. Rosen was excited. And when Rosen got excited about something, he threw himself into it totally, learning all he could about the field.

There were myriad technical problems to overcome for the electronics, propulsion, and power systems needed to get a satellite that high—nearly twenty-three thousand nautical miles above the Earth—keep it there, and make it usable.

If anyone could get this satellite built, Rosen believed he could, but first he would need to rally his talented colleagues at Hughes to his vision. From there, he'd have to work on Hughes's conservative upper management and then the government bureaucrats who had the ultimate say on whether the project would get off the ground.

Rosen had known since he was fourteen that he wanted to be an engineer, following a visit to the New York World's Fair in the summer of 1940. It was on a quick stopover from a train trip between New Orleans, where he was born and raised, and Montreal, where his Russian Jewish parents had emigrated from in the 1920s. The family often spent summers in Canada with their relatives. While both Rosen and Lemay would have been in Montreal around the same time, there is no evidence they ever crossed paths, though their lives would ultimately become entwined through their chosen professions.

Rosen ranged through the vast grounds at Flushing Meadows in Queens centered around the Trylon and Perisphere, massive modernist structures in the shape of a steel spire and a sphere. It was at the fair, appropriately themed "The World of Tomorrow," that he saw a television for the first time. At the Westinghouse building, he got to play the Nimatron, an early computer device that allowed people to challenge a machine at the mathematical strategy game Nim. The experience so deeply affected Rosen that by age seventeen he was already a senior in electrical engineering at Tulane University. His studies were interrupted by a two-year stint in the navy at the end of World War II. He never saw combat, but he did go from being a student at a military electronics training facility to teaching there.

When it came time for graduate school, a *Life* magazine article brimming with tanned teens frolicking on a Southern California beach helped him decide between Harvard, where he'd already been accepted, and Caltech. Who wanted to suffer through freezing New England winters when you could have fun in the sun and still be part of a university with a stellar reputation in the sciences, especially engineering and physics? And thanks to the G.I. Bill, he could go for free. Although he would miss the food of the city of his birth, especially the famous po'boy sandwiches, and the company of his older sister, Ruth, and younger brother, Ben, Rosen, at twenty-one years old, boarded the Sunset Limited train and headed west.

At Caltech, he studied under Bill Pickering, a pioneering rocket scientist, and worked part-time in the radar department at Raytheon. He also married Rosetta Hirschfeld in 1949 following a chance meeting at a Colorado ski resort. He'd found her upside down in a snowdrift after she'd taken a header. Rosen rescued her and things developed from there. A son, Robert, followed in 1950.

Rosen had planned to stop with a master's degree, but Professor Pickering convinced him to continue his education. Rosen didn't consider himself an exceptional student, and he wasn't a perfectionist, but he often had insights his classmates didn't. "I think you should go on, Harold," Pickering told him. "You have some great potential."

Rosen graduated with his PhD in electrical engineering from the California Institute of Technology in 1951 and was employed at the defense contractor Raytheon developing guided missile and radar systems until 1956, when he went to work as a senior staff engineer for Hughes Aircraft, where he continued to develop radar technology.

The sprawling Hughes plant and headquarters had once been a favored Hollywood film location thanks to its wide, flat wetlands. Howard Hughes himself had filmed part of his 1930 epic war film *Hell's Angels* there. A World War II bomber squadron named itself after the film's title. Later it would be co-opted by the infamous outlaw biker gang.

The site, which would eventually encompass more than one thousand acres, comprised various structures, including the world's longest private runway. Howard Hughes used it during his ill-fated 1946 test flight of the experimental XF-11 plane, which crashed in nearby Beverly Hills, nearly killing him, a bad omen of things to come.

Hughes Aircraft had gone through many changes since Hughes founded the company in 1932. One of the biggest shake-ups occurred in 1953. That year, the U.S. Air Force's top brass, the company's primary client, forced Hughes, whose erratic behavior led to his top executives leaving the company, to divest control.

Hughes split off Hughes Aircraft from Hughes Tool Company and handed sole ownership of Hughes Aircraft over to his new nonprofit Howard Hughes Medical Institute to avoid taxes and (eventually) fund medical research. In its early years, the institute amounted to little more than a giant tax shelter. Hughes also ceded direct control of the aircraft company but kept the title of president. Lawrence "Pat" Hyland, Hughes Aircraft vice president and de facto head, joined the company the next year, bringing stability and growth.

By the late 1950s, Rosen had become obsessed with building his communication satellite, but it took a devastating blow to Hughes Aircraft, and especially his department, to provide Rosen the foothold needed to make his dream a reality.

Near the end of September 1959, Hyland received an air force colonel in his office, who brought devastating news. The military was immediately scrapping the XF-108 Rapier, a long-range interceptor jet fighter that had been in development since 1957 and included a radar system designed and built by Hughes Aircraft. The air force had shifted its focus to long-range guided missiles instead of interceptors.

Hyland had an inkling this was coming, but the news still hit him, and the radar department where Rosen worked, hard.

Hyland, who had a grandfatherly air but ruthless business acumen, called the heads of the various departments together and told them to begin layoffs and develop action plans for new projects as quickly as possible.

Rosen's boss, Frank Carver, tasked the young engineer with coming up with new directions for the radar department to help keep their nearly two thousand workers employed.

Space was on everyone's mind in light of the Soviet Union's continued dominance over the United States, but domestically another Space Race was also brewing. Hughes competitors AT&T and RCA were champing at the bit to get into the satellite business and had a head start. What Rosen had in mind differed greatly from what either of these companies were proposing. He knew that with his idea, Hughes could win this other Space Race. He just had to get the right people on board.

At the time, international communications were in a terrible state. You had to schedule an international phone call sometimes weeks in advance and transoceanic television was impossible. Rosen believed his twenty-four-hour satellite would revolutionize the way the world communicated. All he needed to do was get a satellite into geosynchronous equatorial orbit, GEO for short. Unfortunately for him, the prevailing wisdom among engineers was that such a satellite was little more than science fiction, an impossibility due to the current state of technology.

Their concerns weren't unfounded. After all, an actual science fiction writer, Arthur C. Clarke, best known for his novel *2001: A Space Odyssey*, was the first person to propose the idea back in 1945 in an article for the magazine *Wireless World*. Clarke's version focused on manned space stations in geosynchronous orbit—rather than satellites—that would act as relay stations beaming telephone, radio, and television to Earth. He didn't explain in his article exactly how the crafts would be stabilized.

When Rosen began his research, he was unaware of the Clarke proposal, but had come across a paper by an older, well-respected engineer named John Pierce, who worked for Bell Labs, the research arm of AT&T. In the paper, Pierce and his fellow engineer Rudolf Kompfner discussed the various types of communication satellites. They included GEO satellites, but dismissed the idea as impractical, believing it would take years to develop the technology needed for this type of high-orbit satellite. Pierce and AT&T planned on putting their efforts and money into a fleet of low-altitude satellites. They aimed to launch somewhere between 40 and 120, enough, they believed, to provide communications services for nearly the entire Earth.

Rosen begged to differ with Pierce on the practicality of creating GEO satellites. He believed Hughes Aircraft could do it and could do it right then, not years in the future. His time working at Raytheon designing high-performance antiaircraft guided missiles had given him special insight into what guidance and control systems this type of satellite would require. He knew he could come up with a practical design using technology that was already available or could quickly be developed.

Rosen knew weight was one of the biggest issues he would have to deal with. His satellite couldn't weigh over thirty-five pounds since the only type of U.S. rocket then in use—the Scout A—wasn't strong enough to propel anything heavier such a long distance. Sputnik 1, which had none of the equipment a communication satellite required and traveled in a much lower orbit, weighed in at 180 pounds.

Rosen's satellite would need miniaturized electronics, not an easy fix in the era of bulky transistors. It would also need a lightweight means of stabilization to prevent drift once in orbit. But if it could reach a geosynchronous orbit, the satellite could provide coverage for one third of the Earth.

Rosen turned to two colleagues for help, Tom Hudspeth and John Mendel, whom he considered brilliant. Both men had independently suggested the company pursue the development of communication satellites.

Hudspeth was a communications engineer and ham radio enthusiast seven years older than Rosen and had been at Hughes a decade longer. He was quiet and humble but had a prolific ability for inventions. He mostly thought of these as "dumb little ideas that seemed to come naturally to me," showing just how self-effacing Hudspeth could be. In high school he wanted to become a scientist—he especially loved bacteriology—but had a practical turn of mind and chose engineering since he was good at making things work and felt it would be a decent way to make a living.

Hudspeth was in his late thirties, trim and fit, with a receding hairline. He considered himself a "solder jockey" who loved to get his hands dirty.

Mendel was two years younger than Rosen and had worked for Bell Labs before joining Hughes Aircraft. He was born and raised in Palo Alto, California, five hours north of the Hughes plant in Culver City. Mendel, short and wiry with thick black hair, was a Stanford graduate who had quickly become friends with Rosen even though they worked in different departments. They had similar senses of humor and shared a deep abiding love for their profession.

Mendel was heading up the development of advanced, lightweight traveling wave tubes that could amplify radio waves received over vast distances, the very thing a GEO satellite would require.

Rosen also brought a third colleague into the small circle that would form the nucleus of the team. Don Williams was a Harvard-educated physicist and a mathematical genius whom Rosen had convinced to come back to Hughes after he'd quit two years earlier.

Williams left Hughes to work at a start-up specializing in a new automated method of detecting foreign objects in recycled glass milk bottles. For months afterward, Rosen tried to lure his former coworker back with promises of having him join their small, advanced development group to work on space projects. Williams had turned him down cold.

Rosen knew Williams had the precise mind and mathematical chops for the immense number of calculations needed to get a satellite into the highest orbit ever attempted. Exasperated, he asked Williams what it would take to get him to come back. The answer: twenty-two thousand dollars a year, the equivalent of more than two hundred thousand dollars today, which was a substantial pay increase for Williams. Rosen ran it up the chain of command without much hope. Surprisingly, John Rubel, the head of the Airborne Systems Lab that oversaw the radar department, agreed to Williams's demands, and he was soon back at Hughes.

Williams had already begun developing the concept for a navigational satellite, and while Rosen wasn't interested in the application—it was communication, not navigation, that obsessed him—it was a geostationary design. Williams had also analyzed the mechanics of the orbit enough to prove how little propulsion was required to change a satellite's orbit.

At Caltech, Rosen had taken a physics course with the Nobel laureate

Carl D. Anderson. He wanted to learn about the stabilizing effect against external influences that spin had on things like a football, so he and the professor worked out computations on the comparative effects of external torques—the measure of twisting forces—on bodies while spinning and when static. Rosen realized the same principle could be applied to his satellite. Spinning the satellite on its axis like a gyroscope would not only keep it in its proper orbit but also help keep the satellite's weight down to the absolute minimum.

All that was required was a single thruster using spin-phased impulses—small bursts of power during specific phases of the satellite's spin cycle—to maintain a proper orbit if the satellite's spin axis was parallel to the Earth's axis.

The idea came to Rosen in part from a memory of a trip he'd taken with his mother to Covington, Louisiana, just across Lake Pontchartrain from his hometown of New Orleans. He recalled seeing a small boy standing on a sidewalk spinning in a circle while urinating, the stream jetting out as the boy whirled in delight and the boy's mortified mother tried to stop him. This image kept coming back to Rosen as he thought of a way to control his spinning satellite and keep it from slowly drifting out of orbit due to various environmental factors in space. The spinning boy and his jet of urine helped Rosen visualize the idea that a small radial thruster could nudge a satellite back into its proper orbit if it drifted.

They also needed a way to keep the satellite facing Earth so its antenna could be in direct line of sight with a ground station. By placing small axial thrusters on the satellite—Rosen figured on four—they could keep the satellite pointed toward Earth.

Rosen brought his plan to Williams, who walked out of the room without a word. Rosen figured his friend and colleague didn't like the idea. Williams soon came back with calculations for an even simpler idea based on Rosen's proposal that further cut down on the satellite's weight. A single thruster could control the attitude and another the orbit. With just two thrusters, the satellite could move in any direction, an elegant solution to one of their major problems.

Rosen knew a spin-stabilized satellite wasn't without downsides.

There was the problem of the antenna. Because the satellite would be in a high orbit, it would need a high-gain antenna (one with a strong, narrow beam), and incorporating it into a spinning satellite would be problematic. The solar array used to power the satellite was another issue. They couldn't use solar panels that stayed facing the sun since the entire satellite spun. But because they intended the GEO satellite to be exceptionally light, Rosen believed a cylindrical solar array that went around its entire circumference would provide adequate power.

Even with the problems they needed to work out, Williams enthusiastically endorsed Rosen's idea. The two began filling in the details of exactly what they'd need to get the satellite off the ground and into orbit.

As their plans developed on paper, they added a fifth solid rocket to the Scout A, the vehicle that would get the satellite into space. A smaller sixth rocket attached to the satellite, known as an apogee motor, would push it into its final orbit.

They soon realized that even if they could keep the satellite's weight down to a bare minimum, they didn't have the rocket power to get it into a true geostationary orbit directly above the equator. It would be geosynchronous, following the Earth's twenty-four-hour rotation and remaining at a constant longitude. But it would appear to move in an elongated figure-eight pattern around the equator, requiring ground stations to track it to stay in constant communication.

For Rosen and the small team he'd cobbled together, it was a time of high excitement about what they were creating. It would soon turn to frustration.

Rosen, Mendel, Hudspeth, and Williams were all using discretionary funds that wouldn't take them much further than the drawing board. They would need money, real money, to actually build the satellite and even more to launch it.

Rosen and Williams worked on their satellite presentation assiduously, and by September 1959 they were finally ready to give their pitch to Allen Puckett, a Hughes executive high up the food chain and just below the big boss, Pat Hyland.

The two men—data, charts, and various diagrams in tow—entered

Puckett's office. Rosen was less nervous than keyed up; he knew Puckett was vital to getting the company on board and also knew Puckett had become deeply interested in communication satellites. If Rosen could convince Puckett, they'd be one step closer to getting the money they needed.

Puckett was aware of Rosen and Williams's proposal. Their immediate superior, Frank Carver, had already briefed him on what it entailed. He was skeptical. The proposal included a lot of "what ifs" and "could bes" to Puckett's mind.

Puckett, in his forties, his hair only a few shades darker than his yachtsman's deep tan, was energetic and precise and expected the same from his employees. Like Rosen, he was a Caltech graduate. Puckett had a PhD in aeronautical engineering. He'd come to work for Hughes Aircraft after being lured there by Hyland a few years after Rosen.

Puckett sat behind his desk, ready for the pitch. He wasn't smiling. Rosen leapt right in. The twenty-four-hour satellite would weigh only thirty-five pounds and would be launched from Jarvis Island, an uninhabited U.S. possession close to the equator, using a low-cost Scout rocket supplemented with a bit more in the way of power by extra booster engines.

"Why Jarvis Island?" Puckett asked.

Rosen answered that launching as near to the equator as possible would mean it would take less power to get the satellite into position. He described the other key aspects of the proposal, including the control system and a lightweight traveling wave tube Mendel was working on that would amplify communication signals to and from Earth. Puckett occasionally interrupted Rosen with more questions, for which Rosen believed—hoped—he offered satisfactory answers. Then came the real sticking point: the cost.

Rosen paused briefly before tossing out the number. "We believe it would cost no more than five million dollars." This was the equivalent of more than forty-nine million dollars today, a big number for an untested concept. His answer was met by stony silence. Rosen filled this void by describing the potential benefits for the company if they moved forward. He pointed out that there was rapid growth in demand for long-distance communication due to increased international business. Additionally, the cost of the satellite was only a fraction of the price for laying submarine telephone cables and could handle much more traffic, up to thirty times more for one-sixth the price. All they needed was a partner like General Telephone & Electronics, which was then trying to break AT&T's stranglehold on the domestic communication business. Best of all, if Hughes became its own satellite company, instead of building satellites for someone else, they could reap more of the economic benefits. Rosen believed he'd given his best pitch and wrapped up the presentation. Puckett thanked them for their time but offered little in the way of encouragement. "I'll get back to you," was all he would say. It wasn't the answer Rosen and Williams had hoped for, even if it was the one they had expected, and they left in low spirits. Rosen knew it was hard to generate enthusiasm about something so novel. He had hoped Puckett could see his vision. Now, he wasn't so sure.

After Rosen and Williams left, Puckett picked up his phone and put a call through to Homer Joseph Stewart, the director of NASA's Office of Program Planning and Evaluation. NASA was then a fledgling organization. President Dwight D. Eisenhower created the agency in 1958 to develop and oversee civilian space activities. Puckett, who knew Stewart from Caltech, gave him the rundown on the project.

"Well, what do you think?" Puckett finally asked.

"It's certainly interesting," Stewart answered before continuing. "The proposal is basically sound."

They chatted for a bit longer before Puckett rang off. He sat back in his chair and considered all he'd heard from Rosen and from his friend Stewart, whose opinion he held in high regard. Puckett decided the best course of action was to wait and see how things played out. He wouldn't get in Rosen's way as the engineer worked on his satellite, but he wouldn't actively support the project financially either.

While Puckett's lack of enthusiasm frustrated Rosen, he didn't let it dampen his own. Rosen and Williams continued plugging away on the satellite's design and their promotional campaign among Hughes management in an attempt to gather a groundswell of support.

Days turned to weeks, and September turned to October with no official word. Rosen and Williams had put their proposal on paper, and it was circulating among the executives. Momentum was building. Finally, Rosen got some good news of sorts. Upper management had decided to create an internal task force that included Rosen to assess the satellite's potential and its pitfalls. It meant they were over the first hurdle, and Rosen was one step closer to his dream. What it didn't mean was that funds would be forthcoming. Even if the task force came back with a ringing endorsement, they would still have to convince Pat Hyland, the man who held the purse strings.

Near the end of October 1959, Hyland received the task force's report. "It is the unanimous opinion of the Task Force working members that the satellite communication system proposed by Dr. H. A. Rosen is technically feasible, is possible of realization within close to the estimated price and schedule, has great potential economic attractiveness and should not encounter too serious legal or political obstacles," he read.

Hyland believed Hughes Aircraft needed to look for new opportunities to branch out beyond its main business as a defense contractor, especially considering the air force's finicky attitude of late, but a geosynchronous satellite seemed like a huge investment for such a theoretical concept, especially coming off the loss of the air force contract.

Even with the enthusiastic support of the task force, Hyland wasn't convinced, although he agreed to meet with Rosen and Williams that December to hear them out.

The two engineers came into his office with an easel, charts, and a large pad of paper on which to further illustrate their plans. Rosen and Williams took turns running through the proposal, which they had refined after various discussions with the task force. Like in their earlier meeting with Puckett, Hyland asked many questions that the pair answered, helped along by diagrams they sketched out for him.

Hyland believed he understood the science behind their ideas but didn't feel Rosen and Williams understood probable costs and thought the pair implied that those details fell squarely on Hyland.

When they'd finished, they both looked at Hyland expectantly.

Hyland's mind raced as he looked for an out. He understood these men were not just bold dreamers but had the technical chops needed to make a geosynchronous satellite a reality. He didn't want to lose their respect or enthusiasm. However, he didn't believe this was the time to undertake such a large, unanticipated investment.

He explained that although the future of the company looked bright, at present Hughes was a long way from having the reserves necessary to invest the kind of money needed to develop and produce a prototype. He encouraged the pair to seek financial support from the U.S. government.

It was a hard blow for Rosen after the enthusiastic response of the task force. If he wanted to make his dream a reality, he'd need to move from office politics to national politics, a jump akin to going from a schoolyard tussle to a championship boxing match.

7

Idling, Grounded

FOR ROSEN, 1960 BEGAN IN SALESMAN MODE AS HE AND Williams tried to convince NASA to back their geosynchronous satellite. They'd prepared a slick brochure describing their design in loving detail. It didn't matter. The organization had made a deal with the Department of Defense (DOD) in November 1958, just a month after NASA formally began operating, to pursue only passive communication satellite balloons, while the DOD focused on active communication satellites like Rosen's. NASA dismissed the project out of hand and made it clear they had no wish to fund the proposal.

Rosen, Williams, and Hudspeth weren't willing to give up, and they pursued funding sources outside Hughes Aircraft and the U.S. government, beginning that February. Rosen was especially motivated since his bosses at Hughes had him working on lasers, a field he wasn't particularly interested in.

They scraped together ten thousand dollars (about ninety-eight thousand dollars today) each in seed money and went looking for investors to put in one million dollars, the amount they believed was needed to fund the project. Mendel decided not to throw in with the others, considering the enormous sum of cash and the risk involved. He told his coworkers he just wasn't gutsy enough to join them.

It was hard to get any traction for their project in a time before venture capitalists when the television news regularly showed images of rockets blowing up on the launchpad or careening wildly through the sky, billowing huge plumes of smoke after misfiring. The navy's Vanguard satellite launch of December 1957, in which the rocket made it all of two feet off the ground before disintegrating into a giant fireball, remained a vivid memory for many.

The banks said no, as did the private investors the group approached. Rosen and the others were getting desperate. At one point, Rosen went to Mattel, the toy company, where a friend of his was an engineer. He'd hoped that Mattel, which had recently become flush with cash thanks to the release of the Barbie doll the year before, might be interested in a good investment. They weren't. As he would later quip, "They invested in Ken instead."

Hudspeth worked his contacts, with similar results. A friend briefly led him on concerning his company's interest in the project before admitting they weren't actually going to fund it.

Rosen stewed. He knew the satellite was a worthy investment, not only for the trailblazing technology inside of it, but also as a huge money-maker in the international communications business—telephone and television—for anyone bold enough to see it.

In early March 1960, he finally called Tom Phillips, a friend of his and executive at Raytheon, where Rosen used to work. Phillips quickly set up a meeting. Rosen, Williams, and Hudspeth flew to the company headquarters in Waltham, Massachusetts. Mendel declined to join them.

Rosen sensed Raytheon was taking the satellite proposal seriously when he walked into the meeting and Charles Francis Adams, the company's president, greeted them. The vice president for engineering and research, Ivan Getting, was also in attendance.

The team gave their presentation. It was nearly rote after the many times they'd given it before. But unlike the blank stares or shifty looks from most of their earlier meetings with executives, bankers, and government men, the looks on the faces of the attentive audience were those of intense interest. Phillips explained that they loved the satellite system. The only problem was they wanted to pursue it as a Raytheon project rather than as private-venture investors. Rosen and his two friends would have to move east and become company employees.

The three men had a lot to think about on the trip back to California. Rosen felt that while it wasn't exactly what they'd hoped for, it was probably the best outcome they could get. He loved living in Southern California, but he loved his project more.

The next day, he went to see his supervisor, Frank Carver.

"I'm going to take Tom Phillips's offer and go back there," he said.

"No, you can't quit, Harold," Carver said, looking shocked. He immediately took Rosen to Puckett's office, where the higher-up executive also begged him not to leave.

"We've really been considering this, and we really want to do it, and Pat Hyland really wants to do it," Puckett told Rosen. It looked like Rosen had forced Hyland's hand without even knowing it. Still, after all the difficulties and roads taken that ended up in dead ends, it wasn't until Rosen actually met with Hyland that he allowed himself to feel elation.

Hyland had been thinking about the satellite project since their meeting in December and began to seriously consider the project when he learned that the engineers were looking for outside private funding. He'd met with the company comptroller, gone over their R & D budget, and decided to invest $2 million (more than $19.5 million today) of company funds in developing a prototype. He would also move forward with financing Mendel's traveling wave tube project.

While Rosen and his coworkers wouldn't have a financial stake in the synchronous satellite, at least it would become a reality. Still, Williams, not known for being dramatic, barged into Hyland's office and slapped down a check for ten thousand dollars—his life savings—and told Hyland he still wanted to invest his own money in the project. Whether Williams was merely letting his boss know how serious he was about the satellite, or he really wanted to have a financial stake, it didn't matter. The move impressed Hyland. He handed Williams his check back with the promise that he would do everything within his power to get the project up and running, but explained that it would be a hard road ahead since they'd have to deal with NASA and other federal agencies.

Carver gave Rosen, Williams, Hudspeth, and their small teams lab space to work on the project in the radar department while Mendel continued to work on his project with his team in the company's microwave tube lab.

For the transmitter, Mendel designed the lightest traveling wave tube (TWT) created at the time. This vital piece of technology amplified radio signals to and from Earth. In its simplest terms, it was an elongated vacuum tube with an electron gun on one end that shot an electron beam—focused more tightly through the use of external magnets—down its length into a helix-shaped circuit that collected the electrons at the other end. After the TWT was connected to a power source, a radio frequency input and output, and a few other components, it could produce high-powered microwave signals that could reach Earth. This device was known as a traveling wave tube amplifier, or TWTA (*tweet-uh*).

While Mendel hadn't invented the TWT, he improved on it, making it small and light enough for a synchronous satellite by replacing a single thirty-pound magnet that was used to keep the electrons in a tight beam with a series of magnetic disks and by replacing the glass tube with one made out of metal and ceramic, allowing him to also shorten the device by a foot.

Hudspeth designed a lightweight communication system that incorporated the TWTA as well as everything needed to monitor and control the satellite from Earth. He also came up with an omnidirectional high-gain antenna with a narrowly focused pancake-shaped beam pattern to improve its bandwidth.

Williams improved on Rosen's idea of using small, controlled pulses to easily move the spinning satellite back into its proper orientation if solar radiation or another disturbance caused it to move out of place.

Initially, Williams, who was a firearms aficionado, thought they could use a gun-like apparatus that would shoot bullets, with the recoil providing the needed thrust to get the satellite to move where they wanted it.

But using bullets meant they could use the system only a limited number of times before running out of ammunition. Then one of their colleagues, Bob Roney, spoke up. "Why are you using bullets?" he asked. "That's so crude. Why not use compressed gas for the control?" He mentioned a new type of pneumatic valve that would allow them to use bursts of compressed nitrogen to move the satellite when and where they needed it.

Williams also designed and built a V-beam solar sensor in his garage that could collect data from the sun and transmit it to a ground crew to determine the current and desired orientation of the satellite.

In April, Williams successfully demonstrated the attitude control system in the lab. Successful tests of the other systems followed. Rosen's geosynchronous satellite was quickly moving forward. The team was ecstatic, but Hughes still didn't have a partner, either governmental or in the communications business, and incredibly this aspect of the project would prove harder to come to fruition than creating the myriad new technologies for the satellite.

* * *

Rosen turned thirty-five in March 1961, and things were looking bleak for his beloved synchronous satellite. Several major U.S. corporations were attempting to design and launch their own communication satellites or work with the government to make it happen.

Hughes had approached General Telephone & Electronics to partner on the satellite project, and it initially looked as if they would bite. The technical side of the company was all in, but upper management nixed the plan. Hughes had even reached out to their competitor, Bell Labs, but the company was dead set against geosynchronous satellites, preferring to work on low-orbit versions.

Their last hope lay with the U.S. government, but the various federal agencies were also competing with one another. NASA, the army, and the air force all had satellite projects in various stages of development.

Puckett, who initially had been hands-off on Rosen's satellite concept, became an enthusiastic cheerleader for the project, marshaling his connections within the government, hoping to get the project funded.

Rosen and Williams made the rounds of the various agencies to once again present their proposal.

In addition to the aforementioned deal between NASA and the DOD, restricting the former from working on synchronous satellites, a major sticking point with getting government backing for the Hughes satellite was the DOD's project Advent, a geosynchronous communication satellite being built by General Electric and headed up by the army. In the works since 1959, the project budget kept ballooning while the production timeline kept getting pushed back. Even so, the army continued backing it.

While Rosen impatiently waited for the government or a commercial partner to latch on to the satellite project, Pat Hyland sent Rosen and Hudspeth to France that spring to show off the working model of the satellite at the Paris Air Show.

First held in 1909 by French aviation enthusiasts to highlight early airplanes, hot-air balloons, and engines, it had become an international event, held every odd year at Le Bourget Airport. The 1961 show, which commemorated the thirty-fourth anniversary of Charles Lindbergh's famous 1927 transatlantic flight, drew hundreds of thousands of visitors and hundreds of exhibitors from around the world showing off the latest air and space technology along with dramatic aerobatics demonstrations.

That year, dubbed the "Salon Extraordinaire" by the French press, presented a microcosm of the Cold War. Among the many cutting-edge aircraft on display were the Soviet Tupolev Tu-114, the fastest prop-engine passenger plane in the world, and the American Convair B-58 Hustler, the first bomber jet able to hit Mach 2.

Overhead, fighter jets whisked across the Paris sky in precision formation as the crowds stared upward agog, mouths open in awe of the aerial tricks. Smoke billowed out from behind the planes as they barrel-rolled and looped the loop. Unfortunately, on June 3, the B-58 Hustler, which only days before had set a new speed record by crossing the Atlantic in just three and a half hours (it took Lindbergh thirty-three and a half), crashed in flames in an open field after streaking low above the grandstand and disappearing over the horizon, killing three U.S. airmen.

Compagnie Française Thomson-Houston, a sister company to General Electric, hosted Rosen and Hudspeth's demonstration of the satellite's ability to relay television signals from the top of the Eiffel Tower.

As Rosen rode the elevator up the Eiffel Tower, a French passenger looked at the model of the satellite Rosen was holding, sniffed scornfully, and told him that this was as high as the satellite would ever get.

The demonstration involved transmitting a signal from the model to a booth on ground level that displayed pictures of passersby on a television screen. The team then took Polaroids to pass out as souvenirs.

The satellite turned out to be a hit at the air show but was overshadowed by the Hughes-built Falcon missile, and no European government showed interest in investing in Rosen's project. It didn't help that he wasn't particularly diplomatic. He couldn't stand the mealymouthed doublespeak of government bureaucrats who stood in the way of progress. He did like John Rubel, though.

Rubel was a former Hughes executive who'd left in February 1959 with Hyland's blessing and recommendation to pursue a government career. A *Time* magazine article about Herbert York, who had been named the first head of the DOD's Research and Engineering Department, had been the catalyst for Rubel. York was looking for six assistants to head up project-driven offices for the far-reaching agency, and by March, Rubel was assistant director of defense for research and engineering for strategical weapons.

In the spring of 1961, Rubel was firmly behind the Hughes geosynchronous satellite project. The year before, an old friend from his Hughes days, Gordon Murphy, had been talking up Rosen and Williams's plan. Their ideas intrigued Rubel. Not long afterward, he was given a tour of the Hughes Culver City complex, and Rosen, instead of discussing laser developments, as he'd been instructed to do, steered Rubel over to the lab where they were working on the satellite.

Williams and Hudspeth were there, and the three of them began demonstrating the satellite's various systems as they crowded around the improbably small machine. Rubel couldn't believe its size, about two feet around and a foot long, and so light you could pick it up, especially compared to Advent, which was the size of a large desk stood on end and weighed several thousand pounds. He marveled at the solar cells covering its surface that powered the satellite and the innovative solid-state circuitry. Advent relied on older vacuum tubes and required a lot of power.

The team demonstrated the system's ability to receive television signals. They walked Rubel over to where an image was being simultaneously rebroadcast on a receiver in the lab. The team then let him play with the controller they'd rigged up to demonstrate the satellite's attitude control system that released little puffs of gas to orient the machine while in space.

Rubel twisted the dials and imagined himself controlling a satellite almost 22,300 miles above the Earth, hovering over the Atlantic Ocean near Brazil. "A Walter Mitty moment," he laughed to himself, recalling the hero of James Thurber's famous 1939 short story and the 1947 screen adaptation starring Danny Kaye. Mitty would drift off into vivid fantasies of exciting adventures accompanied by the sound of whatever machine his fantasy revolved around, whether hydroplane or flame thrower—*pocketa-pocketa-pocketa*.

"At last a machine that really goes *pocketa-pocketa*," Rubel said aloud to chuckles from the engineers. Rosen and the others could see he was hooked. Rubel believed he was staring at the solution to geosynchronous communication satellites. He asked to see Pat Hyland, Hughes's head, but he was out of town on business. It would have to wait. Rubel went back to D.C. to figure out how to make the Hughes satellite a reality. Rubel lacked confidence in the Advent project, whereas Rosen's proposal impressed him with its lightweight design that worked within the confines of available rockets. Advent relied on rocket technology still in development.

By the time of Rubel's visit to the Hughes facility in the spring of 1961, he and Keith Glennan, the NASA administrator, had made an initial breakthrough in the bureaucratic stalemate between the DOD and NASA that had prevented the space agency from developing active satellite projects, but this didn't solve Hughes's dilemma. Since the DOD already had a synchronous satellite project in the works, NASA didn't want to duplicate efforts. Instead, NASA moved forward with plans for a series of low-altitude satellites, similar to the kind AT&T was working on, called the Relay program.

NASA had issued a request for proposals for Relay in late 1960, and to Rosen's chagrin, Hughes Aircraft bid on it even though it meant coming up with an entirely different design. Nothing about Rosen's satellite was built for a low orbit.

In May 1961, NASA awarded Relay to RCA. Rosen was pleased by the decision since it meant RCA, whom he considered able competition, would be tied up with low-orbit satellites, leaving the path for a synchronous one for Hughes to pursue. Advent didn't worry him since he believed it would never make it past the design stage.

By the spring of 1961, a lot had changed. John F. Kennedy, who came into office at the end of January, prioritized the space program, and while his primary goal was getting to the moon first, he included communication satellites in his plans since the program dovetailed with his international outlook.

Kennedy appointed James E. Webb as NASA administrator. Webb was in his fifties and had a hint of Southern drawl but spoke quickly, like a New Yorker, and could be blunt. He was smart, energetic, and knew his way around Washington, having previously served as director of the Bureau of the Budget and undersecretary of state under President Harry S. Truman.

Webb swiftly changed NASA's policies regarding communication satellites, announcing that the agency would no longer force the industry to fund its own satellite R & D. From now on the space agency would be directly and fully funding upcoming satellite projects. He earmarked ten million dollars (ninety-six million today) for this purpose, a move that was sure to supercharge the burgeoning industry.

Then, on April 12, the Soviets once again shocked, embarrassed, and roundly beat the United States in the Space Race when Yuri Gagarin blasted off in Vostok 1 to become the first human to orbit the Earth. Since the Soviet's launch of Sputnik 1 in October 1957, and Sputnik 2, which carried a dog named Laika—the first animal to orbit the Earth—a month later, the United States had struggled to keep up.

The United States launched its first satellite into space on January 31, 1958. Explorer 1 was a joint army and air force project designed by Caltech's Jet Propulsion Laboratory under the leadership of Rosen's old professor and mentor, Pickering. The small satellite, shaped like a zucchini, was a little over eighty inches long and the first satellite to detect the Van Allen radiation belt. Despite that milestone, the nation continued to lag behind the Soviets.

On May 5, just days after Gagarin's achievement, the United States launched Project Mercury's *Freedom 7* with Alan Shepard aboard, making him the first American to travel in space.

This was the boost Kennedy needed to get Congress to loosen the purse strings for NASA. Later that month, on May 25, the president went before a joint session of Congress and gave his "Moon Shot" speech. He walked into the House chamber to loud applause and proceeded to the House rostrum, stopping to shake the hand of Vice President Lyndon B. Johnson, who was heading up the National Space Council, and Speaker of the House Sam Rayburn, before starting his speech.

"These are extraordinary times," he began. "And we face an extraordinary challenge . . . If we are to win the battle that is now going on around the world between freedom and tyranny, the dramatic achievements in space which occurred in recent weeks should have made clear to us all, as did the Sputnik in 1957, the impact of this adventure on the minds of men everywhere, who are attempting to make a determination of which road they should take . . . Now it is time to take longer strides—time for a great new American enterprise—time for this nation to take a clearly leading role in space achievement, which in many ways may hold the key to our future on Earth."

At this point in his speech, he began thrusting his right arm downward to emphasize his words. He asked Congress for between seven and nine billion dollars to be allocated over five years for the space program.

Kennedy pushed hard for his dramatic plan of "landing a man on the moon and returning him safely to the Earth" before the decade was out. He believed "no single space project in this period will be more im-pressive to mankind, or more important for the long-range exploration of space." He didn't forget other, arguably more important, if less sensa-tional aspects of the space program in his speech. He asked for fifty mil-lion dollars toward "accelerating the use of space satellites for worldwide communications."

He knew the country needed a bold goal to jump-start its efforts, and communication satellites wouldn't do it.

That same month, the House Committee on Science and Astro-nautics—a standing committee with the exclusive responsibility to re-view and study all laws, programs, and government activities of federal nonmilitary R & D—held a two-day hearing that included represen-tatives from AT&T, RCA, GE, Lockheed, and other major players. They came there to discuss the future of communication satellites and to pitch their pet projects. The consensus was that a synchronous sys-tem would ultimately be best for international communications but that it was years away from becoming a reality. AT&T, which had thrown its lot in with a low-orbit system, flatly rejected synchronous satellites. Rubel testified in favor of a twenty-four-hour system and Puckett sent a written statement also backing it.

While the debate continued on which type of satellite system would win the day, Kennedy pushed for a comprehensive national policy for uni-fying their development and operation. He wanted this new technology up and running for the benefit of the globe as quickly as possible. Kennedy asked Vice President Lyndon B. Johnson to formulate a national policy on everything from who would own the satellites to how to coordinate pri-vate and public interests and international cooperation.

Kennedy favored private ownership and operation of the U.S. portion of the system with government oversight, but many in the administration, including Johnson, along with a cadre of powerful Democratic congress-men, opposed the proposal.

The communication companies and their allies wanted to own and operate their own satellites without government control, while others believed the system should be completely in the hands of the U.S. government. It would take more than a year to hash it out.

By the summer of 1961, AT&T's Telstar low-orbit satellite system was moving apace, and it looked as if it would be up and running before Hughes even got out of the starting gate. But Rubel continued to work behind the scenes. A few months earlier, he'd learned that NASA's deputy administrator, Hugh Dryden, opposed Hughes's twenty-four-hour satellite project, believing Congress might consider it to be in direct competition with the DOD's Advent program and a duplication of efforts. No matter what Rubel did, it seemed the competing fiefdoms of the various agencies continued to stymie his attempts at getting Hughes's synchronous satellite green-lighted. Since the plan was to have NASA sponsor the project and the DOD provide logistical support, Rubel knew he needed Dryden and the rest of NASA's administrators fully on board. He called Roswell Gilpatric, the U.S. deputy secretary of defense and one of Kennedy's handpicked appointees at the Pentagon, and secured his backing. Gilpatric wrote Webb, NASA's head, explaining that the DOD considered the Hughes project "complementary to, not duplicative of, the military Advent." Rubel actually wrote the letter, which Gilpatric signed. "You have my assurance of support in the event that, in your judgment, their proposals should be adopted," the letter read. NASA now had the DOD's backing, and Webb quickly jumped on the synchronous satellite project.

On July 21, 1961, Kennedy, surrounded by various Congress members, his vice president, and NASA administrators, signed HR 6874 into law, which provided a massive influx of funding for NASA, including the fifty million dollars Webb had requested for communication satellite research and development. Less than a week later, on July 27, Webb directed the Goddard Space Flight Center to begin a preliminary project development plan for Hughes's synchronous satellite. The same day, NASA and AT&T entered into agreements to launch Telstar.

The next month, on August 11, 1961, NASA contracted Hughes to build three synchronous satellites. NASA would supply the launch vehicles and the DOD the ground stations used to telecommunicate with the satellites.

Rosen and his team were exuberant. The dream they'd fought so long and hard for—against their own company, fellow engineers who didn't think it was possible, and government red tape—was about to be put to the test.

PART 2

Highs and Lows
in Florida

(Winter 1962–Summer 1965)

*Syncom 1 was designed to be the world's first
geosynchronous communication satellite.
NASA/Wikimedia Commons.*

8

A Big Break

BÉDARD, HOBBS, AND THEIR DETECTIVES WERE WORKING HARD
on the bank burglary, but it was a bit of dumb luck that cracked the
case. Detective-Captain Armand Morin, a handwriting expert, had
spent months meticulously poring through all the handwriting samples
of known criminals on file with the police. His efforts paid off. On January 4, 1962, Lajoie had been arrested in Montreal for forging checks.
Morin matched his signature with that of J. P. Villeneuve, the alias Lajoie
used to lease the office across from the bank.

Lajoie, who had four kids by two different women and lots of debts, had
burned through his share of the burglary's spoils—the equivalent of more
than seventy thousand dollars today—in less than a month. For a while,
he was getting a little money each month from André Lemieux, who felt
bad that Lajoie had gotten stiffed by Lemay. But that allowance dried up in
December 1961. He turned to other means of support, including working
with a young burglary crew—he was nearly twice as old as two of the others
in the gang—in the Laurentian Mountains north of Montreal, breaking
into the type of chalets his old boss Lemay owned. They broke into so many
unoccupied vacation homes in the fall of 1961 that Lajoie lost count.

Detective-Sergeant Robert Leblanc, a heavyset French Canadian with blond curly hair, brought Lajoie to see Morin. They asked him to copy out a written page that they handed him. When Lajoie finished, Morin studied it closely. It matched the name on the lease. They had him.

Leblanc laid it out for him. They knew he was involved in the bank burglary and there were the forgery charges as well. If he came clean, it would go easier on him.

"What's going to happen to me?" Lajoie asked.

"I don't know," Leblanc answered.

Lajoie knew if he wanted to cut a deal on the other charges and avoid a long prison sentence, he'd have to flip on his accomplices in the bank burglary. It didn't hurt that spilling the details on the Dominion Day break-in meant getting revenge on Lemay for shorting him on his take. The only problem: Lemay scared the hell out of him. But his fear of Lemay wasn't as strong as his desire to avoid a long prison sentence. He told Leblanc everything he knew about the Bank of Nova Scotia heist.

The police response was swift. Bédard and Hobbs coordinated with the Quebec Provincial Police to raid the homes of the Lemieux family in the Sault-au-Récollet neighborhood of Montreal; Primeau's house in Chomedey, west of the city; and Lemay's Laurentian chalet, among others. Bédard had suspected Lemay was behind the crime based on the modus operandi of the thieves but had no evidence to back up his hunch until Lajoie's confession. Lemay had been on Bédard's radar for several years, but the clever criminal, who continued to work for his mother's upscale real estate business even as he pulled off bank heists, was able to pass himself off as a law-abiding citizen with a relatively clean record because he never left evidence behind. Bédard, and many others, still recalled the headlines of a decade earlier when Lemay's wife, Huguette, mysteriously vanished while the couple vacationed in the Florida Keys.

This time, Bédard hoped, Lemay wouldn't be so lucky.

As dawn broke on the clear cold morning of Friday, January 5, forty officers headed north in sixteen cars for the forty-five-minute drive to Saint-Adèle. When they reached the Laurentian Mountains, they broke out of their convoy and headed in separate directions. Leblanc and Bédard led the way to Lemay's chalet near the village of Mont-Rolland. Their car bumped its way along the single-lane road and over the small bridge leading to the vacation home. They were hoping to catch Lemay unawares and arrest him without any trouble. Other officers made their way to five other chalets they believed held clues to the bank heist.

Lise Lemieux had been staying at the chalet since her return from Miami a few weeks earlier. A heavy pounding on the door startled her awake. The seemingly inevitable had come to pass. The police were at the door. She let them in and was arrested.

Soon the chalet was in shambles as officers stripped the place bare in their search for evidence. In a closet in the master bedroom, Montreal Police Detective-Sergeant Felix Jean noticed a panel that looked out of place. He wrenched it off, and out poured thousands of coins onto the floor. There were more than five thousand rare coins, including two commemorative shillings and nineteenth-century Canadian pieces later valued at more than ten thousand U.S. dollars today, along with jewelry and some paper money, both U.S. and Canadian. He also found a list of figures on a scrap of cardboard that he believed showed how the spoils from the break-in were to be divided.

Detective Leblanc was ecstatic. He'd been hoping to find a tangible piece of evidence tying Lemay to the break-in, and now he had it.

"How did you find our hiding place?" Lise asked when Jean came out of the bedroom with the coins. "It's funny, others already searched the room and didn't find it."

She told the police the coins were a collection she and Lemay had acquired a little at a time. She never mentioned they were stolen.

Meanwhile, back in Montreal, more police went to the Lemieux house and arrested Yvon and André. Officers also took Primeau into custody at his home in Chomedey.

"This is only the beginning," Bédard told a Canadian Press reporter that day.

Primeau and the Lemieux brothers were arraigned on January 9, 1962, on charges of conspiracy and burglary.

By this time the Bank of Nova Scotia had come up with a preliminary figure of the losses incurred in the heist: $528,468 (more than $5.1 million today) but there were still more customers to track down. Not all of the 377 box holders submitted claims, and some of those the bank spoke to weren't forthcoming about exactly what they were storing in their safe-deposit boxes, since they hoped to dodge the taxes due on their property.

Primeau and the Lemieuxs would soon be reunited with Lajoie, only this time Lajoie, who was still being held on his forgery case and wasn't charged with the bank burglary, would be on the stand as the prosecution's star witness.

The judge refused bail for the defendants, including Lise, whom they charged as a conspirator. She was shocked and angered.

News of the arrests and the fact that Lemay was wanted in connection with the heist made headlines across Canada and the United States. In Miami, many an expat Montrealer read the news with great interest. One read it with shock, which quickly turned to fear. He hesitated about what to do.

The Montreal Police contacted the FBI and the U.S. Coast Guard on Tuesday, January 9, informing them Lemay might be in Florida or in the Caribbean. The Coast Guard searched the Florida coast but turned up nothing. Then the Miami Police Department received a call about exactly where they could find the *Anou*.

The Montreal Police sent Detective-Sergeant Léon St. Pierre to Miami, where he met Miami Police officers Charles Alexander and Sergeant Paul Rosenthal and assistant state attorney Roy Wood. St. Pierre, who looked more like a businessman with his horn-rimmed glasses and conservative dark suits than a cop who specialized in fraud cases, was disappointed to learn that surveillance of the *Anou* had failed to turn up Lemay. The yacht was locked up tight at the Ocean Ranch Hotel docks.

Lemay was nothing if not a careful operator. The boat was registered under Primeau's name. The paper trail showed that Lemay's sister, Rita Lemay-Guimont, was the yacht's previous owner and had sold it to Primeau in October. Lemay's sister, however, was unaware that she had ever been listed as the *Anou*'s owner. It was just one more way Lemay shielded himself from government oversight and attempted to hide anything that might lead back to him.

With a warrant in hand, St. Pierre and the other men boarded the *Anou* on the afternoon of Thursday, January 11. Their search turned up little useful information and none of the missing loot. Lemay's clothes were gone, and so was he.

The trip wasn't a complete waste for St. Pierre. The person who contacted the authorities about where to find the *Anou* was an old friend of Lemay, a mechanic named René Morin (no relation to the police handwriting expert with the same last name). St. Pierre paid Morin a visit at his home and learned a little about Lemay's movements following the Bank of Nova Scotia burglary and where the thief may have headed. He also recovered the *Anou*'s shortwave radio and the walkie-talkies used in the heist.

Morin mentioned he and Lemay had opened a joint account at a local bank. St. Pierre and the Miami Police officers went there, but Lemay had already cleaned it out earlier in the week. He always seemed to be a step ahead of the law.

While St. Pierre pursued leads down in Miami, fifteen investigators led by Bédard and Hobbs descended on Primeau's home in Chomedey with cameras to document the basement, where they found evidence that the gang had tested out the drills and saws used in the bank heist. They wanted to have physical proof that would back up Lajoie's written confession.

The investigators also went back to Lemay's Laurentian chalet to look for anything that might have been missed during the first go-round. The police returned to headquarters with color photographs as well as a garbage can full of trash they planned to sort through, hoping to find more evidence.

* * *

On Tuesday, January 16, Primeau and the Lemieux siblings had their initial hearing to determine whether there was enough evidence to go to trial. Lajoie was the star witness against them, repeating what he'd told

Leblanc in his written confession under questioning by Deputy Chief Crown Prosecutor Claude Wagner. Speaking in quiet measured tones from the witness stand, Lajoie named Lemay as the heist's mastermind and walked the court through how they'd pulled it off, including the prodigious use of dynamite.

"Didn't they make a noise?" Judge Armand Cloutier asked the witness.

Lajoie, relaxed and jovial, wryly answered by telling the judge about the beat cop who passed down Saint-Alexandre Street during an explosion and didn't hear a thing.

There were a few other witnesses, including a woman who identified some of the valuable coins found hidden at Lemay's chalet as having belonged to her dead husband. The hearing dragged on for a second day, in which the prosecution revealed enlarged photos of the two fingerprints they found at the rented office space across from the bank. Lemay, it seemed, had given his stern warning against removing gloves to the wrong team members. He'd reminded Lajoie and André, but the fingerprints the police recovered belonged to Yvon.

The court found that there was plenty of evidence that the gang was behind the burglary. Judge Cloutier again held them all without bail. The four defendants sat in jail while they waited for the cases to wend their way through the justice system.

While none of the witnesses directly tied Lise to the heist, the judge turned down her attorney's request for a dismissal of her charges or even for bail.

"It would be in the best interest of society and of herself for her to remain in custody," the judge said.

The next day, Wednesday, January 17, it was Lajoie's turn to go before the court for his role in the heist. Raymond Daoust, Lemay's former brother-in-law, took on Lajoie as his client at trial. It showed exactly what he thought of Lemay, who he still believed knew more about the disappearance of the defense attorney's sister Huguette a decade earlier. Representing the man he hoped would put Lemay in prison would be a small measure of justice for his lost sister.

Lajoie pleaded not guilty and was returned to jail for further court action. His decision to turn against the others was already paying dividends. Lajoie was being held forty miles southwest of Montreal at Valleyfield, a minimum-security facility opened in 1959 that had once been an army base. His private cell was in the women's section and was never locked. The jailers allowed him a television and radio and even regular conjugal visits with the mother of three of his children. Life was pretty good, and all he had to do was promise he'd testify against the others.

* * *

In the early morning hours of Sunday, March 11, dark ribbons of smoke and an eerie orange glow filled the sky just above the small island near Mont-Rolland where Lemay's chalet was located. By the time the local volunteer fire department arrived, the home, worth at least three hundred thousand dollars (in today's valuation), was engulfed in flames and was ash within two hours.

By the next morning, when the Quebec Provincial Police from Saint-Jerome began their investigation, all that remained of Lemay's former home was a stone fireplace standing amid smoldering timbers that were quickly being covered in snow.

Investigators had to shovel the snow away before they could sift through the rubble for bodies and clues, neither of which were found. By the afternoon, the police had to leave before another vicious winter storm arrived.

The police could tell it was arson, but like every other investigation related to Lemay, they had lots of theories and few facts.

The police interrogated Jean-Guy Richer and his wife, Lise's brother-in-law and sister, whom Lemay had left in charge of the property before going into hiding. The couple had been in Montreal for the weekend when the fire broke out, they said.

Richer told the police he didn't even hear about the fire until Sunday afternoon while still in Montreal and had no idea how the blaze started.

Lemay, police discovered, didn't even own the property.

He'd paid twenty thousand dollars for the island in 1957. Less than a year later he sold it for one dollar to his brother-in-law, Bernard Parent, a doctor and radiologist who lived two hours away in Hull. Again, Lemay was covering his tracks.

Rumors were circulating in the Montreal underworld that Lemay was dead, murdered like Petrov had been nearly five years earlier, but the blaze quashed this idle gossip. Everyone now believed Lemay had managed to sneak into Canada and burn down his old home to destroy whatever evidence may have been missed by the cops and to recover the last of his hidden loot.

* * *

If he was going to make the charges stick, Prosecutor Claude Wagner needed more than the testimony of Lajoie, who had a long criminal record. He was also eager to see Lemay, the man who'd planned the heist, behind bars.

On March 19, 1962, Wagner applied to Montreal Superior Court Justice Roger Ouimet to form a rogatory commission to go to Miami to question witnesses in the bank heist and Lemay's disappearance. The commission was tasked with obtaining evidence in the cases involving Lemay's gang and would require the assistance of Florida courts to make it happen. Ouimet quickly signed off. Montreal Sessions Judge T. A. Fontaine would head up the commission, joined by Wagner; two defense attorneys, Léo-René Maranda and Réal Gagnon, who were representing the defendants already rounded up in the case; and a court stenographer.

The commission hashed out questions to ask the various witnesses, a list that included the Miami cops involved in the raid on the *Anou*, two Miami bank employees who'd dealt with Lemay while he was there, and Morin, Lemay's old friend, among others.

The questions were straightforward: "If you are a Canadian citizen, when did you leave Canada?" "Do you know Georges Lemay and/ or Roland Primeau, Yvon Lemieux, André Lemieux, and Lise Lemieux?" "Tell me what you know about the incident at the bank of Nova Scotia on June 30, 1961, and activities before or after this incident, involving the above-mentioned persons."

Witnesses would be subpoenaed and were to testify under oath, just as if they were appearing in court in Canada. The depositions would then be sealed and opened in court during Primeau's trial. He would be the first to have his day in court.

The small group began making preparations to head south, but days before they were to fly to the United States, the commission was scrapped when the witnesses agreed to instead come to Montreal for Primeau's trial, scheduled for mid-April. Wagner, Bédard, and the other Montreal Police investigators hoped it would be the first of many, with Lemay's trial as the centerpiece. First, they would have to catch him.

9

The Gang's All Here

SPRING FINALLY CAME TO MONTREAL, AS DID PRIMEAU'S TRIAL. He'd been held at the city's notorious Bordeaux Prison for three months without bail awaiting his day in court.

On Tuesday, April 10, Primeau appeared before Justice Roger Ouimet in the Court of Queen's Bench. The courtroom was in the imposing granite neoclassical Palais de Justice de Montreal, built in the 1920s with massive copper doors and a Latin phrase—FRASTRA LEGIS AUXILIUM QUAERIT IN LEGEM COMITTIT (He who offends the law shall call upon it in vain)—chiseled into the cornice.[4] The stern warning, like the rest of the building designed by Montreal's renowned son, the architect Ernest Cormier, was meant to make the individual tremble before the might of the law. It didn't work in Primeau's case. It wasn't the thirty-six-year-old's first go-round with the legal system, and he took the trial with a casual swagger and easy smile.

After the chess game that was jury selection between Primeau's attorneys—Dollard Dansereau, Léo-René Maranda, and Réal Gagnon—

---

4. The old Palais de Justice building now houses the Court of Appeal of Quebec.

and Deputy Chief Crown Attorney Wagner, twelve French-speaking men (at the time, women weren't allowed to sit on juries) were finally chosen, and the trial began.

Detective-Sergeant Plouffe, the Montreal Police explosives and forensic specialist, spent two days going over the various tools, wires, and detonators he found at the bank and how he discovered the route the gang took to get into the bank vault.

Primeau seemed undisturbed by the testimony. He smiled and waved at friends who came to see his trial and twice asked the judge for permission to call his wife to update her during court recesses, requests to which Justice Ouimet reluctantly agreed as long as it was to his "wife and not to someone else."

The defense scored an unexpected point when Primeau's brother-in-law, Yvon Bélanger, who appeared as a prosecution witness, inadvertently gave the defendant an alibi for the day of the bank heist. The prosecutor brought Bélanger to the stand to testify about having seen Lemay and the others testing out equipment in Primeau's basement before the bank burglary. Under cross-examination the witness revealed that Primeau had attended a funeral on July 1, the day of the heist. Bélanger's wife also took the stand and confirmed Primeau had been at the funeral but hadn't been home at all the previous night and that he almost made them late to the funeral. She also testified that Primeau had gone over to the home of Lemay's mother the afternoon of July 2.

The next afternoon, the entire court took a field trip to the scene of the crime with Jacques Lajoie, the prosecution's star witness, as their tour guide. Wagner, the prosecutor, made the request after Lajoie spent nearly three hours on the stand describing the break-in. Wagner felt the jury would get a better understanding of Lemay's operation if they could see it firsthand.

The court arrived at the scene in a large black van typically used to transport prisoners.

Outside the bank on Saint-Catherine Street, a phalanx of journalists, photographers, and TV cameras greeted them, along with a growing crowd of curious passersby and workers who came out of the surrounding businesses to watch the scene unfold. The crowd of hundreds of people, including fifty police officers, choked the street in front of the bank.

Lajoie, while attempting to dodge the cameras, demonstrated for the court and jury, with the help of a screwdriver a police officer handed him, how easy it was to open the trapdoor that eventually led into the tunnel under the bank.

Primeau, handcuffed and with a gray overcoat over his head to avoid being photographed, sat on the stairs surrounded by a dozen cops while the court stenographer attempted to take down Lajoie's testimony, balancing a stenotype keyboard on her knees as she crouched nearby.

They also visited the boiler room, the vault, which had by that time been refurbished, and the office the gang rented across the street as their command post. Lajoie provided a running commentary the entire time.

Lajoie wouldn't be so talkative back in court for his cross-examination on Friday, April 13, when defense attorney Dansereau grilled him for seven hours. By this time, Lajoie had been charged with the break-ins at the Laurentian chalets, and the Quebec provincial police had cut a deal with him. They had him for two dozen burglaries, but if he agreed to testify against Primeau, they'd reduce the number to a handful. It was a good deal, if not strictly by the book, since police weren't supposed to outright promise defendants anything for their testimony. The defense was well aware of Lajoie's other charges and hammered him about them while he was on the stand.

Dansereau handed Lajoie a stack of photos, asking him if he recognized them. Lajoie flipped through them, picking out a few. "These strike a familiar chord," he told the attorney.

"Why are they striking to you?"

"They look like some houses I looted," Lajoie admitted. The defense attorney pushed Lajoie to explain that back in December he'd participated in "four or five" burglaries. Dansereau went through the witness's long criminal history, attempting to show the jury the man whom the prosecution had put so much stock in. Lajoie garnered some sympathy from the twelve men when he told them he had lived in fear of Lemay since January, when he testified at Primeau's preliminary hearing.

"You don't know Lemay," he said, looking directly at the jury, "but I do."

On the seventh day of the trial, Primeau took the stand in his own defense. It was a risky move, since Wagner would get to cross-examine him, but Primeau wasn't scared.

He told the jury he'd known Lemay for about eight years and admitted he'd teamed up with him on the Cuban peso smuggling operation in which they'd made a hefty profit the year before. He denied any involvement in the Dominion Day bank heist. Primeau said that the time he spent with Lemay just before the bank heist was to discuss the Cuban business, not the burglary. According to Primeau, he'd been home both weekends of the heist with his wife.

"I'm a homebody," he said with a shrug.

He denied knowing Lajoie and said he had met the Lemieux brothers only a few times.

Primeau held his own during Wagner's cross-examination. He stuck to his story even in the face of a long list of receipts and other documents police had discovered from around the time of the bank heist. Primeau said whatever he'd spent around that time came from the money he'd made on the Cuban peso deal. The defendant discounted his brother-in-law's testimony. He explained that Bélanger was trying to get back at him for kicking him out of his house for being a deadbeat. Primeau said Bélanger had even threatened his seven-year-old daughter. After two days on the stand, the ordeal was over.

The trial ended on April 24. After sitting through eight days of testimony, broken up by the Easter holiday, and nearly forty witnesses, the jury began deliberations. A little more than two hours after leaving the courtroom, the jury sent a note to the judge saying they'd reached their decision.

The twelve men quietly filed in and took their seats. The verdict was guilty. Judge Ouimet, who had made it pretty clear during the earlier jury charge—the point in the trial when the judge explains the pertinent laws before the jury begins deliberating—that he thought Primeau had done it, congratulated the men, telling them he was in "complete agreement" with their verdict. Primeau took the verdict in stride, showing little emotion when it was read in court.

The following day, Wednesday, April 25, Judge Ouimet sentenced Primeau to thirteen years in prison, one fewer than the maximum. Ouimet took the three months of Primeau's pre-trial detention into consideration, but said the defendant had "lived off the fruits of his crimes" for years and was obviously Lemay's "lieutenant" in the bank heist. Primeau's less-than-serious demeanor at trial irked the judge, who urged the police and prosecutor to look into whether they could charge the defendant with perjury. Primeau seemed unconcerned as he was led out of court to head to another courtroom for sentencing on the forgery charges he had already been facing when he pulled off the Bank of Nova Scotia heist. He knew he was going to be serving time for that crime, and his lawyers planned to appeal the thirteen-year sentence, anyway.

He served his sentence at the Leclerc Institution in Laval, a newly opened medium-security prison that housed nearly five hundred inmates eighteen miles northwest of Montreal.

* * *

In April, while Primeau was at trial, Lise Lemieux, pregnant with Lemay's child and in jail since January, was finally given bail. Not that it mattered. The bail amount was huge, and she was facing separate charges in another case.

Her lawyers, Dansereau, Gagnon, and Maranda—the same attorneys representing Primeau and Lise's brothers—tried various legal means to get her out, arguing as they had for months that no evidence tied Lise to the heist, that she "never got in trouble with the police," and that she had given herself up without a fight when arrested. They were stymied at every turn. Wagner, the prosecutor, was steadfast in fighting any bail request. He hoped to keep her scared and in pocket, believing he could flip her. He wanted to use her as a prosecution witness in her brothers' trials and in Lemay's (when and if they caught him). Wagner also feared if Lise made bail, she'd immediately flee and join her boyfriend on the run.

It took the defense attorneys more than three months, four judges, and seven tries before they finally got a Court of Appeal judge to issue a $25,000 bail bond, a sum equivalent to more than $239,000 today.

Lise, along with her father, three of her brothers, and her brother-in-law, were also facing burglary charges in Saint-Adèle, to the north of Montreal. The Montreal Police had discovered stolen property linked to several chalet break-ins in the Laurentian Mountains at her family's house during a raid. The Lemieux clan told police the stolen items belonged to Jacques Lajoie, who'd been storing the goods at their house. The police weren't inclined to believe the family based on their history.

Even if Lise could come up with the huge bail amount, the cops could still hold her on these lesser charges. They alleged she possessed a stolen coat. It was worth only sixty dollars, but like her tenuous role in the bank heist, it was enough to keep her locked up while the cops tried to get her to turn state's evidence. She was miserable and just wanted to go home, but she wasn't going to turn on Lemay or her family.

At the end of May, Lise's case came up for trial. Wagner had planned to force her brother André to testify against her, but André escaped custody before the prosecutor got his chance. The trial had to be postponed.

It was a clerical error that led to André's opportunity to escape from the cells at the Saint-Jerome courthouse and prison building on the evening of May 29. He'd been transported there from Montreal's Bordeaux Jail a day earlier under heavy police guard and arraigned on the burglary charges related to the chalet break-ins. He was being held for a June 4 hearing.

His attorney in this case, Germain Bock, got André released on bond on the lesser charges and showed up at the courthouse jail with paperwork from a local judge along with bail money provided by Lemieux's other sister.

The three guards on duty were unaware that the judge in the Bank of Nova Scotia case had ordered André to be held without bail. They released Lemieux, and he walked out of the building with his lawyer. The last time they saw André he was getting into a car driven by a blond woman.

The very embarrassed provincial police, once they'd discovered the error, launched a massive manhunt across the Laurentian Mountains that stretched on for several days but failed to turn up the escapee.

André's good fortune produced unintended consequences for his sister. In early June, Lise was also being held in a cell at the Saint-Jerome courthouse and prison building. A riot broke out in the men's section when the longer-serving inmates set their bedsheets and other items on fire and caused general mayhem in response to the warden curtailing their privileges in the wake of André's accidental release. To prevent the riot from spreading, the administration transferred a dozen prisoners, including Lise and her younger brother Richard, who was serving a six-month sentence for the chalet burglaries, to Montreal's Bordeaux Prison. Lise's cell in Saint-Jerome had been much better than any of those at the decrepit Bordeaux Prison. It was one more thing to add to her misery.

On June 13, Lise again appeared for trial before Judge Emile Trottier. The tiny brunette with a fiery disposition fought with her attorneys before announcing that she wanted to change her plea.

Her lawyers, Maranda and Gagnon, none too happy, asked the judge to inquire why Lise had so abruptly changed her mind.

Judge Trottier refused, telling them, "We will follow the ordinary procedure." The judge, after reading the criminal complaint aloud, asked Lise if she was sure she wanted to plead guilty. In a barely audible voice Lise simply said, "Guilty."

Wagner, the prosecutor, stood up and addressed the court.

"Justice is not blind; it knows how to separate responsibilities between two sources, even if they are accused of the same offense," he told the judge. "The court should not be of the same severity in every case."

Wagner then used the same arguments the defense had been making for months when asking the court to give her time served, which amounted to about six months: Lise has no previous record, she was never at the scene of the crime, and she obviously suffered from the enormous publicity around her case.

What had gone unspoken by anyone in court was that Lise was by then visibly pregnant. This may have accounted for Wagner's change of attitude, and it was clearly Lise's reason for changing her plea. Had she been convicted after a trial, she would likely have given birth in prison, which was a great motivator for pleading guilty.

Gagnon broke in with a pointed comment regarding the rest of his clients charged in the bank heist. "In front of so much humanity there is only one thing to point out: this humanity should also apply to all other defendants, in the same case."

Trottier ignored Gagnon's comment and instead praised Wagner for his stance in Lise's case, but he stressed that while Lise was neither the "author nor an active conspirator" in the heist, she must have been involved if she was willing to plead guilty and put "her case in the hands of justice."

"Time served," the judge said without hesitation.

"Thank you," Lise replied, smiling.

Unfortunately for Lise, she still faced burglary and possession of stolen items charges in Saint-Jerome. Wagner ordered her transported there the same day. That case dragged on for another week before she was released on a $950 bond.

Finally, on July 10, the visibly pregnant Lise Lemay appeared before Judge Omer Côté, who immediately dismissed the charges for lack of evidence. Lise was finally free and her cases closed. She couldn't wait to meet up with Lemay, who was still on the run. However, she would have to wait longer than she hoped.

André, like his sister, was also free. Unlike his sister, he was on the run and being hunted across the continent.

On May 31, police in Saint-Laurent, thirty miles south of Saint-Jerome, where André had been held, attempted to chase down a driver who'd had a fender bender that morning and sped off. A vacationing Montreal detective named Joseph Girard nearly captured the driver, who abandoned his stolen vehicle and ran across a field. Girard, who was wearing civilian clothes, fired three warning shots into the air. The man kept running. He was gone. The detective believed it was André Lemieux he'd been chasing.

Police warned citizens to lock their doors, and a manhunt ensued but was abandoned two hours later when it became obvious that André, if it had been him, had gotten away again.

On June 5, André's father, Rosaire Lemieux, also facing burglary charges, told the court his son would turn himself in but wouldn't specify exactly when that would happen. Adding to the general confusion, the paperwork that had prohibited André and Lise from being released on bail mysteriously went missing from their files.

The entire situation became untenable for Bock, the attorney representing both André and Rosaire Lemieux in the case in Saint-Jerome. He quit criminal defense work in the middle of the case, leaving Rosaire, who was out on bail, without a lawyer.

André never turned himself in, as his father had promised he would. The police search expanded to include all of Canada, and the RCMP eventually asked the FBI to keep a lookout for the second member of Lemay's gang to go on the run.

* * *

In the spring of 1962, Bédard was running out of time. He planned to retire from the Montreal Police to take a new position as the head of security for the Bank of Montreal and Royal Bank of Canada. Lemay and André Lemieux were still at large, and Bédard's team had recovered very little of the loot from the bank heist.

At the end of May, Montreal detectives received a bit of hope that the key to Lemay's whereabouts was within their grasp when the FBI arrested a mysterious American named Clifford Von Alderbruch, alias Cunningham, in a sting in a North Miami Beach parking lot.

On May 3, 1958, five men had used blowtorches, sledgehammers, and drills to smash their way into the vault of the Brockville Trust & Savings Company in Brockville, Ontario, a small city with an enclave of wealthy citizens on the banks of Lake Ontario. They looted thirty-six safe-deposit boxes, making off with cash, jewelry, and bonds worth more than twenty-five million dollars today.

Posing as a buyer of stolen bonds, an FBI agent busted Von Alderbruch, a Californian, with one thousand dollars' worth of bonds from that heist as well as twenty-one thousand dollars in bonds stolen in the 1957 Outremont bank burglary. Authorities believed Lemay had a hand in both operations. Detective St. Pierre told a reporter from *The Miami News* as much in a 1962 interview.

Because Von Alderbruch was in Miami, where Lemay had been staying for several months, the Montreal detectives believed Lemay was likely still somewhere in the region and that the two men had been in contact.

It was another dead end. Von Alderbruch remained mum about what connections he may have had to the elusive Lemay or where he might be found.

Detectives Leblanc and St. Pierre continued to work the case, which seemed to go nowhere. They still believed the two fugitives would be captured, so they continued hunting for physical evidence to back up Lajoie's testimony when Lemay and André Lemieux's trials became a reality, even as the most tangible relics of Lemay's recent past became unavailable.

Both the *Anou* and Lemay's island chalet had passed into the hands of strangers in the months since he'd eluded capture in Miami.

Primeau, the legal owner of the boat, sold the *Anou* for fifteen thousand dollars (a steal) through his lawyer Maranda to another reputed Montreal underworld figure named Alphonse Lefebre, who paid a Miami-based captain to sail it up to Montreal. Who the money from the sale ended up with was a question the police weren't able to answer. They couldn't seize the yacht or the money from the sale since they had no proof Lemay had originally bought the boat with stolen funds, even though the Montreal detectives had no doubt that he had.

Lemay's brother-in-law, Bernard Parent, sold the island property with the burned-out chalet to a Montreal hairdresser, also for fifteen thousand dollars (another steal). The new owner planned to rename the property Shangri La, but his plans would have to wait. The Montreal Police and the Quebec Provincial Police once again returned to search for clues during Bédard's last week on the job.

It was painstaking and detailed work that involved the use of a tractor, a large pneumatic drill, blowtorches, metal detectors, shovels, picks, and physical labor. The investigators opted for jeans and work shirts instead of their usual suits and hats, except for St. Pierre, who still wore a tie but removed his suit jacket for the job at hand.

The men sifted through the ruins, dividing the debris into piles of ash, wood, and metal. They used metal detectors to search the boulder-strewn property, and when they got a potential hit, they would dig or drill until they found whatever it was.

The officers also tore apart the steel in-ground pool. It was unusual in that it wasn't faced with concrete and had been built directly on top of sand and sod, which got the cops thinking something could be hidden underneath. They cut away the steel plates at the bottom but found nothing unusual.

Detective Plouffe swung his powerful metal detector back and forth as he slowly walked the perimeter of the island, listening through headphones for the telltale electronic tone that would indicate metal buried in the ground. The expensive piece of equipment was intended for mine detection, but Plouffe used it to thoroughly scan the ground and even the trees dotting the property.

According to Lajoie, Lemay had banned his gang from going near a tall white birch at the edge of the property. Investigators went over it inch by inch but found nothing.

Plouffe had been assigned to the search for both his forensic knowledge and his extensive work with explosives, which paid off when he discovered a cache of blasting caps buried in the ground near a massive rocky outcrop.

Near the foot of another tree, the investigators discovered an old lunch box containing sockets used in mechanical engineering that had been stolen the year before during a nearby break-in.

Plouffe wondered if the fire, which he felt had been deliberately set, was started to destroy documents that he or one of the other investigators had missed in earlier searches.

An officer discovered charred banknotes in the chalet's wreckage. They carefully collected the evidence to send it to the RCMP crime lab for chemical analysis.

It was a sweaty, dirty job, but it paid dividends. Besides the lunch box and charred bank notes, they recovered 34 drill bits of different sizes found in the hollow of a tree, 132 blasting caps, and a bag full of driver's licenses stolen in the burglary of a local permit office months earlier. Someone with forgery experience could alter the licenses to help create a false identity, the police believed.

What they didn't find, and had believed they likely would, was more of the loot from the Bank of Nova Scotia heist or from earlier bank burglaries. The investigators also believed they might find the rest of the remains of Petrov, Lemay's former partner who had ended up dead after the Outremont bank burglary.

Four years after Petrov's murder, the police still hadn't found anything other than his severed leg.

Members of the forensic medical office who were on hand determined that what at first appeared to be bone fragments found in the ashes from the fire turned out to be nothing more than melted plastic. The mystery of Petrov's missing remains would have to wait for another day. At least the investigators had found supporting evidence they could use at Lemay's trial once they'd captured him.

The search of Lemay's former property stretched on past a week. One night, three police officers, tasked with guarding the island during the search, caught a young woman in her twenties with dark hair crossing the small wooden bridge leading to the island. They barred her way and questioned her. Her name was Micheline Meunier, and she'd been with Lemay in Miami a few months earlier. She didn't give a clear explanation of what she was doing there. Officers merely sent her away with a warning not to return.

* * *

At the end of May 1962, Bédard went on a monthlong vacation—time he'd saved up and didn't want to lose—and then officially retired from the Montreal Police to step into his new role. His long-suffering wife, Jeannette, was looking forward to her husband settling in to a nine-to-five routine behind a desk after years of dangerous police work. She hoped the new job would mean Bédard wouldn't constantly be putting his life on the line. She was wrong.

His first day on the new job, Bédard didn't even make it into the office. Instead, he shot it out with a violent gang that had just robbed a Bank of Montreal branch in the city's north end and gotten away with one hundred thousand dollars.

Bédard had gotten a call at home about the robbery as he was getting ready for work and wasn't about to miss out on capturing yet another band of criminals he'd been hunting for months. He and his former police coworkers trapped the gang at their headquarters, a small tumbledown shack in the Laurentian Mountains north of the city. When the smoke cleared, one bandit lay dead. The police captured two more as they tried to flee into the woods, though a fourth man escaped. The cops took their prisoners to the hospital for their gunshot wounds.

"Well, I guess I'd better be getting over to my office now," Bédard said after the stolen cash was counted and locked away as evidence. It was 7:45 p.m.

The thrill of the chase and capture of these bandits only helped underscore Bédard's gloom about failing to capture Lemay. While Bédard had helped solve the Bank of Nova Scotia burglary, Lemay remained a loose end that vexed the former detective.

The ten-thousand-dollar reward for his capture offered by the bank—upped in April from two thousand dollars—hadn't helped track down the elusive criminal. Bédard would have to rely on the RCMP, the force he had been a member of back in the 1920s before joining the Montreal Police, to capture Lemay. He had no idea that it would be an electrical engineer in California, and not the Mounties, who had the bigger role to play in the hunt for Lemay.

10

The Highest Highs, the Lowest Lows

WINTER 1962–SPRING 1963

THE HIGH ROSEN FELT, FROM MAKING IT OVER ONE OF THE biggest hurdles he had faced in trying to get his satellite built, quickly dissipated. He and his team were now working with NASA on the project the feds had named Syncom, a bit bouncier than its full title, the Synchronous Communications Satellite.

Hughes's executives named Rosen project scientist and expanded his team to around forty engineers with hundreds of other employees in supporting roles. From NASA, they were joined by Leonard Jaffe, who headed up the agency's communications and navigation satellite programs; Harry Stafford, a Texan who was NASA's project engineer for Syncom; and their team of engineers and technicians.

Hughes named Richard "Dick" Bentley Syncom's project manager, rather than Rosen, in what some saw as a move by upper management to have a public face for the project who was a bit more diplomatic than Rosen. He may not have been diplomatic with the money men and bureaucrats, but Rosen was beloved by the engineers who worked under him. He always challenged his employees to achieve their full potential without resorting to negativity. He always led by example and had a great sense of humor, which put others at ease.

Syncom was based on Rosen and Williams's design, but moving from a prototype to an actual satellite capable of withstanding the harsh environment of outer space, such as being bombarded by photons from the sun, would take months more work and even more creative thinking, especially with the changes Jaffe, representing NASA, insisted on.

One major issue that arose early was the launch site. NASA nixed Rosen's choice of Jarvis Island. The tiny uninhabited coral island in the South Pacific, about halfway between Hawaii and the Cook Islands, had no infrastructure and no navigable harbors. NASA decided it made more sense to launch from Cape Canaveral at Launch Complex 17, a dual launch area the air force built in 1956 to test Thor ballistic missiles. By 1962, the government was transitioning the site from missile development to space operations.

The launch vehicle chosen by NASA to put Syncom into orbit made Rosen happy. When he and Williams originally drew up their plans, they'd chosen the Scout rocket, the first solid-propellant rocket capable of launching payloads into space, as their launch vehicle. They had been unaware of the air force's Thor-Delta rocket launch vehicle program underway in the late 1950s. The Delta rocket was more powerful than the Scout. The added power allowed them to include redundancies for both the communication and control systems, which could mean the difference between success and utter failure for Syncom 1 once it was thousands of miles above the planet with no way to fix anything that might break.

But even with the extra power the Delta provided, because NASA insisted on launching from Florida instead of nearer the equator, Syncom 1 couldn't reach a geostationary orbit. This meant that while Syncom 1 would be the first geosynchronous satellite in orbit, if all went right, it would not be the first geostationary satellite since it would appear to move in an elongated figure eight at 33 degrees north and south of the equator when viewed from Earth. This north-south motion would require the ground stations to track the satellite as it moved through its orbit.

Another change from Hughes's original plans was the frequency the ground stations would use to communicate with the satellite. Rosen and Hudspeth had chosen the frequency at random, since at the time the government hadn't yet designated any for satellite use. Syncom would use the ground stations built by the U.S. military for the Advent program, requiring Rosen and his fellow engineers to develop another piece of equipment to change the frequency of the original signal.

That the DOD was allowing Syncom to use equipment meant for its Advent program may have been a clue that the military had finally run out of patience with its bloated, mismanaged synchronous satellite project. Advent was the amalgamation of several military projects that were eventually rolled up into one, but by the spring of 1962, Rubel and his DOD colleagues decided to pull the plug on the program that had stymied Rosen's efforts for so long.

Meanwhile, Pierce and Bell Labs moved ahead with their plans for Telstar, which was on course to be the world's first active communication satellite.

The first passive communication satellite, meaning radio and radar signals merely bounced off of it, was Project Echo, a massive mylar balloon with a one-hundred-foot diameter. Pierce spearheaded the project, which was launched by NASA in August 1960.

Pierce had spurred on his main competitor in the race to get a commercial communication satellite into space without even knowing it.

On October 2, 1960, Rosen had met with some of the Bell Labs engineers—including Pierce, whose seminal 1959 paper on satellite technology inspired Rosen—at the company's sprawling campus in Murray Hill, New Jersey. Pierce, a wiry scientist with prominent cheekbones and a receding hairline whom *The New York Times* once described as "wispy," adjusted his rimless glasses as Rosen excitedly explained his plan to a less-than-enthusiastic reception. Pierce thought Rosen was young and reckless—a "whippersnapper"—with an idea that wouldn't work, a dreamer willing to promise the world to get his satellite built. Rosen got no traction with Pierce or Bell Labs.

While Rosen respected the older scientist, he also believed his own knowledge of guided missile systems from his Raytheon days trumped

Pierce's background working on ground systems. Rosen walked away from that meeting thinking of Pierce as an adversary. From that moment, the race was on not only to get a working satellite into orbit but also to see which of these two systems would prove to be superior.

Pierce continued to dismiss GEO satellites as unworkable given the current technology and believed Bell Labs's low-orbit Telstar system made more sense than Rosen's geosynchronous satellite. At least initially, he appeared to be right.

Two years after that fateful meeting with Rosen, Telstar 1 rocketed heavenward on July 10, 1962, from the same launch pad NASA planned to use for Syncom. The next day, it broadcast the world's first transatlantic images to the tracking station in Pleumeur-Bodou, France.

Rosen, never one to be intimidated, felt that while Telstar demonstrated the potential for the use of satellites for television broadcasts, its low orbit—a mere 3,687 miles above the Earth—meant it was limited to a twenty-minute window every two-and-a-half hours when both the Andover Earth Station in Maine and its French counterpart used to track the satellite had Telstar in sight. Illustrating Rosen's point, Telstar's initial television test consisted of little else besides images of the American flag outside of the Andover station broadcast to France before having to sign off.

Less than two weeks later, the first public transatlantic television broadcast took place using Telstar 1. Narrated by Walter Cronkite, the program relayed live television events to Europe, including snippets of a news conference featuring Kennedy; a Chicago Cubs and Philadelphia Phillies game; a Canadian Shakespeare festival, where actors rehearsed *Macbeth*; and an interview with astronauts at Cape Canaveral, among other brief images. The next go-round, Europe returned the favor with shots of the continent's cultural masterpieces, including the Louvre, the Sistine Chapel, the Tower of London, and other sites, before the broadcast abruptly ended when Telstar went out of range of the Maine station.

Bell Labs may have gotten an early lead, but soon it would be Rosen and his team's turn to show Syncom's capabilities. Meanwhile, AT&T's plan for a constellation of Telstar satellites to provide global coverage was being derailed.

The U.S. government had been deliberating on what kind of entity could best oversee the burgeoning satellite communications industry ever since Project Echo's launch in the summer of 1960. This need had become ever more urgent with the newer satellites being built and nearing launch readiness. In the fall of 1961, the Kennedy administration established an informal interagency group—made up of Rubel, representing the DOD, and other administrators from the State Department, NASA, the Space Council, and the Justice Department—to study the matter. They proposed the creation of the Communications Satellite Corporation (COMSAT), a federally funded private-public partnership charged with developing a communication satellite system. The administration believed the bill would sail through Congress. They were wrong.

By January 1962, there were three competing communication satellite bills. A compromise bill easily passed in the House in May, but it sparked raucous debate on the floor of the Senate. The going was so rocky that many feared a satellite bill might not make it out alive before the end of the year.

"When this bill first started out I thought it was as crooked as a dog's hind leg," proclaimed Democratic Senator Russell B. Long, of Louisiana, who opposed the bill. "I am now convinced that that would be a compliment. This bill is as crooked as a barrel of snakes."

Kennedy's plan faced off against a bill presented by Estes Kefauver, a staunch antitrust advocate who headed up the Senate Antitrust and Monopoly Subcommittee. Kefauver was driven by the belief that AT&T had a stranglehold on the country's communication capabilities. His bill called for a satellite system owned and operated by the government. After all, the development of such an important natural resource as space should be firmly in the hands of the government, not private enterprise, he explained. He called Kennedy's plan "the biggest giveaway in the history of our nation" since it would "grant to a favored few the right to exploit this resource for their private financial gain."

The Democrat from Tennessee had become famous a decade earlier when he took on organized crime, heading up the Senate Special Committee to Investigate Crime in Interstate Commerce, which quickly became known as the Kefauver Committee. The committee, which traveled to fourteen cities, held televised hearings that made both Kefauver and the Mafia famous.

He had clout and the backing of some other heavy-hitting Democratic senators in his fight against Kennedy's communication satellite proposal.

Among his principal arguments for government ownership was one that was especially good for Rosen, Hughes, and Syncom. The senator argued that if AT&T and the other major players had their way, the corporation would focus on low-orbit satellites instead of geosynchronous ones, which would delay the creation of what he believed would be a superior satellite communication system.

"I have, of course, pointed out that if a Telstar system is agreed upon and is initially put into operation, I find in the bill no effective way of us getting quickly to a Syncom system when that better system proves to be feasible, as undoubtedly it shortly will," the tall, bespectacled Kefauver told his fellow senators during a hearing on April 10, 1962, before the Committee on Commerce. He emphasized that Syncom was being built by Hughes for the government, the type of relationship that could continue to work without corporate control.

"We are going ahead full steam with the development of the Syncom high-altitude satellite . . . All of the going ahead full steam is being done by the government or by private industry under government control," he said in his understated Southern accent.

He later introduced an amendment that would have forced Kennedy to decide immediately on which system, low- or high-orbit, to pursue. It was shot down in a fifty-four-to-fourteen vote.

A competing bill, shepherded by Oklahoma Democrat Robert Kerr, chair of the Senate Committee on Aeronautical and Space Sciences, would give ownership of the new corporation to AT&T and the other communication companies—RCA, Western Union International Corporation, and International Telephone and Telegraph—with minimal government interference, which could keep Hughes and a commercial version of Syncom from becoming a reality for many years, if ever, because of their focus on lower-orbit satellites.

For weeks the hearings dragged on and continued onto the full Senate floor once they'd hammered out a compromise bill in the summer of 1962, similar to the one passed in the House. The debates became rather acrimonious with unfounded allegations tossed around that the communication companies had attempted to bribe senators for their support.

Kefauver and his allies filibustered against the Kennedy bill for four days until the bill's supporters cobbled together a two-thirds majority to invoke cloture, the first time it had been used since 1927, ending Kefauver's filibuster.

The Senate passed the Communications Satellite Act on August 17, 1962, and among its provisions, it authorized the establishment of the for-profit Communications Satellite Corporation (COMSAT) with ownership evenly divided between publicly available Class A stock at one hundred dollars a share, and Class B stock, reserved for approved communications carriers. A fifteen-person board of directors oversaw COMSAT. The U.S. president got to choose three members; six came from the Class A stockholders, and the last six from the commercial carriers, elected annually. In order to keep the carriers from gaining control of the corporation, the act limited the amount of stock that could be owned by the companies to 50 percent of the voting stock outstanding, and it couldn't exceed the total number of shares purchased by the public, among other measures.

The Federal Communications Commission would oversee the corporation with NASA handling technical aspects and dealing with the telecommunication administrations of foreign governments.

Kefauver and Congressman William Ryan, of New York, called on House members to reject the Senate version of the bill that had returned to the House for final approval. The attempt failed.

On August 31, 1962, Kennedy, surrounded by members of Congress and his administration, signed the bill into law, handing out souvenir pens and saying that the new system would "contribute to world peace and understanding." Of the controversies surrounding its creation and the worries of Kefauver and others about COMSAT, the president said, "no single company or group will have the power to dominate the corporation."

The creation of COMSAT obliterated AT&T's hopes of owning and operating its own fleet of Telstar satellites. They'd invested millions of dollars, and now the best they could do was buy the maximum stock they were legally allowed to in COMSAT and hope they could convince the corporation to focus on low-orbit satellites.

The path was now clear for Rosen and his Syncom satellite to prove that a high-orbit system was not only possible but better than a Telstar-style constellation of low-orbit satellites. The government, industry, press, and public waited impatiently for liftoff. But first, another contender blasted off. On December 13, 1962, the RCA-NASA Relay medium-orbit satellite reached orbit 4,623 miles above Earth, but technical problems kept it from coming online for two weeks. Rosen wasn't really worried. Relay, like Telstar, didn't have Syncom's capabilities. Rosen couldn't wait to show a world in awe of his competitors' satellites just what he and Syncom could do.

In October 1962, as Rosen and his team made final preparations for Syncom's launch scheduled for early 1963, the United States and the Soviet Union stumbled toward the edge of nuclear war. On October 22, Kennedy addressed the nation, telling its citizens that the Soviets had secretly begun installing nuclear missiles in Cuba. The president reported that he had ordered a naval blockade around Cuba and that military action was on the table.

"We will not prematurely or unnecessarily risk the costs of world-wide nuclear war in which even the fruits of victory would be ashes in our mouth—but neither will we shrink from that risk at any time it must be faced," he told the country during the speech, in which he showed little emotion.

Like many Americans, Rosen was shocked and scared by the news. Unlike many, though, who were in denial or suffered paralysis in the face of potential annihilation, Rosen and his son Robert, not yet a teen, attempted to do something about it. They went to a nearby beach and filled sandbags with sand, which they put on the roof of their house, hoping it would act as a barrier against nuclear fallout.

A week later it was all over. Soviet Premier Nikita Khrushchev blinked and agreed to remove the missiles if the United States agreed not to invade Cuba. The United States also secretly agreed to remove its missiles from Turkey. The two superpowers slowly inched away from the edge and the Cold War returned to being just that. With the crisis averted, Americans got back to their everyday lives, and the engineers at Hughes continued finalizing plans for Syncom 1's launch.

On February 14, 1963, Rosen veered from nervousness to excitement, while retaining his razor focus, as Syncom prepared to liftoff at Cape Canaveral, from Launch Complex 17B.

The site, then run by the air force, was just south of a stretch of land nicknamed Missile Row where launch sites ranged along the thirty-four-mile-long coast of the barren barrier island lying between the Banana River and the Atlantic. Steel and concrete had become more plentiful than the scrub brush and palmettos that had dotted the beaches before the U.S. government transformed the cape into the epicenter for the country's push into space.

Rosen and the other Hughes engineers gathered to watch the launch from Hanger AE Control Center, a single-story warehouse-style building where NASA technicians hunched over the various telemetry instruments that would monitor the launch vehicle as it guided Syncom into geosynchronous orbit.

The seconds ticked down and with a ground-shaking roar, the rocket spit fire and smoke, streaking upward into the night sky, a fiery star moving ever upward. It was 12:35 a.m. on Valentine's Day when the rocket lit up the dark over the Atlantic Ocean heading toward its new home. Everything had to be precise. If the Delta rocket didn't get Syncom high enough, the satellite wouldn't reach the correct orbit, which meant it wouldn't be synchronous—too close to Earth and it would be in less than a twenty-four-hour orbit, too far and it would take longer to complete its journey around the planet.

The Thor-Delta B rocket performed flawlessly. A perfectly choreographed ballet of complicated technical maneuvers followed and put the satellite close to its destination in an elliptical transfer orbit. About seven minutes after blastoff, Syncom 1 was set to spinning at around 150 revolutions per minute and released to coast toward the transfer orbit's apogee—its farthest point from the planet—when another rocket attached to the satellite would launch it toward its final twenty-four-hour orbit near the equator between Madagascar and the coast of East Africa.

After years of struggle, Rosen and his team were elated. NASA engineers ran tests on the spacecraft and for five hours everything worked as it should. The next stage involved a twenty-two-second burn of the satellite's apogee kick rocket to place Syncom into its final orbit. At 5:42 a.m., the rocket fired as planned and burned for twenty-one seconds, then suddenly all the signals disappeared. The tracking stations lost radio contact with the satellite. The room went quiet. Something had happened. Something terrible. The tracking station in Johannesburg, South Africa, and the USNS *Kingsport*, anchored at harbor in Lagos, Nigeria, tried their best to locate a signal but had no success.

The team surmised some possibilities of what had gone wrong: perhaps the satellite's temperature was too hot and this was interfering with its communication equipment, or it could have failed to reach its intended target and was hurtling through space in an elliptical orbit lower or higher than it was supposed to be.

In the coming days more ground stations around the globe joined in the hunt for Syncom. The satellite's apparent disappearance made international headlines.

It was a devastating blow to Rosen and the rest of Hughes. For years afterward when Rosen discussed the launch, he would tear up. The disappointment was nearly unbearable. A few weeks later, they received the news they'd dreaded. The Baker-Schmidt telescope-camera located at the Boyden Observatory in South Africa had captured an image of the dead satellite tumbling end over end more than twenty-two thousand miles above Earth. The head of the Harvard Observatory, Donald Menzel, compared the feat to photographing a golf ball in San Francisco from New York City.

As gut-wrenching as the news was, Rosen knew he didn't have time to mourn. He needed to focus on Syncom 2. He couldn't fail a second time. The 350 other Hughes employees involved in the project were relying on him and his satellite.

11

René Roy

RENÉ MORIN HAD BEEN SURPRISED AND HAPPY TO SEE LEMAY when he unexpectedly showed up in Miami on a yacht in early December 1961. With Lemay was a beautiful singer, her brothers André and Yvon, and a tall, heavyset man who looked like he was no stranger to trouble.

Morin's old friend hadn't changed. He was still charming, jovial, and flashy—he seemed to have an endless supply of cash—and still had a love for the nightlife, even though he wasn't a big drinker. Lemay was still in great shape despite his love for Montreal's famous smoked meat sandwiches, which he swore he could live on.

Soon after Lemay arrived in Miami, he asked Morin to open a safe-deposit box for him at a local bank. Lemay deposited a fat stack of cash and an equally enormous amount of traveler's checks. Whether it was out of loyalty, fear, or the belief they would eventually see some financial gain, the friends and family of Lemay and his gang were more than happy to open bank accounts for them when asked.

Toward the end of December 1961, Lemay flew back to Montreal and picked up his jet-black Pontiac convertible with a blood-red interior and drove it back to Miami, a dark-haired twenty-four-year-old woman named

Micheline Meunier in the passenger's seat. Micheline was Morin's cousin. He had promised to get her a job waiting tables in Miami, but the position fell through since the young woman didn't have proper working papers. She was happy enough sunning herself on the deck of the *Anou* and playing companion to Lemay for a few weeks.

On Friday, January 5, 1962, Lemay's contacts in Montreal warned him within hours of the police raids on Lemay's chalet and the arrest of his gang. It was time to leave Miami.

He called the Lemieuxs' brother-in-law, Jean-Guy Richer—whom he'd left in charge of his chalet—at his auto repair shop in Saint-Adèle. Richer owed Lemay three thousand dollars and wouldn't dare avoid a call from the Lord of the North.

"What's going on up north?" he asked Richer.

"André's been arrested."

"So it's true."

He hung up and thought about his next move.

By that Monday, January 8, when the Montreal Police issued a warrant for his arrest, Lemay had finished his business in Florida and was ready to leave. He'd cleared out his safe-deposit box at the First National Bank that Morin had helped him open and said goodbye to the boat he'd had so many memorable times on. Lemay hated to leave it, but he knew the cops would have an easier time catching him on a luxurious and very conspicuous yacht than in a car. He could always buy another boat.

That evening, as Lemay prepared to leave, an employee from the Ocean Ranch Hotel stopped him.

"Hello, Mr. Lemay," the man called, hurrying over to the French Canadian who always seemed to have a cigarette dangling from his mouth and walked with his hands behind his back. "When is Mr. Primeau expected back from Montreal?" Primeau had asked about renting a suite at the hotel.

"Unfortunately, he's been detained in Montreal," Lemay answered in his accented English. "I also have to go back to Canada."

The employee said he understood and wished Lemay the best. Lemay's little joke about his associate being "detained" was lost on the man.

Lemay left the *Anou*'s keys with Morin, telling him he was leaving town for a while. He asked him to look after the yacht and told him he would phone with more instructions soon. A few days later, Lemay called Morin from the road and asked him to remove two suitcases from the boat and deliver them to a motel. He also asked Morin to do something else on the *Anou*, a request that left the mechanic wondering what he was getting himself into.

Following Lemay's orders, Morin went onto the *Anou* and removed a radio and two walkie-talkies. From a trapdoor in the ship's master cabin, he also pulled out some expensive-looking jewelry, including a medallion and several pairs of bejeweled earrings. He gave the radio and walkie-talkies to his kids to play with and threw almost all the other items off the South Miami Avenue Bridge. Against Lemay's orders, he kept a valuable ring that he later sold.

Once the news broke about Lemay's role in the bank burglary, Morin called the U.S. Coast Guard to report where they could find the yacht. A Montreal detective, Léon St. Pierre, showed up at his house a few days later. Morin told the detective what he knew and turned over the radio and walkie-talkies. He didn't mention the ring he'd kept.

By the time St. Pierre got a warrant to search the *Anou* with the help of the Miami Police, Lemay already had a four-day head start. He was speeding across the country on the open road, the top down, the wind in his hair, and a beautiful raven-haired woman in the passenger seat.

Lemay and Micheline stayed together for a week in New York City before she returned to Montreal. Lemay spent the next few months traveling around the United States, with longer stopovers in New York City and in Las Vegas, where he would return often, lured by the siren song of the gaming tables. Lemay frequently returned to Montreal without being detected. In 1962, a passport wasn't required at the porous border between the United States and Canada. All that was needed was a driver's license, and Lemay had a fake one that worked nicely.

* * *

Yvon, the youngest member of Lemay's gang, spent his twentieth birthday behind bars at Montreal's Bordeaux Jail waiting for his trial. Finally, on

October 26, 1962, he appeared in court represented by the same lawyers who defended his siblings and Primeau. The attorneys had worked out a plea deal with Wagner, the prosecutor. If Yvon pleaded guilty, he'd get four years minus the ten months he'd sat in jail waiting for trial. The prosecutor gave a flowery speech to the judge on why Yvon deserved leniency, very reminiscent of the one he gave for Yvon's sister, Lise, a few months earlier.

"It's often repeated that justice is a woman with veiled eyes, but that's not the case," Wagner said. "She is always clairvoyant, lucid, objective. She knows how to divide responsibilities."

Wagner called Lemay "an evil, diabolical genius" who was the mastermind of the heist, used Yvon as an "instrument," and had managed to escape justice so far. Yvon, on the other hand, knew he was guilty, was ready to take responsibility for his actions, didn't have a criminal record, and was quite young.

Maranda, one of Yvon's defense attorneys, thanked the prosecutor for his "impartiality and great spirit of justice" and enjoined in asking the judge to go easy on Yvon, which he did compared to what Primeau received for the same crime.

That same month, Lise gave birth to a daughter she named Josée. Lemay would see his daughter as soon as he was able, Lise knew.

* * *

In May 1963, Jacques Lajoie was again on the witness stand. This time he was in Saint-Jerome selling out his accomplices in one of the many crimes stemming from his burglary spree in December 1961. Lajoie had already pleaded guilty to the charges for these break-ins in March, and he hoped it was the last hurdle he'd have to jump through before the Crown prosecutor resolved his bank burglary case and the forgery charges that landed him in jail.

He was testifying against two members of his burglary crew, Marcel Paquin and Jean-Guy Richer, for the break-in of a business in Saint-Adèle and theft of a safe they found inside.

Richer was the brother-in-law of the Lemieux brothers and was responsible for watching Lemay's chalet and keeping him updated on happenings in Montreal. Together with Lajoie, Paquin, and Richard Lemieux, the youngest of the Lemieux siblings, Richer had hauled the three-hundred-pound safe to a friend's basement, where they used an acetylene torch to cut it open.

It was a sad haul for all the work they put into the break-in. Inside there was little more than one hundred dollars and a bunch of checks they couldn't cash.

The cops later found the pieces of the safe half buried in a pile of scrap metal and dirt at Richer's auto garage, which the gang used as a meeting place and hideout during their burglary spree that winter.

The authorities added these charges to the couple dozen others they'd piled on Lajoie and his crew.

Lajoie had grown quite fat in prison, waiting for his cases to be resolved. He'd continued to enjoy a host of privileges, including a special menu that he ate separately from his fellow inmates. Detectives Leblanc and St. Pierre chauffeured him to a Montreal Police station where he could spend time with his girlfriend, Claudette. His cell door continued to be kept unlocked. Even so, he was depressed, so much so that he saw a psychiatrist while in jail. He also had to have hemorrhoid surgery. While in the hospital in Sherbrooke, one hundred miles east of Montreal, he wasn't guarded and could roam the halls freely.

Finally, after spending nearly two years in jail, on Friday, September 20, 1963, Lajoie, now forty-two years old, appeared in court in Montreal and pleaded guilty to the Bank of Nova Scotia burglary.

Wagner, who only days before had become a judge, appeared for the Crown and praised Lajoie's cooperation in the case against Primeau.

Judge Roger Ouimet, who presided in Primeau's trial and had given him a severe sentence, was lenient in Lajoie's case for helping the police "clear up this matter." He gave Lajoie one day in prison and ordered him to pay a $950 bond that he'd get back in two years if he committed no crimes during that time. All of Lajoie's outstanding cases—bank heist, chalet burglaries, and check forgeries—had been wrapped up in a neat little bow and disposed of. Lajoie was now a free man but knew his work for the cops and prosecutors wasn't over. The judge ordered Lajoie to keep in contact with the court. He would also have to testify against the other members of the gang, André Lemieux and Georges Lemay, if the cops ever caught them.

Primeau was the unluckiest of the bunch. In February 1963, the court threw out his appeal. He would serve all of his thirteen-year sentence. The Court of Appeal panel, made up of five justices, stated in its report that Primeau acted as Lemay's lieutenant during the break-in, collaborating with the others, and used his experience to help pull off this "diabolical" crime. When caught, he didn't help "justice," instead he "persisted in denying" his guilt. For this, the justices decided that there was no probability Primeau could be rehabilitated and therefore would serve his entire sentence.

* * *

Lemay had been working on getting a false passport for an extra layer of security, and with the help of his sisters in Canada, he finally got one in early 1963. He was then staying in Manhattan, where a doctor examined him as part of the paperwork needed for his passport. It was the only authentic document he submitted to the Canadian government in his application. Everything else was forged.

By January 1963, Lemay no longer existed. He was now Joseph-René Roy, and he had a valid Canadian passport issued in Ottawa, the capital, by the federal Department of External Affairs, to prove it. The real Roy was a French Canadian charter-boat captain in the Florida Keys, who had no idea another man was running around using his name.

Lemay grew tired of bouncing around from place to place, so after getting his new passport, he headed to Vancouver.

Vancouver in 1963 was, like Montreal, in the middle of a building boom. High-rises sprang up downtown amid the push for "urban renewal." The population nearly doubled from 1960 to 1970, from 620,000 to 1.05 million. It had the largest port in Canada and an international airport that was Canada's western base for flights and port of entry for travelers from across the Pacific. In 1963, the city, at 726,000 residents, was roughly a third of the size of Montreal, a provincial outpost by comparison, yet it had a wider, open feel to it that made it seem vast in comparison to the narrow, crooked streets of Lemay's hometown. Montreal had an old-world quality, while Vancouver, which was founded more than 240 years later, felt as if you expected the West to feel: wild and expansive and free.

The North Shore Mountains loom over the city, which is bordered by the Fraser River to the south and the Burrard Inlet to the north, where you can soak up the sun at English Bay Beach or wander through the thousand-acre Stanley Park with its aquarium, seawall, and wild array of flora, one of the largest urban parks in North America. To the west is the Strait of Georgia and Vancouver Island, which protect the city's flank from the vastness of the Pacific.

Plus, the city's nightlife was stellar. Downtown, neon-drenched Granville Street held clubs and cabarets and upscale eateries. There were also dives, diners, and low-rent strip joints. Further north, in West End, was the slightly older Cave Supper Club, where fake stalactites hung above a hangar-like space that hosted everyone from Josephine Baker to Lenny Bruce. At Isy's Supper Club you could see everything from Bobby Darin to burlesque. Lemay loved jazz, and the Cellar, an underground club, brought in some of the best acts around, including Ornette Coleman, Charles Mingus, and Stan Getz.

It was all a short distance from British Columbia's vast wilderness, where the hunting and fishing in the myriad lakes, rivers, and streams couldn't be beat.

Lemay liked Vancouver enough to settle down for nearly a year. But in the summer of 1964, he headed back to Florida, crossing the border at Blaine, Washington, with his jazz record collection. Having grown bored with life on land, he was looking to buy a new yacht. He'd reconnected with Lise and had finally met his daughter, Josée, and was thinking about the future.

12

International Manhunt

FALL 1963–FALL 1964

BY THE FALL OF 1963, WHEN GEORGE B. MCCLELLAN, A ramrod-straight officer who sported an impeccably groomed mustache, stepped into the role of commissioner of the RCMP, a four-continent manhunt had been in full swing for months with no success, and McClellan wanted results. He had been in the Mounties for thirty years and had risen through the ranks to become assistant commissioner to Clifford Harvison. Harvison had retired after having helped tighten the force's relationships with other police agencies, such as the FBI and Interpol—not that it helped with Lemay, who had been on the loose for more than two years.

Where Harvison was all about relationship building, McClellan brought a focus on intelligence gathering to the role. Back in World War II, he'd worked closely with British intelligence on Camp X, a secret British counterintelligence training center near Toronto that instructed covert operatives, including members of the FBI and OSS, the precursor to the CIA, in sabotage techniques, intelligence gathering, explosives training, the art of silent killing, and unarmed combat, among other paramilitary skills.

Under McClellan's tenure, the RCMP expanded covert intelligence

116

gathering, especially on French Canadian separatists, Communist Party members, and organized crime.

He also expanded the force's Identification Branch, responsible for collecting and annotating criminal and missing person records. Their new system used criminal identification cards, color-coded index cards that organized their ever-growing list of known criminals by the type of crime they specialized in. At a time before national computer crime databases, this system provided a way for investigators to identify fugitives and share information on crimes. McClellan also beefed up the Crime Detection Laboratories, the forensic arm of the RCMP. He increased the number of police stations with Telex teleprinter systems, electromechanical devices used to send and receive typed messages, and he increased the use of mobile two-way radios.

The improvements meant that the Mounties, whose official role in the Lemay case began just days after a Montreal judge signed his arrest warrant in January 1962, were poised to take the manhunt to the next level. Working with the FBI and Interpol, the RCMP hoped to throw a worldwide net in which to trap the slippery bank burglar.

Through Interpol, the RCMP got in touch with the Haitian National Police after an alleged sighting of Lemay in Pétion-Ville, a city just south of the capital, Port-au-Prince, in February 1962. He was reportedly with an Italian from Montreal who was a "thug of the first water" and was "loaded with money." The RCMP sent wanted posters, but to no avail.

The interagency collaboration wasn't without its hiccups. In February 1962, Interpol planned to issue an international wanted circular to be sent to all eighty-five member countries, but the Montreal Police dropped the ball on getting the needed paperwork done. It took a sternly worded RCMP letter to the Montreal Police in order to get the forms to Interpol, which then issued the wanted circular in May 1962.

In the meantime, the Mounties distributed their own circulars written in English, French, and Spanish to authorities in Argentina, Cuba, and Australia, but no leads panned out, even after they raised the reward money from two thousand dollars to ten thousand dollars (seventy-five thousand dollars in today's U.S. currency).

In January 1963, the RCMP received information that Armand Duhamel was traveling from Honolulu to Tokyo. Duhamel, a big-game hunter and one of the biggest fences for the Montreal Mafia, was one of Lemay's known criminal associates. He was involved in the 1957 Outremont bank burglary. Duhamel's traveling companion was Raymond Daoust, Lemay's former brother-in-law and by then a famous defense attorney with ties to both the Mafia and the Castro regime. According to the informant, Duhamel was supposed to make contact with Lemay in either Japan or Hong Kong. The agency contacted the FBI and Interpol in Tokyo, Hong Kong, Rome, and Paris, advising them to be on the lookout for Lemay. Nothing came of this tip either.

When McClellan became commissioner in November 1963, he believed a shake-up was in order. The longer Lemay was free, the worse it reflected on the RCMP, especially considering McClellan's new focus on intelligence gathering.

Days stretched into weeks, then months with nothing in the way of progress in capturing Lemay. The FBI provided the bare minimum in help, perhaps because Lemay wasn't wanted by U.S. authorities.

Back in Montreal, the police had bigger problems to deal with.

By May 1964, the Lemay case was no longer a top priority. The city remained the bank robbery capital of North America, and the police focused on current crimes, not those from three years earlier in which most of the culprits were already behind bars.

Besides the run-of-the-mill crooks and mafiosi that plagued the city, a new and much more frightening crime wave gripped Montreal and the rest of the province beginning in the spring of 1963.

The first hints of what was to come happened on March 7, 1963. Someone planted Molotov cocktails at three army barracks in Montreal and Westmount, an affluent suburb. The devices failed to explode, but the leaflets that fluttered through Montreal's streets that night announced a truly explosive event: the birth of the Front de Libération du Québec (the Quebec Liberation Front, or FLQ), a paramilitary French Canadian separatist group that hoped to create a French Canadian homeland free from the rest of Canada. The nine-by-twelve-inch pieces of paper distributed by the FLQ sported a crudely drawn flag—one side featured a blue field and the other a red star on a white background—in crayon and a manifesto. The leaflet, written in French, warned that "suicide-commandos" planned to destroy, by systematic sabotage, "all the symbols and colonial institutions (federal), in particular the RCMP and the armed forces; All the information media of the colonial language (English) which holds us in contempt; All enterprises and commercial establishments which practice discrimination against Quebec people, which do not use French as their primary language, which have signs in the colonial language (English);" and "All the factories that discriminate against French-speaking workers."

From April to June, the FLQ bombing campaign kept the police on high alert and nearly shut down Montreal as the violence swept across the city and the province like a shockwave.

Detective Leo Plouffe became nearly a one-man bomb squad in charge of a small, inexperienced team, forced to dismantle the more and more complex explosive devices as the FLQ graduated from defective Molotov cocktails to time bombs with multiple sticks of dynamite.

Plouffe was on twenty-four-hour call through May. After working long shifts, he would collapse on his living room floor, too tired to even make it to bed, only to be called back to duty a few minutes after drifting off. Some days he didn't sleep at all. His longest stretch was a mind-numbing fifty hours, a dangerous situation to be in for a job requiring a steady hand and alert mind. Somehow, he made it through, and on June 1, 1963, the Montreal Police arrested eight suspected FLQ members in a surprise raid.

The reign of terror that killed one civilian, maimed and nearly killed an army bomb disposal expert working with Plouffe, and damaged numerous federal buildings, was over. For the moment.

Always a tinkerer, Plouffe invented an insulated box filled with liquid nitrogen that could freeze a bomb's timing mechanism and reduce the explosive to powder once dropped inside. He also invented a portable shield with blast-resistant gloves. In addition to disarming bombs, Plouffe continued making a name for himself in forensic science. Among his many cases, in October 1961, he tied a bank robber to the vandalism of several masterpieces at the Montreal Museum of Fine Arts through paint stains found on the scabbard of the man's knife.

By the spring of 1964, the forty-one-year-old detective was exhausted. A second wave of separatist violence, consisting mostly of raids and bombings on federal armories, had arrived in the fall of 1963.

In the early morning of May 19, 1964, an anonymous phone call alerted police to a bomb on the Victoria Bridge, spanning the Saint Lawrence River and linking Montreal to Saint-Lambert on the south shore. Plouffe was again summoned. His fellow officers were busy quelling student demonstrations downtown that resulted in eighty-five arrests, traffic jams, and headaches for the city's cops.

Plouffe examined the device, an old army shell casing filled with explosives and wrapped in plastic, and he determined the bomber had created it with the intent to maximize the amount of shrapnel. If it went off, it would tear him to pieces. His solution was to simply drop it into the river. He was so tired.

* * *

On May 29, 1964, the RCMP sent a letter to the director of the Montreal Police, J. Adrien Robert, pointedly mentioning that there had been no communication concerning Lemay between the two agencies in nearly a year. The letter inquired about whether the ten-thousand-dollar reward was still active and mentioned that the RCMP was then considering putting Lemay on the Most Wanted List, believing "this matter is of sufficient magnitude to be included" among Canada's top fugitives.

Canada's Most Wanted List hadn't been updated in two years. There were only two fugitives on the list, a murderer who killed his father back in 1949 and then went on the run and a bank robber who'd made a daring escape on his way to trial in Toronto in 1957.

Given what the Montreal Police were up against, it took two weeks for them to respond to the RCMP's inquiries, and the letter came from Assistant Director Romeo Longpré, not Director Robert. Longpré's response stated that the reward was still valid, that there was nothing new

to report on their end, and that they "heartily" endorsed the plan to include Lemay on the Most Wanted List.

In July, the RCMP officially added Lemay to the list. Lemay was said
to be "possibly armed and should be considered dangerous." The publicity
surrounding Lemay making the Most Wanted List and the ten-thousand-
dollar reward generated a slew of leads from across Canada that police
had to look into, no matter how ridiculous they seemed.

* * *

On the night of August 14, Corporal R. Pypper, attached to the RCMP
substation in Gleichen, Alberta, received information that someone
had seen Lemay shopping at the Safeway grocery store a week earlier in
Banff, 135 miles west of Gleichen. He was described as having a mustache and wearing dark glasses, a deep V-neck black sweater, and a yachtsman's cap. He was nicely tanned and was in the company of an attractive
petite brunette with heavy makeup and a sallow complexion. After shopping, they left the parking lot in a light-green Pontiac station wagon.

The RCMP sent out a telex to all its regional subdivisions the next
morning and conducted inquires in Banff, a resort town in a national park
within the Canadian Rocky Mountains, but no employees at the large
supermarket, where there were around two hundred shoppers on the afternoon in question, remembered seeing the suspect.

The investigators had similar results with their two-day-long search
of the campgrounds near Banff and those farther into the national park.
Officers slowly drove their cruisers past campsites jammed with tents,
kids, and campers during the height of the summer season; checked the
registration information for the campgrounds; and questioned all the
staff, showing them a photograph of Lemay, all to no avail. The same went
for all of Banff's major hotels, from the historic Banff Springs Hotel, a
glamorous castle-like hotel with sweeping views, to the brand-new Voy-
ager Inn with its modernist design. Everyone from the doormen to the
hotel security guards stared at the photo of Lemay without a glimmer of
recognition. No one had seen the mysterious man with a mustache and
yachtsman's cap.

Supposed sightings of Lemay farther west held some promise.

One older woman, "by no means doddering," in her own words, sent a two-page letter to the RCMP detailing a conversation she said she had with Lemay as she was out walking one afternoon in May 1964. The woman lived in Victoria, British Columbia, a forty-five-minute ferry ride from Vancouver, and she described everything from the "gorgeous" weather to the "rocky sea front" she alleged she'd strolled along with Lemay.

She recalled that the man wore a "jacket, sports shirt, slacks, and thick rubber-soled shoes, all of fine quality" and chatted about how he was traveling around by yacht.

"I've been seeing a lot of the United States," he told her. "In the past two years I've been to twenty-four states."

While they walked, the woman noticed that although "he chatted with an easy patter," he remained vigilant of his surroundings—"plainly awake and knew what he was doing"—and she suspected he was a criminal of some sort.

At one point they stopped to look at the rising smoke of a driftwood fire on the beach. He lightly put his hands on her shoulders. She flinched and moved away slightly.

"You are very sensitive," he said.

"Why do you say that?"

"Well, you gave a little jump when I touched you," he responded.

"Oh, I'm highly nervous."

"What makes you nervous?"

"Oh, I am just that way, although I don't look it," she said. "I have had a lot of illness."

After this exchange, the woman felt nervous and left, walking hurriedly to a nearby shopping center, leaving the stranger behind.

"I would adjudge him to be a clever, capable man—not intellectual, but very perceptive," she wrote to the RCMP.

She didn't give her name in the correspondence, instead signing it "For Law and Order" because she had "a great distaste for publicity in connection with crime." The letter was long on purple prose and short on useable information. Inspector G. N. Jones, of the RCMP Criminal

Investigations Branch at the headquarters in Ottawa, found that the woman's account wasn't "consistent with Lemay's general description." Even so, since Lemay was "urgently being sought by all police forces and all leads must be followed," he requested the Victoria, B.C., "E" Division follow up with inquiries to establish whether Lemay was on the West Coast, especially considering another report from farther in the interior of British Columbia that had recently surfaced.

A truck driver eating a quick breakfast at a Monte Lake diner on August 10 couldn't help noticing two men sitting nearby discussing the best type of lures for various fish. One man was slightly on the short and stocky side and was wearing a sports shirt and dark trousers. He was with a man who looked a little younger and was slim and muscular. That night, when the trucker was back home in Vernon, forty miles southeast of where he'd eaten breakfast, he sat down to read the local paper. The front page included a picture of one of Canada's most wanted criminals. This Lemay character looked just like the man he'd seen that morning. He called the Mounties to report the sighting.

Similarly, a man traveling on August 17 by bus from British Columbia to Alberta swore he saw Lemay and another man sitting a few seats away from him. He recognized the criminal when he read a newspaper account of the RCMP manhunt centered on Kamloops, B.C., thirty miles from Monte Lake.

The newspapers had gotten ahold of the story after the Mounties sent out a press release, but reporters bungled the facts. Multiple newspapers reported that Lemay had been seen with an escaped convict named Adolphe Karchesky, who had been serving a life sentence for more than a dozen armed robberies before his escape from a Kingston, Ontario, prison. The news reported that the two men were "living off the woods" in the interior of British Columbia near "a remote lake." Karchesky had been added to the country's Most Wanted List at the same time as Lemay, and reporters apparently conflated this with the man allegedly seen with Lemay. The search in British Columbia turned up neither Lemay nor Karchesky.

But back in Quebec, Detective Leblanc had better luck. He caught

Karchesky in Montreal in August after a citizen recognized the fugitive. With guns drawn, Leblanc and two other Montreal cops burst into the apartment where Karchesky was staying. The fugitive was in the middle of making coffee and went quietly. He'd been in Montreal since his escape, laboring as a construction worker. He hadn't been on the West Coast with Lemay. The court sentenced him to an additional year and sent him back to the prison he'd escaped from four months earlier. With Karchesky's arrest, Lemay became the number one most wanted criminal in Canada.

The RCMP was still no closer to catching him. Sending out wanted circulars through the various police departments was a laborious and costly process, and even the press they'd managed to generate through newspapers only went so far. They needed something big, something new that could generate worldwide interest and reach a mass audience in one fell swoop. Until that day arrived the RCMP would have to continue doing things the only way they knew how.

They sent the Vancouver Police photos of Lemay in time for the city's annual fifteen-day summer fair celebrating the region's industry, agriculture, and domestic arts. First held in 1910, Vancouver's Pacific National Exhibition drew hundreds of thousands of visitors "not only from British Columbia, but Western Canada, and the U.S.A., as well," according to Superintendent C. E. Speers, the RCMP officer in charge of the Criminal Identification Branch for the region. It was an especially busy fair that year since the Beatles performed there in August. The RCMP hoped that with all those visitors in one place, someone might recognize or have information on the fugitive. Nothing came of it.

"E" Division finished up its report in September. They weren't able to track down the "Law and Order" woman who wrote the anonymous letter and concluded that since "there has been no information at this office in the past indicating that Georges Lemay is on the West Coast," he must not have been in the area. They were wrong; he'd been there, but by September, when they finished their report, he was already back in the United States buying a new yacht after a trip to Las Vegas with Lise. Once again, Lemay was several steps ahead of the RCMP. The publicity generated by Lemay's inclusion on the Most Wanted List, instead of help-ing capture him, only resulted in more dead ends.

Rosen and his team at Hughes had also met with dead ends that year. Even as they recovered from the tragic loss of Syncom 1 and tried to fig-ure out what could have gone so wrong, they were already preparing for another attempt to reach the highest heights.

13

Stationary

SPRING 1963–FALL 1964

ROSEN AND HIS TEAM DETERMINED THAT THE LIKELIEST CAUSE for Syncom 1's demise was the apogee motor exploding, a burst nitrogen tank, or a problem with the wiring. Rosen favored the apogee motor as the culprit and changed manufacturers for the part. To cover all the possibilities, however, the team also addressed the other two potential problems. They were going to make damn sure there wouldn't be a second failure.

Four months after the disastrous first launch, on July 8, 1963, Hughes shipped Syncom 2 to Cape Canaveral for a launch scheduled later that month.

NASA technicians put the satellite through its paces, testing its various systems for every conceivable scenario, even those Rosen felt were "imaginary problems." Parts of the satellite that failed to operate to these new exacting standards were swapped out, which pushed the launch back a few days. Everyone involved knew there was no room for failure.

By July 22, NASA had cleared the satellite for launch. The apogee motor was attached. It had been married to the booster and was sitting on Pad 17A, across from Pad 17B, where Syncom 1 had blasted off to its fate.

The rocket looked like a giant syringe with the thicker first stage—a

Thor missile—at the bottom, tapering up to the second-stage Delta B rocket. An Altair solid-fuel rocket comprised the third stage. Syncom sat at the launch vehicle's tip, safe under a protective nose fairing.

The launch day countdown began at 5:51 p.m. As the minutes ticked down, NASA ran the first spacecraft function test. There was a problem. The test revealed one of Syncom 2's transponders, a vital instrument used for receiving and transmitting radio signals, was oscillating wildly, causing feedback that could make it impossible to communicate with the satellite. The rocket was already fueled and ready to go. Removing the satellite so Rosen and his team could troubleshoot the problem was impossible.

To diagnose the issue, Rosen and Hudspeth hauled an unwieldy spectrum analyzer weighing nearly one hundred pounds over to the launch site and took the elevator up the gantry seven stories. They had to walk up a final three floors to reach the satellite. A folded antenna was sandwiched between the satellite's body and the malfunctioning receiver. Hudspeth shoved his hand in between the antenna and the receiver, and the feedback stopped. They realized they'd never tested the system with the antenna retracted, since it would be used only after it had been extended and Syncom had reached its final orbit.

The pair figured there wasn't really a problem, but they needed to prove this to the NASA engineers. Thankfully, they had a prototype satellite back on the ground to demonstrate how the oscillation disappeared once the antenna was opened. They received the go-ahead, and the launch was rescheduled for 9:32 the next morning.

They stopped the launch countdown several more times for technical reasons, including a blown valve on the satellite's hydrogen peroxide axial jet. A technician had inadvertently fired the jet during the final test of a different system. This pushed the launch back yet again. It was maddening. Like Plouffe and the Montreal Police that same summer, Rosen and his team were exhausted from lack of sleep and from chasing down all these small problems.

Rosen and the other engineers, joined by several of the Hughes upper management, huddled in the Delta Mission Control Center in Hangar AE. Tensions were high and Rosen was looking for good omens. One came when the building's soda machine went on the fritz and started passing out free bottles of Coca-Cola. Rosen took it as a good sign of things to come.

Finally, on July 26, at 9:33 a.m. Syncom 2 lifted off. As with the first launch, the Thor-Delta B rocket got the satellite to its transfer orbit with no problems. Syncom 2 separated and spun at nearly 150 rpm as it traversed its transfer orbit toward the apogee.

Five hours and thirty-three minutes after liftoff came the most anticipated, and nerve-wracking, part of Syncom 2's journey. It was time for the apogee rocket to ignite, the piece Rosen blamed for the earlier disaster because it was at this point that the first satellite met its demise. No one breathed. The seconds ticked as the rocket burned for twenty seconds, creating a sixty-six-mile-long fiery plume before going out. The tracking station at Olifantsfontein, South Africa, captured the scene in a series of photographs with its telescopic Baker-Nunn camera. This time, the satellite survived the burn and entered its twenty-four-hour orbit. Everyone in the room seemed to exhale at once. The mission, at least this part of it, was a success.

Less than a week later, on July 31, technicians at the Goddard Space Flight Center in Greenbelt, Maryland, began guiding the spinning Syncom 2 through a series of reorientation maneuvers using thousands of small puffs of hydrogen peroxide and nitrogen gas to position the satellite to exactly where they wanted it, with the antenna facing Earth as it soared around the planet nearly twenty-three thousand miles high, mimicking Earth's own rotation. The satellite could communicate with the Earth stations twenty-four hours a day. Webb, NASA's head, called the maneuvers used to get Syncom 2 into position "one of the outstanding feats in the history of space flight."

Tests of the communication system began even before Syncom 2 had separated from its launch vehicle, just twenty-eight minutes after takeoff. The USNS *Kingsport*, a World War II–era navy cargo ship that the government converted into the world's first satellite communication ship, was docked in Lagos, Nigeria. Using its large parabolic stabilized antenna protected by a massive plastic dome, it acquired the satellite and began receiving range data. When the spacecraft reached ten thousand nautical miles, *Kingsport* received a pretaped recording of the national anthem along with crystal-clear voice and teletype signals. A second test when the satellite was in its transfer orbit gave similar results.

During a later test of Syncom 2's telephonic capabilities, Rosen handed his wife, Rosetta, the phone. "Hello?" said a voice at the other end from the USNS *Kingsport*. Rosetta dropped the phone and turned to her husband. "My God, Harold, it works."

Over the coming days, weeks, and months, they ran several thousand more tests and public demonstrations of Syncom's telephone and telefax capabilities. On August 4, the satellite relayed news stories by the Associated Press and United Press International and also sent a photo of President Kennedy to Nigeria from New Jersey. In return, the satellite relayed a story by the Nigerian press and a photograph of that country's governor-general, Nnamdi Azikiwe, to New Jersey. The Associated Press reported the photograph they received was "as clear as a photo portrait." The Nigerians reported the same on their end.

The most historic of these tests came on August 23, when President Kennedy used the satellite to hold a phone conversation with the prime minister of Nigeria, Abubakar Tafawa Balewa. It was the first live two-way phone conversation between heads of state via satellite in history.

"I hope that this is the beginning of much closer communication between Nigeria and the United States and, indeed, between the whole continent of Africa and our continent, our hemisphere. I think that this can be a very important means of providing for closer understanding among our peoples and also, of course, among the people of Africa," Kennedy told Balewa. "I think what we are doing today shows what can be done through the peaceful use of space."

Nigeria, newly independent from Britain, had recently signed on, along with the Soviet Union and more than one hundred other countries, to the Partial Test Ban Treaty, which prohibited testing nuclear weapons in the atmosphere, space, and underwater. The treaty, which Kennedy signed in October 1963, directly resulted from the October 1962 Cuban Missile Crisis.

The two heads of state discussed the treaty, Balewa's previous state visit in the summer of 1961, and the possibility of another face-to-face meeting. Unfortunately, both men would be assassinated within three years of each other without meeting again.

Syncom 2's television capabilities were tested on September 29, 1963. The terminal at Fort Dix, New Jersey, picked up a broadcast from channel 3 in Philadelphia, on a home receiver, and transmitted it through Syncom 2 to the Andover Earth Station. The Bell Labs engineers who viewed it said the picture they received was of "motel quality," which they considered to be very good.

As the satellite continued to perform exceptionally, Rosen rightly felt he and his fellow Hughes engineers had ushered in a new age in communications. Hughes's star was rising, as was universal acclaim for high-orbit satellites.

AT&T launched a second Telstar in May 1963. It would be the last. The company's plan for a constellation of low-orbit satellites was dead. They had lost the battle for supremacy in the heavens, but the war to determine which system, low- or high-orbit satellites, COMSAT would adopt was far from over.

On August 19, 1964, NASA launched Syncom 3, also known as Syncom C, from Cape Kennedy, which had been renamed for the president less than a week after his assassination in Dallas, Texas, on November 22, 1963. The shocking murder shook Rosen and the others in the aerospace world, especially since Kennedy and his administration had been instrumental in developing the satellite industry.

Even while riding high from the acclaim of Syncom 2's achievement as the first geosynchronous communication satellite, Rosen hoped to prove that a Syncom satellite could be geostationary as well. To do this, they used the brand-new Thrust-Augmented Delta, also known as the Delta D launch vehicle, which had three solid-rocket boosters ringing the first stage to provide more power, a nearly 2.37 thrust-to-weight ratio at takeoff, and a larger third-stage rocket motor.

The satellite also went through some improvements, including changes to the control units and solar panels; the addition of more temperature sensors; and a new apogee rocket that could be fired by ground command. They also increased the bandwidth of one of the satellite transponders with a channel exclusively dedicated to television tests.

In order to get Syncom 3 into geostationary orbit at the intersection of the International Date Line and the equator, above the mid-Pacific, the team needed not only the extra power provided by the Delta D, but some tricky maneuvering as well.

The new launch vehicle performed as expected and pushed the satellite toward its parking orbit on the morning of August 20, 1964. From there, Syncom 3 drifted toward this orbit's apogee, at which time the third-stage rocket fired, boosting the satellite into a wide transfer orbit that swung from about 700 to 23,675 miles above the planet over a nearly twelve-hour period. Back on Earth, the technicians waited for the satellite to pass through the transfer orbit three times. With each pass they slowly reoriented the craft in the proper direction. As it reached apogee for the third time above the equator in Borneo, twenty-nine hours and two minutes after liftoff, they fired the apogee motor, sending Syncom 3 into synchronous equatorial orbit. Over the next ten days, they maneuvered the spacecraft using Rosen and Williams's control system, puffs of gas pushing it to its new home above the intersection of the equator and the International Date Line, 22,236 nautical miles high.

Where Syncom 2 moved in a figure-eight pattern, symmetrical about the equator when viewed from the Earth, Syncom 3 appeared to remain stationary when seen from the ground. Ground stations could acquire the satellite and lock their antennas in place, eliminating the need for the expensive tracking systems required by lower-orbit systems.

After years of being told his idea was a science-fiction fantasy that would take decades to achieve, wouldn't be reliable, or would cost too much to build, Rosen and his team had done it. Syncom 3 was an undeniable reality as it soared around the Earth at nearly seven thousand miles per hour, in sync with the planet below. You could look up into the night sky with a telescope and see it.

A few months later, on October 10, 1964, Syncom 3 again made history when it beamed a live broadcast of the opening ceremony of the

Tokyo Summer Olympics, the first held in Asia. Rosen knew the first live international telecast of the Summer Olympic Games would shine the world's attention on the immense capabilities of geostationary communication satellites in a highly dramatic way.

It was a warm, sunny, cloudless afternoon in Tokyo as the Olympic parade got underway on Saturday, October 10, 1964, at 3:00 p.m. The parade consisted of nearly six thousand athletes, led by the Greek delegation, many wearing their countries' traditional clothing. Martial music mingled with the roar of the crowd.

Speeches followed and then Yoshinori Sakai, a student born on the day the atomic bomb detonated in Hiroshima—August 6, 1945—came running into the new Olympic stadium with his torch held aloft and made his way through the crowd of eighty-three thousand spectators, including Japanese Emperor Hirohito and the Empress Kōjun. He ascended the 163 stairs to light the Olympic cauldron in a symbolic call for world peace.

Gymnast Takashi Ono, a twelve-time Olympic medalist, representing all the athletes, took the Olympic oath as thousands of doves flew into the air. The ceremony ended with five Japanese jet planes forming the Olympic rings high above the stadium.

At the same time, on the U.S. East Coast, it was one in the morning and avid sports fans, insomniacs, journalists, and the merely curious were up watching history unfold. Rosen was among them. He was at the NBC studio in Burbank when the broadcast came through. As Syncom 3 relayed the opening ceremony, he couldn't help but feel a sense of awe and pride at what he'd achieved. What was once merely a dream that he and his fellow Hughes engineers had been forced to fight so hard for was now made visible in crisp black-and-white images coming in from halfway around the world.

"The live telecast of the opening ceremony of the Olympic Games in Tokyo without doubt will rank as one of the truly memorable experiences in viewing," columnist Jack Gould wrote in *The New York Times* afterward. "The quality of the images relayed across the Pacific by the satellite Syncom 3 were of such magnificent quality that the person at home had difficulty in adequately comprehending what he was seeing—that the element of time no longer separated one's home from Asia."

Gould echoed what those lucky enough to have gotten the chance to see the telecast were feeling, calling the broadcast "the dawning of a new era in international communications" that "suddenly became a tangible and exciting reality." Syncom 3 was a sensation.

COMSAT coordinated the Olympic broadcast as a nonprofit venture with funding from the Canadian Broadcasting Corporation and Eurovision. The broadcast wasn't just a test for Syncom, but also for COMSAT, which had just spawned the International Telecommunications Satellite Organization (Intelsat), an international intergovernmental consortium dedicated to establishing a global commercial communications network with COMSAT at its head. Within weeks more than thirty countries had come aboard.

Over the next two weeks, Syncom 3 beamed both live and videotaped coverage of the Olympics shot by the Japan Broadcasting Company and sent from an Earth station in Kashima, fifty-six miles northeast of Tokyo, to a large ground antenna at a naval installation at Point Mugu, California.

The antenna at Point Mugu, located less than an hour from the Hughes facility where Rosen worked, was originally built for the military's Advent program. Hughes engineers modified it for better television reception. From Point Mugu, the signal was sent via microwave link to Canada, where the sporting events were recorded on video and flown by jet to Europe for distribution to twenty-one countries.

Canadian viewers benefitted the most from the satellite with a total of nearly fifteen hours of live coverage of the games.

In the United States, NBC, which held exclusive broadcast rights for the country, preferred film and video of the Olympics flown over from Japan each day, mainly because of the large time difference between the two countries, and better image quality than what a live broadcast could achieve.

NBC used the satellite only for the live broadcast of the opening ceremonies on the East Coast. The company didn't even bother to show it on the West Coast, deciding to stick with its normal television schedule for contractual reasons. Washington, the Japanese Embassy, and COMSAT were livid, as were American viewers. COMSAT sent a telegram to NBC charging them with breach of contract.

In his piece for *The New York Times*, Gould groused about this decision, calling NBC's move "far larger than rationalization of contractual provisions," rather "a commentary on American values" since the corporation made "a moment of history subordinate to the fate of a cluster of advertising spot announcements in California."

Scathing editorials aside, commercial concerns were always part of Rosen's vision for Syncom. By the time the satellite was broadcasting the pomp and circumstance of the Olympics, Hughes had already inked a deal with COMSAT for a commercial version of Syncom, mainly based on the performance of Syncom 2.

Rosen and his team had come far, but they weren't at the finish line yet. While COMSAT was sold on the capabilities of Syncom, they still remained uncommitted on whether their emerging communications system would rely on geostationary or low-orbit satellites. It seemed no matter how well Syncom performed, it was never quite good enough.

14

Dead Ends

FALL 1964–SPRING 1965

THE ONGOING HUNT FOR LEMAY YIELDED REPORTED SIGHTINGS across Canada, in South America, and in the Caribbean, but all leads came up empty. Meanwhile, Lemay, using his alias Réne Roy, traveled back and forth from the United States to Canada frequently, always one step ahead of the police.

In September 1964, police in Kenora, a small city in Northwestern Ontario that originally had the rather unappealing name Rat Portage, ended a monthslong investigation into a man named Roger Goyette.

Goyette arrived in town that May with his wife and five children. He was quickly hired on as a mechanic at a local garage, but after seeing Lemay's photo in the newspaper, the garage owner's wife began snooping around. She suspected Goyette was Lemay. When she questioned Goyette about his past, he seemed to get nervous. The next day, he and his family disappeared, and their home showed signs of a hurried departure. They left children's clothing and shoes behind, and the numerous bills Goyette had run up around town never got paid. Police eventually identified the man. It wasn't Lemay, but simply someone who didn't like having his boss's wife dig into his past.

* * *

Running out of leads, the RCMP asked the Montreal Police in September to spy on attorney Raymond Daoust, Lemay's former brother-in-law. Investigators were following up on old reports that Daoust had traveled to Asia in January 1963 with Armand Duhamel and had possibly contacted Lemay while there.

But this, too, proved to be a dead end.

In the intervening year and a half since the Mounties received the information, Duhamel had died while Daoust was representing him in court on conspiracy charges. The police had caught Duhamel with close to thirty thousand dollars in stolen bonds linked to the Brockville and Outremont bank heists of the late 1950s.

On Christmas Eve 1963, Duhamel fell from a second-story balcony while being held at Bordeaux Prison and died from a fractured skull. The police called it a suicide, but rumors circulated that he'd been murdered or even that Duhamel had faked his own death.

Nevertheless, Superintendent Edward Martin of the RCMP Criminal Investigation Branch continued pursuing the angle. He had received information that it was "highly probable" Daoust knew of Lemay's whereabouts and was likely in periodic contact with him. It was unclear if the RCMP knew Daoust held a grudge against Lemay over the disappearance of Huguette, his sister and Lemay's former wife, and was unlikely to be regularly chatting with Lemay.

Martin suggested the Montreal Police examine any toll calls from Daoust, which "might lead to Lemay, or you might be successful, with contact through other telecommunications media, to establish the present whereabouts of Georges Lemay." They weren't successful.

* * *

That fall André Lemieux was sentenced to six years in prison. He'd been on the run for nearly two years and was going by the alias Jean-Paul Brisson when the police finally captured him in Hamilton, Ontario, in April 1964.

After he burned through his heist money, André began burglarizing houses to stay afloat. Local police in Hamilton caught him with a stolen stamp collection worth two thousand dollars. The cops who apprehended him suspected André was one of the men responsible for the now infamous Bank of Nova Scotia heist. They contacted the Montreal Police and discovered they were correct.

The two jurisdictions wrangled over who should get André first. The red tape dragged on until May, when André pleaded guilty to the breaking-and-entering charge in Ontario and was sentenced to two and a half years in prison. The authorities in Ontario and Quebec struck a deal that allowed André to serve his sentence at Saint-Vincent-de-Paul, an imposing nineteenth-century stone prison in Laval, Quebec, where the Montreal Police had easy access to him for interrogations and from where he could more easily make his court appearances in Montreal.

The Montreal bank burglary case dragged on until October 14, when André, now twenty-eight, took a plea deal. In court, the prosecutor called André the "muscle man" of the operation and Lemay the mastermind. He asked the judge to sentence André to six years in prison, to which the justice agreed, finding it "just and adequate."

André entered prison as another Lemieux exited it. His younger brother, Yvon, was released from prison in November 1964 for good behavior after serving about two years.

Lemay would be the last of the gang to face justice, if the cops could only catch him.

* * *

On March 2, 1965, a resort owner named Lucien Rivard made a daring escape from Montreal's Bordeaux Prison, setting off a massive manhunt and one of the biggest political scandals in Canada's history. Rivard's jailbreak would also become entangled in the RCMP search for Lemay and nearly destroy the career of RCMP Commissioner McClellan in what would become known as the Rivard Affair.

Rivard was more than just the owner of Domaine Idéal (Ideal Estate), a Laval-West beach resort on the Rivière-des-Mille-Îles known for its "wenching and drinking," according to a contemporary newspaper report. He was one of the largest heroin smugglers in Canada with deep ties to the Mafia. Rivard was the linchpin between Corsican heroin suppliers in Marseille, France, and the Montreal Mob in an international drug operation known as the French Connection, immortalized by the 1971 eponymous film. The RCMP believed he had deep ties to Lemay as well.

On the evening of his escape, a guard allowed the stocky, dark-haired Rivard, and another prisoner, a convicted armed robber named André Durocher, to water the ice-skating rink within the jail complex, even though it was well above freezing that day. The guard took the two men to the boiler room, where Rivard grabbed two hoses. Durocher then pulled out a gun and ordered the guard to put his hands up.

"Don't joke around," Durocher told the guard when the man jumped at him and reached for the weapon. "We're serious."

Two prison workers wandered in just then. While Durocher held the three at gunpoint, Rivard broke into another room, where he found some wire with which he tied up the men, but not before he made the guard strip.

Now dressed in the jailer's uniform, Durocher walked up to a guard on the catwalk of the lower of two walls surrounding the massive prison. The convict knocked the guard down and tied him up as well. Rivard, still hauling the two hoses he'd taken from the boiler room, grabbed the guard's rifle while Durocher went to look for a ladder. The two men made it over the interior wall with the ladder and continued to the twenty-five-foot outer wall. They scurried up to the top of the wall, tied off the hoses, and climbed down to freedom. The prisoners tossed the rifle and ran through a field headed west.

The guards later found Durocher's pistol where he'd abandoned it in the jail courtyard. It was made of wood and had been blackened with shoe polish.

The escape took all of forty minutes. Once outside the jail, they walked up to a car that had stopped for a traffic sign a few blocks from Bordeaux Prison. They told the driver they were armed but didn't brandish any weapons as they slid into the car. Rivard took the driver's seat and Durocher the passenger seat, sandwiching the man into the center.

"Don't be foolish and you won't get hurt," muttered Rivard, hitting the gas. "We just escaped from Bordeaux Prison."

As they drove through the twilight streets of North Montreal, their prisoner, an accountant, spoke up.

"I thought prisoners there only served two years or less?"

Rivard, guffawing, told the man, "I'll get more than two years. I'm fifty now and when I get out I'll be seventy, so I took a chance. I'm not going to tell you I'm innocent—I'm no angel—but I'm not guilty of all the things they say I did."

For ten minutes straight, Rivard unburdened himself, telling the stranger he'd known what it was like to have "lots of everything," but that the only things he cared about now were his wife and his mother.

The prisoner asked Rivard to slow down. Speeding, he reasoned, would attract police attention, and he feared a stop by the police would inevitably lead to a gun battle in which he might be hurt. Rivard obliged.

The man also suggested they let him out, but Rivard ignored this request.

They continued heading north for another few miles before Rivard finally stopped the car and deposited the man in the neighborhood of Saint-Michel, about four miles from where they'd hijacked the car. Rivard gave him cab fare, got his phone number, and later called him to tell him where he and Durocher had abandoned the car.

Police located the vehicle where Rivard said it would be, but he was long gone. The hunt for Rivard would drag on for months.

At the time of the jailbreak, Rivard was fighting extradition to the United States on charges related to a massive heroin bust in Laredo, Texas.

Customs agents stopped Montreal gambler Joseph Michel Caron and his wife, Marie Ida, during a routine check at the border crossing at the International Bridge on the morning of October 10, 1963. They discovered seventy-six pounds of heroin with a street value of $35 million ($330 million today) hidden under the back seat and behind the door panels of their 1962 Chevrolet. At the time, it was the biggest heroin bust at the Mexican border in history.

Caron flipped on his partners, giving up several big names, including

Paul Mondoloni, a Marseille-based Corsican mobster known as Monsieur Paul who was a key player in the French Connection; Jorge Moreno Chauvet, a large-scale Mexican drug trafficker; and Rivard, whom Caron called the "mastermind" of the operation.

A probe involving the U.S. Customs Service, the RCMP, and Mexican and French authorities turned up connections between Rivard and both New York's Gambino crime family and Montreal's Cotroni organization, a branch of the Bonanno crime syndicate that ruled the Quebec underworld.

The RCMP arrested Rivard on June 19, 1964, and held him at Bordeaux Prison. Attorney General Robert Kennedy had personally requested the extradition.

Daoust, Lemay's former brother-in-law, represented Rivard in the extradition proceedings. Daoust also represented Joe Bonanno, the head of the crime family that bore his name, who was also fighting extradition that summer.

Rivard and Daoust's relationship went back at least to 1959, when Rivard was running a string of Havana nightclubs for the Mob and building a drug- and arms-dealing business. Rivard was playing both sides of the Cuban revolution, paying off Batista and his cronies while simultaneously involved in gunrunning for Castro and his rebels. It caught up with him in 1959, when Castro took over and rounded up all the foreigners involved in the casino and cabaret businesses and held them at Trescornia detention camp.

Rivard was especially in danger, as he'd become well known in Cuba and had been tight with the Batista regime. There was talk of making an example of him, even if he had provided much-needed arms to Castro.

Jack Ruby, the Dallas nightclub owner and Mob associate who killed Kennedy's presumed assassin, Lee Harvey Oswald, had flown to Havana and tried unsuccessfully to get the men released.

Daoust had better luck thanks to his connections in the Canadian government and a personal association with Castro—he helped organize Castro's first visit to Canada a few months earlier. The lawyer persuaded the Cuban government to deport Rivard instead of prosecuting him.

After Rivard's arrest by Canadian police in June 1964, Daoust again stepped in to help his old client, aided by well-placed government officials. Rivard's connections went beyond mobsters, heroin suppliers, and Batista officials to high-ranking members of Canada's Liberal Party, which at the time was the minority government under prime minister Lester B. Pearson.

Rivard had been a big donor to the Liberal Party in the past, and now his friends promised the party sixty thousand dollars (nearly half a million dollars today) in campaign contributions if they quashed his extradition to the United States.

On July 14, 1964, Pierre Lamontagne received an urgent phone call from Raymond Denis, the chief of staff for the minister of immigration and citizenship, asking him to come to Ottawa that day. Lamontagne was a Montreal lawyer hired by the U.S. Justice Department to handle the extradition proceedings against Rivard and his French Canadian coconspirators. The twenty-nine-year-old rising star in the legal profession was perplexed, as Denis wasn't specific about the "urgent matter." He went anyway, since they were good friends.

They met in Denis's office and began discussing the Bonanno extradition case, but before long, Denis pivoted to discussing Rivard. He offered Lamontagne twenty thousand dollars if he'd agree to release Rivard on bail.

Lamontagne, shocked by the proposition, asked Denis why he was doing this.

"Rivard is a good friend of the party," he answered. "There may be elections shortly, and his help will be required in the future. The party would benefit from his release on bail."

Denis also told Lamontagne that the charges against Rivard were "trumped up."

Lamontagne refused the bribe and went back to Montreal. He had already been told by the Americans to oppose bail at all costs because they believed Rivard was a flight risk. Now, his close friend was offering him a huge bribe—more than $140,000 today—to work against the wishes of the people who hired him to help an alleged drug runner. It was crazy.

Six days later, on July 20, Lamontagne was visiting his parents in Chicoutimi, north of Quebec City, when he received a phone call from Daoust asking him when he should put in his bail application for Rivard.

"I understand everything's been fixed in Ottawa," he told Lamontagne.

Lamontagne, confused and surprised that Daoust even knew where to reach him, didn't answer for several seconds.

"I don't know what you're talking about," he finally stammered.

Daoust told him to call later so they could straighten things out. They hung up.

A few minutes later, Lamontagne received another call from a man calling himself Bob Gingras, who said he was a friend of Denis. He threatened Lamontagne if he didn't play ball.

"I know about that trip you took," the man said in French that was heavy on slang. "And I know you wouldn't want your wife to find out."

Lamontagne hung up on him. Gingras called back again later that night making similar threats.

Gingras was actually Robert Gignac, Rivard's friend, who'd promised he could deliver bail for the drug kingpin.

Daoust called back the same night. Lamontagne refused to discuss the matter but was getting worried. The situation seemed to be spiraling. He called Denis the next morning.

"Tell your boys to leave me alone or I'll go to the RCMP," he angrily told his friend. His next call was to a Mountie he knew. Lamontagne told him about the mysterious phone calls but didn't mention the bribe Denis had offered him. He asked the investigator to keep it to himself.

In the following weeks, rumors began circulating around the Montreal courthouse that Lamontagne took a bribe in the Rivard case.

Lamontagne also began getting more phone calls from various government officials, including Guy Rouleau, a member of Parliament and prime minister Lester Pearson's former parliamentary secretary, and two aides to federal minister of justice Guy Favreau, all trying to get him to allow bail in the case.

Lamontagne, sick of the harassment and more and more frightened by the pressure campaign, contacted the U.S. Justice Department about the situation, and on their advice he finally brought the RCMP into the loop on August 10.

McClellan received a report on the RCMP interview with Lamontagne two days later. He brought it to minister of justice Favreau, who told him to conduct a "full investigation" into the matter.

McClellan gave the order that lead investigator Inspector Paul Drapeau would be constrained by a "step-by-step" process requiring him to keep in close contact with his superior officers and seek permission on whom he could interrogate.

Several missteps hampered the RCMP investigation. In a decision that would later come back to haunt the RCMP and McClellan, although he hadn't given the order himself, a non-French-speaking officer, Sergeant Joseph McLeod, assisted in the investigation, which almost exclusively involved French speakers. It would seem impossible that McLeod could corroborate any testimony given during interviews in a language he didn't understand.

Inspector Drapeau wanted to interview Marie Rivard, the wife of the man at the center of the entire affair, but was told she was off-limits. Later, Drapeau listened in on a phone call between Lamontagne and Denis but wasn't told to tape the call. One of the officers took a few notes during the phone conversation. The RCMP later destroyed the notes without explanation.

Drapeau's report to McClellan, given on August 28, concluded he would need to interrogate more of the people involved for a complete picture of what happened, but that "in compliance with your instructions no action in the latter respect is being taken by the writer and consequently this matter will be considered closed unless otherwise instructed."

It took more than a week before Drapeau finally got permission to interview the suspects, though none were recorded and he'd been ordered not to examine their bank accounts.

The RCMP's summary of Drapeau's investigation, which Drapeau hadn't written, made some questionable leaps of judgement, concluding there was no evidence that corroborated Lamontagne's allegation that Denis offered him a bribe, and that members of government had applied political pressure against the lawyer. The RCMP hadn't looked for circumstantial evidence that might back Lamontagne's allegations.

The summary also discounted the political pressure placed on Lamontagne, chalking it up to a normal occurrence in "political circles."

McClellan brought the minister of justice the case file but failed to point out some important details, specifically parts of Denis's interview that showed he was lying.

McClellan concluded Lamontagne wouldn't have made baseless allegations. "There was no doubt that representations had been made in view of obtaining bail" for Rivard and that Denis "had his part to play in these representations," he told the minister.

He also believed that many of the people they interviewed had been in touch with each other to get their stories straight before being interrogated by the RCMP. But, he concluded, "unless further channels of investigation open up, we can see at the moment little hope of obtaining the necessary legal corroboration of Mr. Lamontagne's statement to prefer charges against Mr. Denis."

"Are you satisfied that there is sufficient evidence to prosecute Denis?" Minister of Justice Favreau asked.

McClellan responded that he strongly suspected that Denis was guilty, but that there wasn't enough evidence to go forward with the case.

McClellan felt that Lamontagne had destroyed any credibility he had as a witness. Instead of coming straight to the RCMP after Denis offered him the twenty thousand dollars, he waited nearly a month and came forward only after he heard rumors that he'd taken the bribe and was getting harassing phone calls from "fringe racketeers."

"No, I don't think so at this time," he answered Favreau.

That was the end of the case until November, when the opposition party got wind of the affair. The Conservatives in Parliament, smelling blood, went after Minister of Justice Favreau hard. He was a rising star in the Pearson cabinet, and the Conservatives hoped that taking him down would bring the rest of the Liberal Party with him.

Denis was the first to fall. Under pressure, he'd stepped down from his position on October 15.

Favreau set up a commission to look into the Rivard Affair, headed by Chief Justice Frédéric Dorion, who presided over the Superior Court of Quebec. The story blew up, snowballed, and ended in the destruction of several careers, including Favreau's. The Pearson government teetered but didn't fall.

McClellan appeared before the commission on March 3, 1965—a day after Rivard escaped Bordeaux Prison—where they grilled him for two days about his recommendation not to press forward with criminal charges against Denis.

He told the commission that the RCMP was interested only in whether Denis had committed a crime. "Impropriety was not our business," he said. While on the stand, he wheeled around and angrily asked a commission lawyer what he'd just said after mishearing what he thought was a snarky aside. He later had to apologize. McClellan's outburst left the room stunned.

The Dorion Commission's official report flayed McClellan and the RCMP's handling of the bribery investigation.

For McClellan it was a hard lesson in the game of national politics. The report stated that McClellan and the RCMP had bungled the investigation. The police file "didn't contain all the facts" and McClellan's opinion on the case created "a doubt" in Favreau's mind as to whether to pursue criminal charges against Denis.

The commission's scolding of the RCMP's language barrier in investigating the case—Dorion called it "so extraordinary that it is hard to believe it has happened in our times"—especially stung. In the year since he'd been in charge of the Mounties, McClellan had been trying hard to increase the number of bilingual officers but was having trouble finding enough French speakers to join their ranks.

As the hunt for Rivard dragged on, the RCMP investigated reports that the fugitive may have hooked up with Lemay. The Mounties believed the two knew each other through their Montreal underworld connections. It was a positive development for McClellan, who was sorely in need of some good news after being used as a political cudgel between rival parties. Mounting pressure meant more resources were put toward finding

Lemay in the hopes that catching him might mean getting Rivard in the bargain, or vice versa.

It also meant thinking outside of the box. As Rosen and his team at Hughes Aircraft pushed themselves to complete a commercial version of Syncom three thousand miles away in California, a revolutionary new tool in crime fighting was also being born.

15

Early Bird

SPRING–SUMMER 1965

ON TUESDAY, APRIL 6, 1965, NASA'S DELTA MISSION CONTROL Center in Hangar AE at Cape Kennedy, Florida; the Goddard Space Flight Center in Greenbelt, Maryland; and the COMSAT Control Center in Washington, D.C., were in constant communication as the minutes ticked down to launch. The Andover Earth Station in Maine had the key role of relaying command-and-control instructions to the spacecraft.

The world's first commercial geosynchronous communication satellite had the official designation of HS-303. Hughes referred to it as Public Satellite No. 1. But Matthew Gordon, COMSAT's director of information, gave it the name that stuck: Early Bird. The name came in part from COMSAT's Early Capability Program, of which the satellite was the heart. The other was from the slang used in the industry for satellites, which they called birds.

An Associated Press journalist and friend phoned Gordon about what COMSAT was calling this new satellite, and Gordon responded without thinking, "I guess you could call it the early bird." And they did. They would eventually change the satellite's name to Intelsat 1 in honor of the new international organization, but by then it was impossible to dislodge its earlier press-friendly appellation.

At eighty-five pounds, Early Bird was about ten pounds heavier than Syncom 3. It was also the heaviest payload the Delta D launch vehicle could handle. The added weight translated to two and a half times the power and bandwidth as Syncom 3 and 240 voice circuits. The Syncom satellites, by contrast, had been capable of carrying only a single two-way telephone conversation. Most crucially for law enforcement, Early Bird also had one two-way television channel. This capability provided an opportunity to spread the names and faces of criminals who were wanted by the various police forces across the globe and had managed to outwit and outrun them. It was one thing to have a wanted poster with a blurry photo hanging from a post office wall and quite another to have this brand-new technology disseminate the information to millions upon millions of people across two continents. The world was about to shrink for Lemay and other fugitives who had thus far managed to remain under the radar.

On the evening of the launch, a closed-circuit television line at the new COMSAT headquarters on L Street Northwest, in Washington, D.C., provided an intimate view of the launch taking place in Florida.

The guest list for the exclusive event included Arthur C. Clarke, who first dreamed up the idea of a synchronous communication satellite system more than twenty years earlier; U.S. Vice President Hubert Humphrey; Senator Walter Mondale, from Minnesota; the COMSAT upper management; representatives from AT&T, ITT, and the other carriers; and a cadre of international reporters.

Leo Welch, COMSAT's chairman and CEO, cut through the low buzz of conversation from the attendees sitting close to one another in wooden chairs, and the reporters and cameramen standing in the rear of the crowded room.

"We hope you are not going to be disappointed," he said, in what he might have intended as a bit of levity, though he couldn't hide an undercurrent of genuine fear. Notoriously conservative in business, he remained skeptical about the geosynchronous satellite he'd agreed to back.

A lot was riding on the Early Bird's success for COMSAT, and its president, Joseph Charyk, felt the tension of the moment rippling through the room. COMSAT's reputation in the United States and internationally was at stake. They'd convinced the members of the new Intelsat organization, now forty-seven nations strong, that they could get Early Bird into a geostationary orbit and that its communication system would work and work well. A failure now would be "a solid negative blow."

Even more rode on the satellite for Hughes. Their fees and reimbursement for Early Bird were contingent on its performance and promised life span of eighteen months, to say nothing of the implications for commercial synchronous communication satellites should Early Bird fail.

For Rosen, who was at Cape Kennedy for the launch, the commercial success of geostationary communication satellites would finally shut the naysayers up for good. It would herald what he believed was a new age for the peaceful use of space and the dawning of the global village.

Millions of dollars, individual reputations, entire companies, national pride, and the future of telecommunication were all resting under the protective nose cone of the Delta D rocket sitting on LC17A. Illuminated by searchlights as the sun sank below the horizon and the launch clock ticked toward zero, the spacecraft looked more like an unmovable obelisk than a vehicle capable of rocketing a satellite into the heavens.

Eleven minutes before liftoff, technicians determined the second-stage rocket engine's automatic fueling system wasn't working properly. They would have to switch to manual, a fifteen-minute process. It was one more thing for the COMSAT execs to fret about. COMSAT paid NASA $3.33 million for the launch, whether successful or not.

At least the satellite itself was covered for any prelaunch damages. COMSAT had taken out the first satellite insurance policy in history with Lloyd's of London to cover any physical damage to Early Bird before liftoff.

This wasn't the first delay Early Bird encountered. The original launch date of March 23 was pushed back by two weeks when several transistors used in the satellite's communication system failed during tests. All transistors of that type needed to be replaced.

Finally, at 6:48 p.m., with a deafening roar and a burst of flame that changed from bright orange to blood red, the rocket hurtled upward into the dusk, a trail of thick smoke snaking out. Attendees watching the flight from Washington burst into applause. Soon after, the three solid-fuel boosters that ringed the first stage sputtered out and fell away as the first stage continued to push the satellite higher and higher until it was completely out of sight.

Welch, feeling better than he did before liftoff, and with obvious relief in his voice, told the crowd, "We will all sleep better tonight." Vice President Humphrey then jumped in, "Now we'll be able to call everybody. I don't know if this is a good thing or not. We have enough telephone calls in the office already." Perhaps realizing the importance of the moment, he then took on a decidedly statelier tone. "It is indeed an early bird and thank goodness it looks like an eagle."

Rosen, witnessing the launch from Hangar AE, watched the fruit of years of trials, setbacks, leaps of ingenuity, and countless work hours hurtle skyward on the nose of a Thor-Delta D rocket. He understood what a leap forward this satellite was compared to the original Syncom he and Williams had first envisioned. With 240 telephone circuits, it had the capacity of nearly all the underwater telephone cables that had been laid. This was going to change the world.

Far above the gathered dignitaries who slowly made their way out of the COMSAT headquarters, the second-stage rocket fired, the first stage dropped away, and the nose section jettisoned to reveal the satellite as it continued its journey. About five minutes after liftoff, the second stage engine shut off, and the launch vehicle coasted for about twenty minutes, performing needed maneuvers to position Early Bird. The satellite then spun up and the third-stage engine fired, sending the spacecraft, now spinning at 152 rpm, into an egg-shaped transfer orbit that swept from about 200 miles near Earth to 22,300 nautical miles high at its apogee.

Thirty-five minutes after liftoff, control of Early Bird passed from NASA to the COMSAT Control Center, at 2100 L Street Northwest, two blocks west of COMSAT's headquarters. It was now up to them to get Early Bird into its final geostationary orbit.

Magnetic tape whirred as an IBM computer spat out the millions of computations to the clickety-clack of printers to determine the exact moment to launch Early Bird into its final orbit. They needed to know the satellite's exact orbit and the orientation of its spin axis to prepare its antenna pointing information. Technicians then checked and rechecked these calculations by hand. COMSAT Control Center was in constant contact with the Andover Earth Station, which resembled an enormous puffball mushroom and was originally built by AT&T for Telstar, where engineers from COMSAT, Hughes, and NASA crowded together to track Early Bird. With little to do until the telemetry data was in, Sid Metzger, COMSAT's head of engineering, suggested they get a jump start on testing out Early Bird's television capabilities. They used a small television camera to film still photos they found in a COMSAT press folder of an artist's rendition of the satellite and a caricature of a bird. They beamed the flickering black-and-white images up to Early Bird and back down to Andover. The unauthorized test worked. The engineers were exhilarated. And they hoped it boded well for the satellite's future.

Finally, COMSAT Control sent the reorientation and velocity correction instructions. At 8:40 a.m. on April 9, the control station in Andover, Maine, sent the signal for Early Bird's apogee rocket to fire as it made its sixth pass through its elliptical transfer orbit and reached apogee. The booster responded and fired the satellite into its final orbit.

In the following days, using the satellite's hydrogen peroxide jets, they nudged Early Bird into geosynchronous orbit at a latitude of 28 degrees west over the Atlantic Ocean. They then corrected its attitude so the antenna's beam faced the Andover Earth station and the European stations at Goonhilly Downs in Cornwall, England; Pleumeur-Bodou in Brittany, France; Raisting, outside of Munich, Germany; and the Italian Telespazio station at Fucino, near Rome.

It wasn't long before the European stations were sharing live television transmission tests with Andover, Maine, to prepare for a live telecast in May that would show the entire world just what Early Bird was capable of and would change the way law enforcement hunted criminals.

While the world was on the verge of changing thanks to Harold Rosen's unbending fight to see a geostationary communication satellite become a reality, his life changed as well. He'd turned thirty-nine two weeks before Early Bird's launch and was already being feted by his fellow engineers with various awards for his work. He was Hughes's communication satellite laboratory manager, not that he ever paid attention to titles, and was fully in his element. Rosen was also getting a lot of press attention following Early Bird's launch. Don Dwiggins, a pilot, author, and freelance aeronautics journalist, called Rosen "the Edison of the Space Age" in an April 1965 article picked up by most of the major newspapers across the country. Rosen wasn't quite becoming a household name, but he was on the rise, as were GEO satellites.

Yet, even after Early Bird's successful launch and the battery of tests that proved the satellite worked as advertised, COMSAT continued to waffle on which type of orbit to use as the framework for its international communication system, which frustrated Rosen.

One of the main objections to geostationary satellites was a 0.6-second time delay in phone conversations due to the distance the signal traveled. Pierce had railed against this since the beginning, but ordinary users seemed fine with it. The delay also caused an echo effect that Rosen and Williams dealt with through the use of echo suppressors. Various tests showed that users, without even realizing it, made a psychological adjustment to the delay within a few seconds.

Luckily, Rosen had an advocate in German-born COMSAT electrical engineer Siegfried Reiger. Before joining the fledgling organization in the spring of 1963, Reiger had managed the Systems Division at the RAND Corporation. There he'd written white papers on the various systems and favored GEO satellites over low-orbit versions. Reiger set about convincing his COMSAT colleagues that geostationary satellites should be the basis for their new international communications system.

Sid Metzger, the manager of the engineering division who'd worked on the medium-orbit satellite Relay while at RCA, agreed. Eventually, Charyk, the COMSAT president, would join them in advocating for GEO satellites.

Yet COMSAT wasn't taking any chances and called for two engineering design studies for low-orbit satellite systems, one from AT&T and RCA, and another from Thompson Ramo Wooldridge and ITT. The studies proved what Charyk and the rest of the COMSAT management finally came to believe: a low-orbit system would be a lot more expensive, and it would take COMSAT a lot longer just to break even if they went with it.

It wouldn't be until the end of December 1965 that COMSAT finally pulled the trigger on choosing geostationary satellites as the framework for its international communication system. Hughes got the contract.

The battle for supremacy between GEO and low-orbit satellites appeared to be over, but the Soviets had their own ideas.

* * *

A few weeks after Early Bird went up, the Soviet Union launched their own communication satellite, Molniya 1, into a highly elliptical orbit that didn't require as much rocket power as a geosynchronous orbit and worked better over the Soviets' polar regions. Unlike Hughes's spin-stabilized satellites, Molniya used three-axis stabilization, the same type the U.S. military had pursued for the defunct Advent satellite.

The Soviet program began in 1960 with the goal of bringing telephone, television, and telegraph capabilities to Russia, but it suffered two failures before successfully launching Molniya 1 on April 23, 1965.

The Soviet Union was highly critical of Intelsat since it brought private enterprise into space communications. The Soviets refused to join the organization but made vague counterproposals of cooperation between Intelsat and Molniya to be coordinated by the United Nations. Nothing came of it. Meanwhile, in the real-world chess game between the Soviets and the United States, Rosen's creations had become pawns.

On January 1, 1965, NASA turned Syncom 2 and 3 over to the Department of Defense just as the conflict in Vietnam was escalating, going from civil war in South Vietnam to proxy war between the Soviets and the West. The satellites saw use as the primary communication links between Southeast Asia and the Western Pacific during the Vietnam War.

The Cold War had come to the other Space Race, just as a groundbreaking international television event was being rolled out to show that communication satellites could bring the world together. And make the world seem much, much smaller, as Georges Lemay would soon learn.

PART 3

Nowhere to Hide in the Global Village

(Spring 1965–Summer 1967)

The Montreal Police Department's wanted poster for Georges Lemay from the fall of 1962. From the RCMP file of Georges Lemay.

Lise Lemay's FBI Wanted Poster from 1966. FBI/from the RCMP file on Georges Lemay.

16

A Novel Idea

SPRING 1965

IT WAS A NOVEL IDEA. FOR THE FIRST TIME IN HISTORY Scotland Yard, the RCMP, and the FBI would use a live satellite television broadcast to hunt down their most wanted criminals.

Early Bird's commercial debut was scheduled for June, and COM-SAT was planning a splashy television special—"This Is Early Bird"—to let the world see what the satellite could do. They would broadcast the show on all three U.S. networks, the CBC in Canada, Telesistema Mexicano in Mexico, and across Europe, including Yugoslavia, the only Eastern Bloc country to see the broadcast.

Av Westin of CBS was selected to executive produce the hour-long show for the three major U.S. networks and the Canadian Broadcasting Corporation. Westin had started out as a "copy boy" to famed television journalist Edward R. Murrow when he was still only on the radio, and he had made a name for himself as the producer for *CBS Morning News with Mike Wallace*, which began airing in 1963. CBS had just promoted him to executive producer of live coverage of major events and of news specials. "This Is Early Bird" would be his first assignment.

Westin envisioned a mixed program of news, science, culture, and sports that would best show off the new satellite's capabilities and illustrate how television unites us all. He also wanted to convey how the satellite allowed mutual participation in both directions by highlighting actual uses of Early Bird, like a news exchange that he believed would soon be a daily occurrence once there were enough satellites up and running.

Thom Benson, newly named head of TV features and special events for the Canadian Broadcasting Corporation (CBC), helmed the Canadian end of the hour-long broadcast. Benson had been with the CBC since its founding in 1952, handling duties both behind and in front of the camera.

One of the show's segments would be as groundbreaking as the satellite itself. They would show the world's most wanted fugitives live on television for the first time in history.

The CBC contacted the RCMP in April to take part in the live exchange of two of Canada's most wanted criminals with the FBI and Scotland Yard.

McClellan loved the idea. Although a by-the-book officer who came up through the ranks of the highly regimented and tradition-bound RCMP, he believed in using the most cutting-edge policing methods available. He was determined to modernize his police force, demonstrated by his order that ended mandatory equestrian training for recruits when he became the RCMP's thirteenth commissioner.

Benson suggested the RCMP feature Lucien Rivard, who was then making international headlines for his escape in March from Bordeaux Prison. But in the midst of the Rivard Affair that was shaking up the political world, McClellan and his senior officers decided against featuring the drug smuggler, a move that would again draw McClellan into the muck of national politics. They wanted to get the most out of the broadcast and felt they had a better shot with Lemay than Rivard.

The Rivard case had also gotten a huge amount of publicity in both Canada and the United States, while the Lemay story had faded somewhat from the public's eye. This would be the perfect opportunity to renew interest in the case.

It was highly unlikely, in the commissioner's opinion, that even if Rivard was living under an assumed name only months after his escape, many people would have had contact with him. Plus, he was wanted on charges in the United States, not Canada, so why should they use this huge opportunity on a deportation case? No, it made more sense to highlight Lemay, who had been on the run for nearly four years, had most likely established a domicile under an alias, and in the course of his ordinary life, would have become known by sight to a number of people, perhaps the milkman or a postal worker. With three hundred million people watching the broadcast, someone would recognize the wanted man, he hoped.

McClellan and his staff also felt it might look bad to include two criminals with French names, considering the ongoing separatist strife in Quebec, so the other fugitive they featured was "Tough Johnny" John Frederick Meagher, an armed robber on the run since 1957.

* * *

On Sunday, May 2, 1965, at 1:00 p.m. Eastern, Weston, his director, Vern Diamond, and technical director Harold Classon, sat in the CBS New York City control room facing a bank of television monitors showing scenes from around the world. Each was labeled in bold white text on a black background and read: CANADA, WASHINGTON, HOUSTON, PHILADELPHIA, TO EUROPE, FROM EUROPE, WIPES, DIRECT, VIDEO TAPE, FILM, and others. In the center was a large clock labeled NEW YORK TIME.

Diamond leaned toward a microphone. "Stand by, Mexico," he growled. "Ten, nine, eight . . ." And suddenly they'd transported television viewers from the United States, Canada, and Europe for the first time live to Mexico City, where a mariachi band performed as a man and woman in traditional clothing began an intricate dance, pounding out a rhythm with their feet. Other scenes from the city followed. The Telesistema Mexicano technicians in a mobile control unit choreographed the cameras and various scenes. It was a microcosm of the CBS control room 2,500 miles away, where Diamond shouted, "Stand by to swipe . . . and wipe it in. Stand by to super . . . and super . . . and wipe all the way through to the bird. Give me live via Early Bird, please."

For the first time in history live television images were relayed simultaneously in both directions across the ocean. The mostly live hour-long program had eighteen other pickup points besides Mexico, spanning the United States, Canada, the United Kingdom, and across Europe.

Mike Wallace, the CBS news anchor, narrated most of the show for the network's audience. Each network covered the special with their own news anchor—Bob Young at ABC and Frank McGee for NBC—all using the same script.

News reports from both continents came next in the program, and then it was time for the most-wanted criminals segment.

Investigators from Scotland Yard in London, FBI agents in Washington, D.C., and Inspector John Eugene Gibbon, at the RCMP headquarters in Ottawa, were all connected via satellite using split screens. Scotland Yard featured four members of the gang that had pulled off the Great Train Robbery. The August 1963 heist netted the thieves the equivalent of about forty-nine million dollars in today's terms.

When it was Gibbon's turn, he described Lemay and the Bank of Nova Scotia heist while the fugitive's mug shot appeared on the screen. Just as Gibbon was about to describe Meagher's crimes and show his mug shot, the scene switched, leaving Lemay as the only Canadian to have his mug shot flashed to millions of viewers.

It was a historic moment in crime fighting. *The New York Times* called it "the ultimate electronic improvement on the posters in the post office."

Besides the exchange of most wanted criminals, the groundbreaking broadcast featured a live heart-valve operation in Houston, coordinated by ABC, that allowed surgeons in Geneva, Switzerland, to watch and ask questions of Dr. Michael Ellis DeBakey, a pioneering cardiovascular surgeon. DeBakey had most recently been in the news for operating on the Duke of Windsor for an aneurysm of the abdominal aorta a few months earlier.

There was a live split screen of the New York World's Fair at Flushing Meadows-Corona Park and scenes from Rome; festivals in Italy, Germany, and Sweden; a test of the Concord's jet engines; and shots of a tunnel being built under Mont Blanc between Italy and France.

There were Russian sailors dancing on a ship in Portsmouth, England; astronaut Alan Shepard, the first American to go into space back in 1961, training at a NASA facility; a bullfight in Barcelona; and a look at an innovative tidal power station being built in France, among other events.

The program ended with bands in Quebec City and Washington, D.C., accompanying thousands of students in Stockholm, and a military chorus in England, singing a rousing rendition of "Auld Lang Syne."

"And so this is the conclusion of our broadcast inaugurating the transmission of regular live television between Europe and North America," Mike Wallace intoned as the song faded out. "Proceeding from the assumption that men are good and decent and that their troubles grow from untruths and misunderstandings. This communication facility will serve mankind well. It will serve by making truth and understanding between people easier to come by. Nations know this little thing or that about each other, but essentially, they are strangers. Their judgments about one another are formed by a caricature, a trait, a look of a face, or the half-told story of a thing that never happened. If Early Bird and the satellites yet unlaunched can help reveal nations to nations and people to people, this will have been a day."

A cheer went up in the CBS control room when the hour-long show ended. Sure, there had been a few hiccups: The scene of the Astros practicing at the Houston Astrodome cut out for portions of the U.S. audience. The narration by BBC announcer Richard Dimbleby, known as "the voice of Great Britain," sounded as if he were in an echo chamber, but at that point the sound was coming in via underwater cable and not Early Bird, so the satellite couldn't be blamed. There were some missing shots from Europe near the beginning of the show. Even so, it had been an enormous success. Westin, the executive producer, was thrilled with the result. The broadcast had achieved its chief aim of showing how, thanks to Early Bird, television now united the world through news, science, culture, and sports. He even had enough material for another whole show from segments they'd been forced to cut to get "This Is Early Bird" in under an hour. The bird had so much potential.

Executives at both CBS and COMSAT were also happy with the program.

"Overall, I think it was an incredible job," Bill Leonard, CBS vice president, later told reporters. Matthew Gordon, who'd been the one who named the satellite Early Bird, called the program "a rather spectacular demonstration."

The next day the press weighed in. The special and its display of Early Bird's potential blew them away. The New York *Daily News* called the program the "most technically astonishing transmission feat since the birth of television."

On Monday, May 3, a repeat of the broadcast aired and a boat repairman in Florida caught it. He stared at the screen, unbelieving.

17

Pride Comes Before the Fall

SPRING—SUMMER 1965

PAUL GOUGLEMAN LIKED THE ROYS. THEY WERE FRIENDLY, interesting, and fun, if a bit wild. Lemay, using the alias René Roy, arrived at the Bahia Mar Marina in Fort Lauderdale on his forty-two-foot yacht, *Triana*, in September 1964. Roy was docked at berth C-12, next to Gougleman's yacht, *Wind Song*, and before long the two men began spending time together. Gougleman was a retired executive from Chicago who managed several commercial properties in the Fort Lauderdale area.

Roy said he was a travelogue film director and had a scrap and salvage business in Ontario. He'd retired early from running the business, he said. Roy liked to go out nightclubbing and had an eye for the ladies. When he left for the holidays and returned with a tiny, strikingly pretty young woman, Elsie, on his arm, whom he introduced as his wife, the news floored Gougleman. Elsie was Lise's alias while in the United States. The Gouglemans had no idea whom they'd become pals with.

Things changed with Elsie around. Roy no longer went out to the clubs. Instead, Gougleman and his wife, Margaret, began going out to dinner with Elsie and Roy, mostly steak houses—Black Angus, Chateau

Madrid, Tropical Acres. Roy loved steak. The couples also spent quiet nights hanging out on one another's boats, sipping wine and chatting.

Margaret was a little confused about Roy's background. Elsie said he came from money and that her brothers worked for him, but also that they were musicians. Perhaps something was lost in translation. Elsie's English wasn't the best.

The Gouglemans believed Roy either was a ne'er-do-well son of a wealthy Canadian family who'd sent him to Florida to stay out of trouble, or was there for a well-deserved rest after working hard for the family business. They never could make up their minds on this point.

Roy told Paul Gougleman that he was thinking about investing in an African American nightclub called the Most, in Pompano Beach. On another evening, after Gougleman complained about his ex-wife and the alimony he was paying out the nose, his new friend said he could take care of the problem for ten thousand dollars. Gougleman assumed Roy meant he could somehow "fix" the judge handling the case and said he might be interested. Roy then told him he had friends in Canada who could make his ex-wife "disappear." Gougleman thought he was joking, chalking it up to the martinis they were drinking.

They continued to spend time together and sailed to the Florida Keys twice. Roy didn't mention his proposal again. Then came the police, photographers, news cameras, and journalists. The Gouglemans' friend Roy had a secret, it seemed.

* * *

Lemay felt safe on the *Triana*, just one of 350 boats moored at the massive marina he'd called home for six months. He felt especially secure with both a driver's license and passport in the name of René Roy. The newspapers had also stopped mentioning him so much, which was a relief. The longer he remained free, the less he felt inclined to look over his shoulder. He could almost believe he was a retired businessman who had taken up a new career as a travelogue director. Almost.

Before arriving in Fort Lauderdale, Lemay spent January to September 1964 in Daytona Beach. There he hired a crew to help him overhaul a yacht he bought from Harold Churchill, a retiree from Weymouth, Massachusetts. The ketch took Churchill more than a decade to build using a design by the famed Boston-based naval architect John Alden.

Lemay had custom cabinets built along with an all-new galley, shower, and bath, and he even had air conditioning installed.

When Lemay wasn't working on his boat, he spent time at the dog track and caught jai alai matches at the Daytona Beach fronton, the special court used in the sport. He loved watching the two players fling the small hard ball at nearly two hundred miles per hour at a wall using a wicker basket, called a cesta, attached to their right hand, and then attempt to catch it and fling it back. It was another sport where betting was part of the fun, and like horse or dog racing, it was a pari-mutuel betting system, so you wouldn't know your exact take until the very end.

Lise had joined Lemay in the United States in the late summer of 1964 as he made his way down the West Coast from British Columbia, where he'd been living for nearly a year. The newly reunited couple stopped in Las Vegas, where Lemay, in one night, lost the thirty-five thousand dollars he'd set aside to buy his new boat. But his luck changed the next day, and they left with more cash than they'd had when they'd arrived.

Lemay christened the yacht *Triana*, Spanish for *love triangle*, he said, in honor of his three loves: Lise, Josée, and his newest paramour, his renovated boat. While Lemay loved his daughter, he didn't think it was a good idea to have a toddler living on a yacht under the circumstances. Lise disagreed, and it was a point of contention between them. Josée stayed in Canada and lived with Lise's family.

In September 1964, the couple sailed away from Daytona Beach on their remodeled boat and headed 250 miles south along Florida's Atlantic coast to their new home in Fort Lauderdale.

The Churchills came to visit their new friends in Fort Lauderdale twice during their annual Florida trip. In December 1964, they stopped in to see Roy (Lemay) for the day. Elsie (Lise) was back in Canada and Roy was about to join her. In March 1965, the Churchills spent more time with the Roys, having dinner on the *Triana* and sailing with the couple a few days later, and then one more dinner out before they returned home.

It was the last time they saw the Roys until they saw their friends' photos in the newspaper and learned their true identities.

In April 1965, after Lise and Lemay spent a delightful two weeks in New York City, a place they both loved, Lise returned to Canada to spend Easter with their daughter. That month, as Lemay relaxed, sailed, and soaked up the sun on deck, high above him Early Bird, after being launched less than two hundred miles away at Cape Kennedy on April 6, was moving toward its final orbital position above the Atlantic Ocean. And in New York City, CBS's Av Westin was hashing out the details of the live exchange of the most wanted criminals between the various police agencies for "This Is Early Bird."

* * *

Had the Fort Lauderdale Police been a little more proactive, they could have caught Lemay nearly nine months earlier. In August 1964, a Canadian tourist from Kenora, Ontario, recognized the fugitive from an article in his hometown newspaper about Lemay being added to the Most Wanted list. The tourist went to the Fort Lauderdale police to report his suspicions. He left the newspaper clipping featuring the somewhat-blurry photo of Lemay with a detective along with his contact information. Captain Bob Smith jotted down a file number on the clipping, filed it away, and promptly forgot about it until he got a call from the FBI on May 4, 1965.

FBI special agent Ken Schiewe, based in Miami, had just gotten a call from a local boat repairman who recognized the mug shot of Lemay featured on a rebroadcast of "This Is Early Bird." Only a few days earlier, the man had worked on the fugitive's yacht, but he knew him as Mr. Roy, not Lemay. That night he wrestled with what to do and called the FBI the next day only at the behest of his coworkers.

The FBI lacked jurisdiction in the matter, so Schiewe needed to coordinate with the local police and the federal Immigration and Naturalization Service (INS). After speaking with Smith, he contacted INS agent James Lisl, and the three met to devise a plan.

Surveillance began on the *Triana*. They studied the mug shot from the *Kenora Daily* newspaper article after catching a glimpse of the boat's owner, and they all agreed the man on the yacht looked like Lemay.

Schiewe decided they needed something more solid than a photo in an eight-month-old newspaper, so he called Washington. The FBI sent Lemay's fingerprints. Schiewe sprang into action.

On Thursday, May 6, at two in the afternoon, Lemay returned to his yacht after running some errands in Miami. He didn't realize he was being tailed the entire trip. He padded up the gangplank and went inside.

While a cadre of police officers in civilian clothing stood guard on the dock, Smith, Lisl, and Schiewe boarded the *Triana* and knocked on the cabin door. Lemay answered wearing only a pair of swimming trunks.

Lisl identified himself and asked Lemay if he was Canadian.

"Yes."

Lisl showed Lemay the newspaper clipping.

"Are you Georges Lemay?"

"My name's René Roy."

"Show me your left hand," an officer demanded. Lemay obliged. Detective-Sergeant Larry Calhoun, a police fingerprint expert who had also boarded the yacht, studied Lemay's outstretched hand, comparing it to the blue piece of paper he was holding.

"You're Georges Lemay," Calhoun said, looking the fugitive in the eyes. Lemay, with a studied casualness, smiled and agreed.

"This is life," he said in English. "Yes, I am Georges Lemay."

The investigators immediately searched the yacht.

"Do you have any weapons?"

"Just that," Lemay answered, indicating a spear gun with the nod of his head.

The officers expected a hardened criminal willing to fight his way out with guns blazing; instead they found Lemay relaxed and completely cool, friendly even.

They also found a stash of nearly one thousand dollars.

"That's my personal money," he told them. "The money that these gentlemen of the police are looking for may be elsewhere."

As the men continued their search of the boat, Lemay asked how they'd found him.

"I never make a mistake," he said.

Smith explained that his face had been flashed on TV during the inaugural Early Bird satellite program.

Lemay couldn't believe it.

"On your honor?" he asked Smith.

Smith said, "Yes, it's true."

"Well, isn't that something! It took a satellite to catch me," Lemay said with obvious pride.

Lemay pulled on a pair of slacks and donned a straw fedora, worn at a rakish angle, before the men handcuffed his wrists in the front.

"The Canadian people have described me as dangerous," he told the officers. "Actually, I'm a very easygoing sort of person. I never do anything to hurt the other fellow."

They took him off the yacht, still bare chested and with a cigarette dangling from his mouth. He'd thrown a coat over his wrists to cover the handcuffs as he made his way off of the *Triana*, flanked by the officers, as the press snapped his picture and peppered him with questions that he ignored.

Back on shore, he turned to look at the yacht he'd lovingly restored.

"It will take time before I see that boat again," he said with a sigh. "Or any boat."

He told his captors he needed to stop at the office to pay for his berth, which they allowed him to do. Lemay peeled off four $100 bills. He owed $375.

"Keep the change," he told the wharfmaster. He asked him whether he knew anyone who wanted to buy a yacht, as he wasn't likely to need one for a long time.

The men drove to the Fort Lauderdale police station, and Lemay put on a shirt and tie one of the officers had retrieved from the *Triana*. He formally identified himself as Georges Lemay. The local officers then booked him at the new Dade County Jail in Miami, which was billed as "escape-proof."

Lemay appeared in federal court in Miami the next morning, where he made it clear he intended to fight extradition to Canada. He wasn't planning on making it easy on the authorities. Lemay hired the high-powered Miami lawyers Harvey St. Jean and Lawrence Hoffman to represent him. Léo-René Maranda, the Montreal lawyer who had defended Lemay's gang, flew down to assist.

St. Jean had defended many high-profile clients, including Jack "Murph the Surf" Murphy, who stole the Star of India, one of the largest sapphires in the world, from New York City's Museum of Natural History in 1964. He also defended Candy Mossler, a Houston socialite accused of murdering her estranged millionaire husband at their luxury apartment in Key Biscayne, Florida, in 1964. St. Jean got her acquitted in a sensational trial in Miami two years later.

* * *

Lise arrived in Miami to see Lemay after his arrest and was promptly apprehended by INS. As a convicted felon—for her role in the Dominion Day bank burglary—she was banned from visiting the United States. INS agents swarmed her hotel room after intercepting a letter she'd sent to the jail telling Lemay she was in Florida and would see him shortly. INS took Lise into custody, but a federal judge released her on a thousand-dollar bond.

Lemay's sister, Carmelle Parent, accompanied Lise to Miami. They attempted to visit Lemay at the Dade County Jail after Lise's release on bail, but authorities refused both women entry. Only family could see prisoners. Lise angrily claimed she and Lemay had married in Mexico the previous fall but couldn't provide a copy of the marriage certificate. Carmelle had to wait for her birth certificate to arrive from Canada before they'd let her see her brother.

Another of Lemay's sisters, Suzanne Poisson, also came to Miami to comfort her little brother. The three women handled all of Lemay's business for him while he sat in jail—negotiating the sale of his beloved yacht for twenty-five thousand dollars in cash, making sure the dapper thief got new clothes for his court appearances, and talking strategy with his lawyers.

Investigators did their best to keep Lise away from Lemay, but on June 1, she appeared at the courthouse during a recess in Lemay's extradition hearing and married him in a two-minute ceremony performed by one of his lawyers, Lawrence Hoffman. The federal immigration director, Robert Woytowich, had vowed to keep the couple from marrying, but the ceremony had been so discreet—the couple whispered their vows—that it was over before anyone could stop it. Lemay's sisters were in attendance, low-key bridesmaids, and it wasn't until Lemay shouted, "Love is stronger than the police," that his guards took notice of what had just happened. The new Mrs. Lemay couldn't be compelled to testify against her husband and now had spousal privileges to visit Lemay at the jail.

* * *

No one from the RCMP had participated in Lemay's capture, so they were flying blind informationally, forced to rely on U.S. officials and newspaper reports for specifics.

A week after Lemay's arrest, the Montreal Police sent Detective Leblanc to Miami to see what he could get out of Lemay. During an interrogation that lasted about three hours, Lemay refused to discuss the bank heist at all. When the detective asked whether it was true Lemay had visited Montreal while on the run, Lemay answered with a smile, "It's your investigation. Try to find out."

Leblanc attempted to determine whether Lemay had been behind another recent Montreal bank break-in. This one took place on the weekend of April 10–11, 1965, at a branch of the Royal Bank of Canada on Van Horne Avenue. The thieves looted four hundred safe-deposit boxes and made off with around one million dollars in cash, bonds, and other valuables. The MO fit Lemay, the Montreal Police believed. Lemay remained mum on the subject.

Leblanc left the jail feeling as though he'd spent the day discussing everything and nothing with the prisoner, so he returned to Fort Lauderdale and, accompanied by INS agents, got a look inside the *Triana*, but found no clues.

"Did you undo the walls of the yacht?" he asked the agents in his accented English. They replied they hadn't and suggested that it would require Leblanc to somehow get the boat back to Canada and into dry dock before that thorough of a search could happen.

Leblanc also interviewed several people who spent time with Lemay while the fugitive was in Florida. Again, he learned nothing of any real value. It was a thoroughly unsatisfying expedition for Leblanc, except for the knowledge that soon Lemay would be back in Canada and on trial for the bank burglary case the detective had worked on for nearly four years. It would be thoroughly satisfying to see the heist's mastermind behind bars.

Leblanc just hoped the U.S. court wouldn't give Lemay bail. If they did, he believed Lemay would again disappear. Leblanc knew he'd have to stick to the thief as closely as he could, but if the court freed Lemay and he made it onto his yacht—well, Leblanc didn't want to think about that possibility.

Unfortunately for the Mounties hoping to snag Rivard alongside Lemay, it didn't happen, though Canadian authorities still believed Rivard could be in Miami or had been at some point. Following Lemay's capture, RCMP superintendent Edward Martin reached out to Paul Grenier in the U.S. Immigration and Naturalization Service about looking into whether Rivard may have been with Lemay after Rivard's prison break in March. The Canadians sent a ream of wanted circulars, and in return Grenier promised his "wholehearted cooperation."

Martin also spoke with Inspector Peter Bazowski, the RCMP liaison officer stationed in Washington, D.C., who was tasked with coordinating Lemay's return to Canada. Martin ordered Bazowski to do some legwork in the Miami and Fort Lauderdale areas. He wanted to know whether any marina attendants or others recognized Rivard as having visited or stayed on *Triana*; who was on board when they arrested Lemay; and whether Lemay kept a boat log showing the various ports he'd visited. Martin also hoped to learn whether U.S. agents had found any correspondence on Lemay's yacht, any evidence about where Lemay had been for more than three years, and if he had a "permanent base of operations." The RCMP hoped if Lemay maintained a hideout somewhere in the United States, Rivard might be using it.

Martin also asked Bazowski to find out who Lemay's associates were and "particularly anything which would give us some indication of where Rivard may be or has been during the past few months."

They were getting desperate.

While Bazowski was contacting both INS and the FBI to learn what he could, Canadian crime reporters inundated the Fort Lauderdale Police Department with phone calls. They fanned out across the city and into Miami, tracking down reports that a mysterious man had been at the marina when Lemay was led away by the police.

"Now, Georges, you take care of yourself," the man supposedly said. "You know what I mean?"

People had seen the man around town with Lemay, and his description matched Rivard's.

A *Toronto Star* reporter tracked down a teenage waitress at a diner near the Bahia Mar Marina and showed her pictures of Rivard.

"Sure, I recognize him," she told the reporter. "He came in about twice a week, had a coffee, and went out the side door toward the basin."

Montreal Detective Leblanc also interviewed the woman, just to cover his bases, but he doubted Rivard would have gone to the United States, where he was wanted for drug smuggling and had escaped specifically to avoid extradition.

Despite the intense scrutiny, no one ever located the mystery man.

After his arrest, Lemay told U.S. Customs investigators he didn't know Rivard and "would have nothing to do with, nor associate with any people in the narcotic business." The investigators who questioned him sensed Lemay was lying. Lemay seemed especially wary of any questions that connected him to Rivard. The Customs agents felt a follow-up interview would reveal an association between the two men. They never got their chance since Lemay's lawyers quashed any hope for further interviews with their client.

* * *

On May 7, during a House of Commons session, Eldon Woolliams, a Conservative from Calgary, stood up. He had questions about Lemay's capture the previous day thanks to Early Bird's broadcast of the Most Wanted segment. But Woolliams wasn't there to praise police for Lemay's apprehension, nor to pontificate on the benefits of space-age technology.

"The Early Bird satellite was successfully used to locate Mr. Lemay, one of the most wanted criminals in Canada, and responsible sources have advised me that Early Bird was also to be used to locate another of Canada's most wanted criminals. Did the government or the minister of justice stop this procedure and, if so, why?" he asked prime minister Pearson. "Is it a fact that Mr. Rivard's picture was to have been flashed over Early Bird but that a minister, or people in high places in the government, prevented this procedure from taking place?"

Pearson replied that he knew nothing about the matter, had had no knowledge of the broadcast before seeing it, and didn't believe anyone would have interfered.

When McClellan learned of the accusation, he was livid. His decision to feature Lemay proved a huge success, but all the politicians wanted was to use Rivard as a weapon against each other and the RCMP.

McClellan, in an interview with the Canadian Press in which he appeared slightly paranoid, said that "sinister agencies" were at work trying to undermine the efficiency of the RCMP and destroy the force.

"This is part of their overall plan to destroy, subvert, and create mistrust in the free world."

He explained his reasoning behind the decision to focus on Lemay and not Rivard during the Early Bird broadcast.

"We were right, but we were still lashed for not showing Rivard," he complained. He would soon be vindicated.

Two months later, on July 16, Montreal Police detectives identified two of Rivard's contacts in Montreal, a pair of bank robbers, whom the police tailed to a cottage only fifteen miles west of the city, near Lake Saint-Louis. The detectives kept surveillance on the property while they called in reinforcements from both the RCMP and the Quebec Provincial Police, more than fifty officers in all. They surrounded the elegant summer cottage in the late afternoon, hoping to find Rivard within. Many of the officers carried machine guns.

When the cops burst through the door, they found the two bank robbers and Rivard in the living room. They were all wearing swimsuits and were about to go for a dip. Rivard went quietly, as did his two companions.

Rivard had mainly been hiding in the Laurentian Mountains during his 136 days of freedom. One of his associates later described how the fugitive often dressed up like a woman, down to a padded bra and girdle, to obscure his identity when not in hiding. Rivard was extradited to Texas at the end of July and given a twenty-year sentence for drug smuggling. He served nine years.

Raymond Denis, the former chief of staff for the minister of immigration and citizenship, was charged with attempted bribery and perverting the course of justice for his part in the Rivard Affair. He was later sentenced to two years in prison.

With the Rivard Affair now behind him, McClellan returned to Lemay.

On June 3, 1965, McClellan wrote a letter to J. Edgar Hoover, the head of the FBI. "The return of Georges Lemay appears imminent," McClellan wrote before thanking the agency for its "quick action and decisive police effort" in capturing Lemay.

The letter may have been premature.

18

The Escape-Proof Jail

SUMMER–FALL 1965

EVERYONE AT THE DADE COUNTY JAIL, EVEN THE GUARDS, liked Lemay. The affable and unflappable French Canadian exercised constantly, smoked cigars, and had begun jokingly calling himself Satellite Boy after learning the Early Bird satellite helped in his capture.

He became friendly with several inmates, including Ronald Fonda, a University of Miami student turned bank robber convicted on federal charges. Fonda was in the Dade County Jail on local charges related to the same heist. Lemay liked to kid Fonda about all the mistakes the student had made during the robbery.

The other prisoners treated Lemay like a star, and the guards were accommodating, almost servile in his presence, so it wasn't hard finding willing accomplices to help with his escape. Lemay spent nearly four months devising and reshaping Operation Tarzan, as he'd dubbed it. The plan was near perfection. He shared only some of the very general terms of his plans with Fonda. Lemay may have been affable, but he knew when to be guarded as well.

The press Lemay was getting made him happy. He felt as though he had the public's sympathy on his side, so if his escape plan didn't work out, he might at least have a decent chance of getting an acquittal at a jury trial.

Meanwhile, his lawyers were dragging out the extradition process, buying Lemay more time to plan. They'd just brought a bail request to the federal Fifth Circuit Court of Appeal in New Orleans after a lower court ordered Lemay held without bond.

After his arrest, Lemay was initially held on the jail's fourth floor in a cell that had a window looking out onto the street. Lemay would loudly converse in French with Lise, but the warden moved him after guards caught him attempting to shout his wedding vows out the window. This was the first marriage attempt, before he and Lise had their two-minute ceremony.

His new cell, 5A4, was a dormitory-style space that didn't have a window to the outside and held eight inmates. It had gray walls, yellow chrome bars, and matching iron furniture. Two steel barred doors in each cell kept the prisoners out of the corridors, which were in turn blocked by more metal doors. A guard in a bulletproof-glass-lined pie-shaped booth controlled the opening and closing of the doors electrically from the center of the floor, which gave a 360-degree view of the prisoners.

Guards stationed on a perimeter walkway could also see into all the cells. The jail had a workforce of more than one hundred guards, including command staff, and new electronic scanning equipment used to search everything coming into the jail. The facility was on Northwest Fourteenth Street near Twelfth Avenue and was attached to the Public Safety Department Headquarters and the county courthouse, which meant reinforcements were close at hand if needed.

The county had opened the ten-story jail facility four years earlier, with the top four floors left empty for future expansion. The state-of-the-art jail took five years to build and cost five million dollars (nearly fifty million today). The jail's architect, Bud Reeder, called the new complex "the best in the country."

"We've incorporated every security measure there is," he told reporters when it opened.

Captain Noah Scott, who was in charge of the new jail, refused to call it escape proof, even if the press did.

"If one man can make something, another man can figure out how to get the best of it," he told the *The Miami News* in June 1960. "But we'll do what we can."

Only one prisoner in four years had escaped: a trustee, an inmate who'd earned special privileges, had scaled an eighteen-foot wall from the kitchen and was quickly caught. Lemay's plan, like its creator, would be the most dramatic. Instead of trying to defeat the jail's modern technology, Lemay focused on the one aspect the designers had no control over: human frailty in the face of a big payoff.

Lemay befriended several of the guards, feeling them out to see which he thought he could manipulate. He chose two: Harold Alger and Peter Jaworski. Lemay loved contingencies, so he worked on both guards simultaneously. Neither guard knew the other was also working with Lemay.

Lemay tested out Jaworski's loyalty by having him pass notes to Lise, which helped solidify the escape plans before the jail began letting Lise visit Lemay after their quickie wedding.

He then offered Jaworski twenty-five thousand dollars in cash to help him escape. The guard quickly agreed and snuck a nylon rope, gloves, hacksaw blades, and a knife into the jail for Lemay. The hacksaw blades Lemay hid behind a shelf in his cell. The rest he stashed in a hole cut in the bottom of his rubber mattress that he then stacked on another mattress.

Jaworski met Lise in the parking lot of a diner in Little Havana, where she handed him an envelope with five thousand dollars in cash to be used to entice any other guards who might be amenable to helping the French Canadian escape. Jaworski brought the cash to work and fanned it under the noses of several guards, who turned him down but didn't turn him in. Jaworski returned the money to Lise afterward.

On the outside, Lise was working on Earl Mixon, a thirty-one-year-old ex-deputy who worked for the bail bond company she had used after her arrest. Mixon had worked at the jail from 1961 to 1963 and had resigned from the Dade County Sheriff's Office in March 1965. Lise first asked Mixon to help with her plans to marry Lemay during a break in his deportation hearing. The authorities had flatly refused to allow the pair to marry and did their damndest to prevent it.

"I'd pay you anything if you can help me with my marriage," she told him in her heavily accented English. They were in the bail bond office where Mixon worked. The petite brunette, who seemed both exotic and approachable, captivated him.

Mixon helped with the paperwork, and she paid him one hundred dollars for his services.

They met a few times for lunch, and at one of these meetings Lise asked whether he knew a certain guard at the jail and whether Mixon believed she could trust the man. She needed a guard to pass French-language magazines to Lemay in jail.

"Nah, he's a fink," he replied.

A couple of days later the pair met again, and Lise mentioned another name, Harold Alger. Mixon had known Alger, a twenty-seven-year-old guard, for several years and believed Lise could trust him. Mixon phoned Alger and asked him to pass the magazines to Lemay. Alger agreed to and didn't even ask for any money.

The next day, Mixon met Alger and handed him a few rolled-up magazines, which Alger passed along to Lemay. It was a test, and both Mixon and Alger passed.

Before he knew it, the ex-deputy was actively helping Lise plan her new husband's escape. He would often get calls at home from "Miss Jeannie," the name Lise gave when calling him. Mixon recruited Alger and promised to split thirty-five thousand dollars with him for helping Lemay escape.

After their quickie wedding, Lise could visit Lemay in jail. They would sit across from each other, separated by a heavy glass partition, speaking to each other in French through an intercom. It wasn't the most convenient way to plan an escape. Mixon made it easier. He was the go-between for Lise, Lemay, and Alger. By late August, the plans were firming up nicely.

On August 23, NASA's TIROS—the country's first weather satellite, built by Hughes's rival RCA and placed into a low-Earth orbit in 1960—photographed a tropical disturbance in the Atlantic north of French Guiana. Four days later, reconnaissance planes picked up a low-grade tropical disturbance 350 miles east of Barbados that was quickly building into a monster storm. They named it Betsy. In the following days, Betsy looped around the Caribbean, gaining and then losing strength. The folks in Florida and all along the Gulf Coast watched breathlessly as the hurricane made an erratic path toward the United States. Lemay focused on his own path, also destined to make headlines.

In early September, a friend of the Lemays', Gilles Lamontagene, arrived from Montreal to assist in Lemay's escape. He stayed with Lise at the Garden State Apartments from September 8 to September 16, when they moved to the Laurel Motel. He drove her around and ran the necessary errands related to the escape plan.

By September 4, Hurricane Betsy, with winds of more than 150 miles per hour, was on course to hit the east coast of Florida. In Miami, businesses boarded up their windows, relief agencies prepared thousands of hot dogs and hamburgers to feed any displaced residents, and the city put emergency plans into action. Betsy finally made landfall four days later in Key Largo as a Category 3 hurricane.

In Miami, there was flooding, power outages, and communication blackouts due to downed power and telephone lines. The jail, which had a backup generator, was unaffected. But on the Gulf Coast, where Betsy again made landfall on September 9, the storm devastated parts of Louisiana, including New Orleans. The city saw the worst flooding in its history until Hurricane Katrina hit forty years later. Betsy flooded nearly two hundred thousand homes, killed between seventy-six and eighty-one people (estimates vary), and caused more than one billion dollars in damage.

* * *

Three days before Lemay's escape, Alger got nervous, perhaps believing Lemay was going to stiff them, and he called Mixon and told him to corner Lise to make sure she actually had their thirty-five thousand dollars.

Mixon ran into Lise at the Metro Justice Building, attached to the jail, and asked about the money. Lise, always cool, opened her purse right there. Inside, Mixon saw a large bundle of cash with a hundred-dollar bill on top. She smiled. He trusted her and told Alger he'd seen the money.

Neither Alger nor Mixon knew exactly what day Lemay planned to make his break or exactly how he planned to get out, only that they had to get him above the sixth floor of the jail.

On Tuesday, September 21, 1965, Lemay made his daring jailbreak. His original plan was to saw through the bars of his cell with the hacksaw blades, but he gave up on that plan early on and decided on something more ambitious.

Around 11:00 a.m., Alger came to Lemay's cell, took the prisoner out, and headed to the elevator.

"What time you want to eat?" Alger asked the other guard on duty, who looked up as Alger hustled Lemay down the corridor. The elevator doors closed, and the two men stepped inside. The other guard didn't even have time to answer the question about lunch.

Alger hit the first-floor button, and they headed down. Once there, he walked Lemay down to a holding cell. He didn't lock the door.

Alger, jittery from what he'd just done—he'd just broken every rule imaginable—left the jail and met Mixon on the steps of the Metro Justice Building. Mixon had been waiting for news of their plan.

"Everything's fine," Alger told him before hurrying off and getting into his car. Mixon met Lise at 1:30 p.m. near the jail to relay the news. She was to look for a signal from Lemay that he was ready to break out. She sat in the car, waiting.

Back inside the jail, Lemay remained in the cell for a few minutes until the coast was clear. He slipped into the hall and snuck onto the elevator. He rode it to the sixth floor, the highest secured floor that didn't require a special key to access. He maintained his cool but knew that at any moment a guard could get onto the elevator and ruin his escape plans.

To access the higher unsecured floors, Lemay relied on a trick he had learned from Alger. Jimmying the elevator door open would bypass the security system and allow the elevator to travel to the higher levels not then in use. Lemay had not managed to bring the rope or gloves with him—it would have been nearly impossible to sneak the items out of his cell—so he needed to come up with an alternative means of escape.

At the tenth floor, Lemay got out. This level was unfinished and completely empty except for construction and maintenance materials. He dragged a hundred-foot-long hose from its storage place, threw it into the elevator, and headed to the seventh floor. He hauled the hose out and tied one end to an exposed pipe. As an experienced sailor, he knew his knots and easily secured the hose without fear that it might slip as he used it to make his escape. Lemay paced the floor, waiting for the right moment. He wanted the sun to be going down, but he didn't want it to be completely dark. He needed to see what he was doing during his dangerous seven-story climb.

Back on the fifth floor, the guards fed the prisoners their lunch. No one noticed Lemay wasn't in his cell. There was a shift change at 4:00 p.m. and still no one noticed Lemay had disappeared.

* * *

Mixon sat in the parking lot of Toby's Cafeteria, in the historically African American neighborhood of Liberty City, waiting for Lise to drop off the thirty-five thousand dollars. It was past 4:30 p.m., the appointed rendezvous time, and he was getting nervous. Alger was in his car parked next to him. Finally, at 5:15 p.m., Lise drove up. She was alone.

She parked and walked over to Mixon's car. Alger came over and the three conferred.

"I still haven't gotten a signal from my husband," Lise said, her brow knitted. "I'm going back to the jail yard to await his signal." Nervous that Lemay had been caught during his escape attempt, she was anxiously awaiting a sign that all was well.

"Your husband's loose in the jail," an agitated Alger told her. "That was the deal. Where's our money?"

"I don't have it with me. It's at the motel, the Frolics Motel. As soon as I get the signal, I'll pick up the package and deliver it. We can do it here or at the motel."

The two men looked at each other.

"We'll meet you at the motel," Mixon answered. "You have to be there by six."

Both men were angry, but what could they do?

Lise agreed. They would meet at Frolics, at Thirty-Fourth Street and

Biscayne Boulevard. She didn't actually plan on making the rendezvous. The two men had served their purpose and they'd been too dumb to ask for the money up front, so they'd suffer the consequences.

Mixon followed Alger back to his house. The guard was still in his uniform and wanted to change. A few minutes later they were back on the road in Mixon's car, heading to the Frolics Motel. It was 5:45 p.m. when they arrived.

Around 6:30 p.m., Lemay kicked out the glass from the unbarred window and flung the rest of the hose out. It was a long drop. He'd spent four months doing push-ups to get his already-muscular upper body in the best shape he could. It would take a lot of strength to shimmy down the side of the jail building, nearly one hundred feet to the ground and freedom. He knew from his time around sailboats that sliding down the hose without the gloves he'd been forced to abandon was likely to result in nasty rope burns, but it couldn't be helped.

Florian Hoban was walking to his car parked in the county health clinic's parking lot, across the street from the Dade County Jail complex, when he heard a crash. He looked up at the jail just as a man began rappeling down the side of the building. He was a long way up, seven floors.

Albertha Horton, a Black teenager waiting for the bus, also saw the escape.

After climbing down the building, the man, who was wearing a white T-shirt and gray pants, landed on a fifteen-foot-high setback. He jumped into the bushes below. He made it and was gone.

Lemay jogged toward a waiting white 1964 Ford Galaxie with white-wall tires in the same parking lot where Hoban's car was parked.

Both Hoban and Horton thought there were three men in the getaway car.

In reality, Lise was in the driver's seat and Lamontagene sat in the front passenger seat. Lemay flung the door open and jumped in just before the car went roaring out of the parking lot and onto the street.

They drove north on Northwest Fourteenth Avenue. Lemay's hands were bleeding badly. As he'd feared, the friction from sliding down the hose had torn the flesh from his palms. The wounds were deep. The adrenaline from the escape had kept him from feeling the pain during the descent, but now they were throbbing.

Hoban, after seeing the escape, ran toward the Public Safety Department Headquarters and spied a man coming out. He was in his shirtsleeves and had a shoulder holster.

"Are you a police officer?" Hoban asked, stopping in front of him, out of breath. The man, a detective-sergeant named Robert Hoelscher, said he was. Hoban told him what he'd seen.

"Go inside and tell the desk officer to get ahold of the shift commander," the officer ordered. Hoelscher ran the one hundred feet around the corner of the building to where Hoban had seen the escapee. He looked up at the dangling hose. It was nearly dark now, and the prisoner was long gone.

Ten minutes later, out rushed several sheriff's deputies, who ran around the yard like ants after someone had kicked their nest. Hoelscher went back to the front of the station and spotted Hoban walking off. The detective caught up to him and jotted down his information. No one had bothered to do so earlier.

Hoelscher also approached Horton, still waiting for the bus. He got her story and personal information as well.

The night shift commander, Captain Richard Gladwell, still didn't know about the escape. He found out only when Hoelscher came upstairs to write out his report forty minutes after Lemay had bolted.

"This guy is really gone," Hoelscher told the surprised captain.

Gladwell looked out the window and saw deputies racing around the yard. He called the hotline to the main jail control booth, but no one picked up. He finally got someone from the booking desk on the line, who told him a prisoner had escaped, but they didn't know who.

Nearly an hour passed before anyone sounded a general alarm. To make matters worse, the authorities sent out incorrect details about the fugitive. They described the unidentified escapee as a trustee wearing blue striped prison clothing. It was a fiasco for the sheriff's office, but a boon for Lemay.

At 6:45 p.m., the jail staff began a full check of the more than 650 prisoners to determine which of them had escaped. It took hours to confirm that it was Lemay.

Mixon and Alger waited at the rendezvous spot until after 7:00 p.m., but Lise never showed. They headed to the jail and drove around it several times looking for Lise's Galaxie, to no avail. Defeated, Mixon dropped Alger at his place, went to a liquor store, bought a bottle, and returned home to drink his troubles away.

He got drunk with his roommate, Russell Lewis, a jailbird he'd been the bail bondsman for on a bad check charge. Mixon was always bringing home strays he'd bonded out.

Lewis said he heard about the jailbreak on the radio. Mixon then filled him in on the details and how Lise had screwed him out of his take. Lewis didn't completely believe the story at first. Mixon was too much of a shrewd operator to let someone get the best of him like that, Lewis thought. But then Alger called, sounding shrill. He confirmed everything Mixon had said. Mixon, too drunk to care at this point, hung up, took a shower, and went for a walk.

Two women showed up at the house shortly thereafter: Mixon's cousin Sandy and a friend of his from the sheriff's office. Lewis told them Mixon had left, but they insisted on searching the house before leaving.

Mixon returned home and went to bed. He woke a few hours later to the sound of his phone ringing incessantly. His old captain, Gladwell, asked Mixon to come over to the jail. Since Mixon had acted as Lise's bondsman, the captain figured he might have some information that could help. Mixon drunkenly agreed and hung up.

Just then, Deputy Donald Deibert, a friend of his, arrived and told him the police believed he was involved in the escape. He tried to sober Mixon up and talk sense to him, but Mixon seemed too far gone. He asked Mixon to show him where Lise had been staying.

"I don't know what you're talking about. I didn't get any payoff," he angrily told the deputy. The latter part was true, at least.

Deibert had known for months that Lemay was planning an escape and that Mixon was tied up in it.

Three months earlier, one of his informants told him two men dressed as INS agents planned to grab Lemay under the pretext of interviewing him and then make their escape in a panel truck disguised as a federal vehicle.

Deibert didn't trust anyone in the sheriff's office, believing most of his fellow deputies were on the take, so he contacted the Miami Police about what he'd learned.

Now, he hoped to get ahead of the situation, perhaps even catch Lemay at Lise's motel room. But getting Mixon, who was barely able to stand, to help him was looking impossible. He waited while Mixon got dressed and then the pair headed outside and got into Deibert's car. Deibert was beginning to think he should just drive his friend to the sheriff's office and wash his hands of the whole mess.

Then a sheriff's cruiser arrived. Deibert argued with the deputy behind the wheel about who would take Mixon. Deibert finally gave up and drove away empty-handed. He went to meet his connection at the Miami Police Department to advise him of what had happened. Mixon had never told him the name or address of the motel where Lise had been staying.

The deputy dragged Mixon into the Dade County Sheriff's Office—his old workplace—at around 12:30 a.m. and questioned him about the escape. He was obviously drunk and denied any knowledge of the breakout. He did provide a description of Lise's car, which matched those given by the two eyewitnesses to Lemay's dramatic get away. Mixon didn't tell them where Lise Lemay had been staying. A deputy drove him home. The agency kept him under surveillance in the hope that he'd lead them to Lemay, but Mixon didn't leave his house that night.

Investigators had already spoken with Alger, who admitted to taking Lemay down to the holding cell on the first floor, but said he locked it and left. Alger claimed he had received a slip of paper with these instructions and thought they came from a superior officer. He said he threw the slip away afterward.

The investigators brought Alger back for a second interview the next morning, and he cracked almost immediately. He admitted everything and gave up Mixon as well. They allowed him to change out of his uniform before booking him on charges of aiding Lemay's escape.

The investigators then brought Mixon back in. When they told him Alger had talked, he cursed his old friend with such vehemence the investigators were too embarrassed to write down the string of invectives he used in their official notes. He, too, was arrested.

In the weeks before Lemay's escape, Jaworski decided not to go through with helping the prisoner, but he didn't tell his superiors about Lemay's plans either. He tried to avoid Lemay, and when he did interact with him, he put him off, hoping the feds would deport Lemay before he had the chance to escape. When Jaworski learned of the breakout, he couldn't believe it. He had no idea Lemay had been working with Alger. The sheriff's office fired Jaworski and he, too, was eventually charged for helping Lemay.

They also fired Don McNelis, a guard Alger had tried to recruit by flashing him the roll of cash. McNelis declined, but he waffled on whether to turn Alger in. McNelis finally decided to confess to his superior officer when he reported for his night shift on September 21. By the time he arrived, Lemay had already made his bid for freedom, and McNelis was out of a job.

Back in May, after Lemay's arrest, a federal immigration agent asked him how he had obtained his fake passport. Lemay prophetically answered, "When you have money, you can get anything."

This escape didn't even cost him that much since none of the guards got paid.

19

Disneyland

FALL–WINTER 1965

THE ESCAPE PLAN OUT OF MIAMI CHANGED OVER MONTHS OF planning. Lise and Lemay considered flying to South America in a small plane or taking a speedboat north on the Intracoastal Waterway. In the end, they decided on something much simpler.

Lise and Lamontagene picked up Lemay in the Ford Galaxie. With its streamlined design and muscular V8 engine, it had speed if needed. Lamontagene rented the car under the name Gilles Lamontagne. This was a bit of a joke as this was the name of a Quebec City politician who was then running for mayor. They drove to the Motel Laurel, in Miami's Morningside neighborhood, where Lise and Lamontagene were staying. They dumped the Ford at the back of the motel and drove off in a white 1954 four-door Chrysler New Yorker Deluxe—a chromed-out beauty with a beast of an engine—that Lamontagene purchased for the escape.

They headed north to Andy's Motel in Opelika, Alabama, a sleepy little city in Lee County, 650 miles from Miami. The two men registered as Paul Martin and Phil Lamonthe.

Lamontagene (Martin) signed them in. The clerk noticed Lise, who was wearing an ice-blond wig and wrap-around sunglasses, but never did get a good look at "Lamonthe," who went straight from the car to the hotel room. It was Lemay.

They stayed for two days, long enough to dump the Chrysler, which was having engine trouble. Lamontagene stripped off its plates and other identifying information and bought a white 1960 four-door Ford Falcon, a less flashy vehicle than the New Yorker, paid for with five crisp hundred-dollar bills.

It helped that Lamontagene was with the Lemays. The U.S. authorities didn't know what he looked like, or even his name, so he took charge of renting the motel rooms, getting the gas, and picking up food. Sometimes they traveled at night, other times when the sun was up. The group focused on avoiding local law enforcement and drawing attention to themselves from nosy clerks and neighbors.

From Alabama they went to Georgia, then Tennessee, Kentucky, West Virginia, Maryland, and New Jersey, avoiding major cities and favoring low-key motels near highways, often staying for multiple days if it seemed safe. It took nearly a month to get to their final destination, New York City, a place both Lemay and Lise loved.

New York was a city so large it wouldn't be hard to melt into the faceless crowds of the 7.8 million residents of the metropolis, or so Lemay initially believed. Even so, he remained cautious about going out in public just to be safe. They dumped the car, took a room at a chic hotel in midtown, and settled in.

Lamontagene returned to Montreal and Josée came to New York to stay with her parents.

Lise was ecstatic the first time Lemay enveloped his daughter in his strong arms. He quickly came to adore the sweet child, who was now three years old. Lise loved to dress her up, a fashionable child to match her equally fashionable parents.

Lemay rarely left the hotel room, afraid that even in a city of millions someone might recognize him. With the brand-new satellite soaring thousands of miles overhead that had already caught Satellite Boy once, even a metropolis like New York City might not be able to hide him. He watched television and read prodigiously, especially his dog-eared copy of master card sharp John Scarne's *Complete Guide to Gambling*, to while away the hours. He still had problems with his hands from the seven-story slide to freedom down the side of the Dade County Jail. Going to a doctor to have them looked at was too big a risk, so it took months for him to recover their normal use.

While the Lemay family hunkered down in Manhattan, patrol cars prowled first Miami's streets, then an ever-widening area. Dade County sheriff T. A. Buchanan coordinated the initial search, but once Lemay could be charged with a federal crime, the FBI would take over.

The sheriff's office put out a BOLO (be on the lookout) for the fugitive, set up surveillance at the Miami International Airport and the smaller ones across Dade County, and covered bus terminals and train stations. They also had eyes on as many of the waterfront areas where a boat might slip out as they could. With so much coastline, it was impossible to cover it all. Dade County was huge, nearly two thousand square miles—bigger than Rhode Island—and stretched from the Everglades in the west to Biscayne Bay in the east and connected to the Keys to the south via the Overseas Highway.

The sheriff's office alerted the Florida Highway Patrol to look out for the white late-model Ford Galaxie. The Coast Guard and Dade County Marine Patrol watched the waterways around Miami for any small, fast watercraft that Lemay might try to escape on. Pilots buzzed random boats, believing Lemay and Lise might be trying to flee to a friendly island nation. Lise had listed Haiti as her preferred place to be deported to on her paperwork, and Lemay had also mentioned Haiti during his deportation hearing.

Deputies handed out copies of Lemay's photo to airline personnel, bus companies, steamship operators, at train stations, and anywhere else someone might reasonably find a way out of town via transportation other than a car.

An inmate who shared a cell with Lemay told investigators the French Canadian planned to borrow the yacht of a Miami underworld figure and head to an undisclosed location in the Caribbean. The Miami Police converged on the yacht moored at Biscayne Bay soon after. The boat was idling and there were several people on board as the police cautiously approached. The engine suddenly cut off and three men scattered before the police even got on board. They didn't identify any of them, much less catch them.

Another prisoner told investigators Lemay was hiding out at the Lennox Hotel in Miami's Allapattah neighborhood with Robert Holland, a con who had recently gotten out of jail.

The morning after the escape, deputies surrounded the down-in-the-mouth Lennox Hotel. They performed a room-to-room search and found Holland and two friends in room 23, but not Lemay. Holland had no idea what the deputies were on about. He hadn't seen Lemay since they were in jail together, Holland told them.

The investigators checked all of Miami's hotels and motels, interviewed guards and inmates at the jail, tracked down the agency that rented Lise the car used in the escape, and spoke with Lemay's neighbors at the marina. They learned a lot about Lemay's life while in Florida and the time leading up to his escape but were no closer to finding their quarry.

Detectives thought they'd gotten lucky when two flight attendants identified the suspects as having been on their flight to the Bahamas on September 22. Further digging by the sheriff's office and INS determined the Lemays had never been on the plane.

The manhunt and surveillance in the Miami area lasted until September 23. Authorities figured the fugitives were long gone by then, but they continued to make spot checks at various locations where the couple could make an escape in case Lemay had been hiding out in Miami waiting for the heat to let off before making a break. The sheriff's office issued warrants for the Lemays, charging them with felony conspiracy to bribe.

The Florida authorities slowed down the FBI's response time by failing to file needed paperwork in a timely manner. Once they did, three days after the Lemays' escape, the U.S. Attorney's Office issued federal warrants for the couple, charging them with unlawful interstate flight to avoid prosecution. Finally, the FBI could turn the full force of its enormous investigative apparatus toward hunting down the fugitives.

U.S. federal agents would soon be able to commiserate with their comrades in the RCMP who had also dealt with a wide-ranging, headache-producing search for one of the most elusive criminals they'd dealt with. It wasn't just that Lemay was so slippery; his flamboyant escape (and personality) attracted media scrutiny like few other FBI cases. Lemay made for good press, which was bad press for the feds.

In the following weeks, the Dade County Sheriff's Office, embarrassed by Lemay's dramatic breakout from its "unbreakable" jail and its deputies' lackluster response, quickly put together a five-man panel to investigate the matter. Besides arresting Alger, Mixon, and Jaworski for helping Lemay escape, they fired two other guards for not reporting what they knew and heard testimony from the various officers involved in the bungled search for Lemay. The commission recommended a more thorough screening process for jail employees and some additional security measures to prevent future escapes.

FBI special agent Michael Crane, a New Jersey native with a law degree who had been part of the D-Day invasion, re-interviewed many of the same witnesses as the sheriff's office. Other agents in the Miami field office tracked down all of Lise's phone calls made during her stay in Florida before Lemay's breakout, dug deeper into her movements leading up to the escape, and looked into who had visited the prisoner at the jail.

Agent Crane sat in an interview room at the jail interrogating several of the prisoners. It seemed Lemay had become friendly with a few of his fellow inmates and shared the details of several different escape plans with them, or at least that's what they said. These men were all looking for something, whether it be a little leniency on a prison sentence or a chance at the reward offered by the Bank of Nova Scotia for information leading to Lemay's capture. They wouldn't get a chance. The boat repairman who turned Lemay in received the two-thousand-dollar reward money.

Crane learned Lemay had told Robert Moret, a French Canadian awaiting trial for murder, that he planned to take a small plane to Tijuana, Mexico, where he would board a waiting boat and head to Venezuela to hide out at the home of a friend in the international shipping business. It was all very vague, but the FBI contacted INTERPOL for help in looking into the story.

Other inmates told of Lemay's plans to take a speedboat north, escape in a panel truck and hide out in an abandoned cocktail lounge, or head to Colombia and become a diamond prospector.

Lemay also looked into having the boat repairman who turned him in whacked, along with Jacques Lajoie, according to various stool pigeons in the Dade County Jail.

Because of this, the FBI contacted the Mounties and the Montreal Police to make sure Lajoie was safe. The Montreal Police refused to divulge where their star witness was currently living and would say only that they were in constant contact with him. Cracks were showing between the various agencies investigating the Lemay case.

The plans Lemay shared with his fellow inmates may have just been a ploy to disseminate incorrect information to confuse the authorities during their search for him. Lemay knew jailhouse snitches were rampant and would rat on a fellow inmate the first chance they got, hoping to wrangle a better deal for themselves. If his idea was to confuse the situation, it worked. After his escape, the FBI was forced to use time and resources following up on jailhouse leads that turned out to be nothing more than Lemay's flights of fancy.

It wasn't just the prisoners who hoped for a reward. On September 29, two women called the Miami FBI field office from their hotel in Nassau, in the Bahamas, to report that they had had cocktails with Lemay at a bar on the island four days earlier. Their description of the man they got smashed with only vaguely resembled Lemay, and since they'd admittedly been drunk, it was a long shot. The women were very interested in any reward money available if it turned out the man they'd been drinking with was Lemay.

Among the various people the FBI interviewed was the real René Roy, who lived down in the Keys. The news that Lemay had stolen his identity shocked him. He couldn't even recall meeting the man but said it was possible that he had taken him out charter fishing at some point.

By the end of September, the agency had tracked the Lemays' movements to Opelika, Alabama, and learned the fugitives had gotten a new car, but the trail went dead from there.

The next month, a clerk at the Laurel Motel, where Lise and Lamontagene had stayed before Lemay's escape, called the Miami Police Department to report an abandoned car behind the motel. He'd waited three weeks before alerting the police about it. The car matched the description of the Lemays' getaway vehicle. The FBI lab identified Lise's fingerprints inside of it, but no one else's.

The trail was going cold even as the search stretched farther across the United States, with field offices from Atlanta to Omaha to Honolulu all chasing down leads. There were reported sightings of Lise working as a nightclub singer near Miami, of Lemay getting down in a dance club in Jamaica, and the couple roller-skating in Delaware. Agents ran these leads down, no matter how far-fetched.

The FBI investigation in Honolulu involved Lise. In September, the field office there received an anonymous package filled with pornographic advertisements for both still pictures and movies from Canada. One model in a glossy color photo, who was reclining on a couch in "an obscene pose" (in the opinion of the FBI), resembled Lise Lemay. Agents tracked down the source of the advertisements and on October 21 interviewed a local nightclub owner involved in the porn business. He revealed the model was a Puerto Rican striptease artist with the stage name Lisa Grey, not Lise Lemay.

In November, the Court of Appeal in New Orleans came back with a decision in Lise's extradition case. She was legally entitled to stay in the United States, not that it mattered now that she was a fugitive.

An RCMP investigator received a phone call from one of his informants on the afternoon of November 16. The source said he'd just overheard a conversation between two brothers, Roger and Maurice Lalonde.

"Georges Lemay arrived in Montreal today," Roger told his brother, Maurice. "He's going to a Montreal bank to cash a check this afternoon. He's going to travel by air with Pat of Wheeler Airlines. I'll call Pat to arrange things."

According to the source, Lemay arrived in Canada earlier that day and planned to go to either Alma, a town three hundred miles north of Montreal, or Roberval, another town to the west of Alma, either on the sixteenth or seventeenth. The information the RCMP received was sketchy, but they quickly mobilized.

Two investigators drove through the beginnings of a snowstorm to the Wheeler Airlines building in Alma. The place was shut up tight, and no one was there. It was nearly 5:00 p.m. They scanned the snow-covered runway, but there were no telltale tire marks showing a flight had left or landed.

The storm was worsening. By 7:00 p.m., snow was coming down so hard that visibility was near zero, and the temperature was dropping fast. No one would be stupid enough to land in this weather. The officers left. After the storm passed, the surveillance continued for several more days. Officers also kept tabs on the Lalonde brothers.

The Mounties found that both the Montreal Police and Quebec Provincial Police were indifferent to the report that Lemay was allegedly in Montreal. They only half-heartedly agreed to help if and when the RCMP located the fugitive. Detective Leblanc was the exception. He had nearly single-handedly kept up with the various reports from the FBI, INTERPOL, and the Mounties, and stayed in contact with the other agencies over the years. Leblanc really wanted to catch Lemay, even as he moved up the ranks and changed assignment from the criminal investigations bureau to the social security fraud squad. He became something of an expert on all things Lemay-related.

On September 17, Leblanc met up with two RCMP investigators and drove around Montreal looking into whether any of the detective's criminal contacts knew anything. No one did.

The three officers then met up with another RCMP investigator and, in two unmarked cars, they kept watch on Roger Lalonde. At 7:00 p.m., Lalonde hurried to his late-model Oldsmobile and jumped in. He headed north, going fast. The roads were slippery that night, and as Leblanc tried to keep up with their target, his car fishtailed. They had a fender bender, and Lalonde got away.

The entire investigation was a bust. The days of surveillance at the airport turned up nothing, nor did the Lalonde brothers angle. It was just one more dead end that drained work hours and morale in the endless search for the mysterious Lemay.

Lemay hadn't been in Montreal in November. He'd been hiding out in a posh Manhattan hotel room. Before Lemay's escape, Lise got false identity papers for her husband sent from Lemay's underworld connections in Montreal. His new name was Robert Bennett. As fall turned to winter, and the second international search for Lemay stumbled, his family enjoyed a little more of what Manhattan offered.

He'd been on the run for close to three months, and along with a new name, he'd changed the way he looked. Lemay had grown a mustache and shaved his head. He looked different enough to go outside and even caved in to taking his daughter to see Santa at Macy's, at Herald Square, during the Christmas holidays of 1965. They went on a brisk November day near the end of the month.

There was something magical about New York during the holidays. There was the massive sixty-five-foot Christmas tree and ice skating at Rockefeller Center and the bold and imaginative window displays in the shop windows of Fifth Avenue, each trying to outdo the other with animatronic characters. That year there was "A Wedding in India," with dancing figures and acrobats swirling around as if by magic; a nearly full-sized carousel with smiling characters and piles of children's toys that whirred past amid a twinkling of miniature lights; a *Nutcracker*-themed display of dancing ballerinas and parading soldiers at B. Altman; and "Arabian Nights" at Macy's. There was the "Forest of Lights" at the Seagram Building on Park Avenue; a giant robot and miniature castle at the Pepsi-Cola Building on Fifty-Ninth and Park Avenue. And then there were the lights that soaked the streets in a rainbow of colors everywhere you looked. It was magical.

The family made their way through the crowd at Macy's toward the line of children and their parents waiting for their turn with Santa. Josée could barely contain her excitement when she finally got her chance to sit on Saint Nick's lap, surrounded by a wonderland of toys—a grinning lion, a large dog with floppy ears, and dolls for days. Her smile was radiant.

Just before Christmas Day, Lemay went down to the lobby of the hotel where they were staying and nearly bumped into an acquaintance from Montreal. A rush of fear went through him at almost being seen.

It would not be a white Christmas after all. Lemay decided the city was just a little too close to the jurisdiction that badly wanted to see him behind bars. So the family headed west the next day, to the city where people had been remaking themselves for years: Los Angeles.

* * *

The FBI's search extended as far as Guadalupe and Saint Martin with the help of INTERPOL, because of alleged Lemay sightings there. What they had no way of knowing was that Lemay had again taken on a new identity and that he and his family were headed to the West Coast. Lemay remained several steps ahead of the FBI, as he had with the RCMP the first time he went on the run.

A few days after Lemay's escape from Florida, the press widely quoted Canadian minister of justice Claude Wagner about his belief that American law enforcement would catch Lemay. "It is deplorable he has momentarily dropped out of circulation," Wagner said. "It may take some hours, some days, some months, but he will be caught. Justice has a long arm."

As the search dragged on with little to show for it, there was a pervasive sense among the Montreal Police that Lemay was slipping through their fingers for good. Detective St. Pierre even told the *Fort Lauderdale News* he didn't believe they had much hope of catching Lemay.

"He loved the South Sea Islands," St. Pierre mused. "He knows them well. It will be harder to get him now—if we ever do."

Even if the Canadian authorities were losing hope, the RCMP continued to follow up on leads. In October an informant told investigators that Lemay had been in Haiti since escaping from Miami. He had supposedly travelled there in a small plane that had also been used in a huge heist in June 1965. Three men wearing Halloween masks broke into a train station in rural Quebec and made off with gold bars worth sixty-four thousand dollars, making their getaway by air.

The informant said Lemay was organizing an international drug trafficking ring from Haiti. At least that was what they were saying in Montreal's criminal circles. The truth was more pedestrian.

Los Angeles suited Lemay just fine. The city had a transient quality that pervaded everything and gave Lemay a boldness he hadn't felt back East.

Lemay was now staying near where Harold Rosen, the man who had unknowingly sent Lemay fleeing across the country, lived and worked. The Hughes headquarters was only ten or so miles away from downtown Los Angeles. The two men whose lives had become intertwined could have passed each other on the street and never even realized it.

The Lemay family settled down in another large hotel where they didn't have to bother with cleaning up or even making a bed. After he shaved his head, people commented on his resemblance to the actor Yul Brynner, then at the height of his career. The family visited Disneyland in Anaheim that January. It was the park's tenth anniversary, which Walt Disney dubbed the Tencennial Celebration, and he spent lavishly on the festivities. Live entertainment included Louis Armstrong, Harry James, Woody Herman, and Duke Ellington, among others.

The park stayed open later than usual on Saturdays that year and was in the midst of a massive expansion with the construction of the It's a Small World boat ride and the Pirates of the Caribbean, among other attractions. There was lots to do and see, including the Jungle River Cruise with its frightening animatronic hippos and lions fighting over a kill; the ultramodern monorail (the first in the country) that quickly and quietly got the Lemays from one part of the park to another; the Swiss Family Treehouse; and the Matterhorn bobsled ride, where you could watch professional mountain climbers scale the face of a fake mountain and rappel back down, just like Lemay had done from the seventh floor of the Dade County Jail four months earlier.

Josée liked Fantasyland with the Mad Tea Party teacups that spun around over and over; Sleeping Beauty Castle; and all those characters— Mickey and Minnie, Pluto, Donald Duck, Tinker Bell, and Snow White. It was magical to a three-year-old.

Lemay even posed for a sketch artist that day. The artist studied Lemay intently for several minutes as his hand reproduced the likeness of the fugitive on paper, never knowing he was drawing the face of Canada's most wanted criminal. Lemay allowed Lise to take a few photos of him at the theme park but only from behind. He felt more comfortable three thousand miles from both Miami and Montreal, but he was still cautious.

While living in L.A., the family also took a trip down to Mexico, where Lemay, an avid photographer, took a series of photos of Josée on the back of a donkey.

That January he celebrated his forty-first birthday.

For Lemay, the only downside to living in L.A. was its proximity to Las Vegas, a city whose siren song called ceaselessly, drawing him to its gaming tables and nightlife. It was torture.

20

Sin City

LATE WINTER 1965–SUMMER 1966

LAS VEGAS WON.

At the end of January 1966, Lemay moved the family to a furnished rental on a quiet street near Las Vegas Boulevard, close to the big casinos on the Strip. Las Vegas was booming. The city's older casinos were getting facelifts, new hotels and casinos were springing up, and the Rat Pack ruled.

The mobsters who held sway there for twenty-five years—as they had once controlled Havana's nightlife—were being pushed out to make way for corporations.

Howard Hughes relocated to Las Vegas permanently in November 1966. He moved into the Desert Inn, where he'd booked the penthouse suite. He ended up buying the hotel and taking the top two floors for himself rather than face eviction by the management, who wanted the penthouse for high rollers rather than to continue to allow an eccentric billionaire to use it as his crash pad.

Hughes had long ago been pushed out of Hughes Aircraft, which by then was dominating the aerospace industry, thanks in part to Rosen's geostationary satellites. His dream of controlling the country's defense industry abandoned, Hughes, ever restless, now spent his time building an empire of a different sort. He went on a buying spree, snapping up the Sands, Frontier, and Landmark. By this time, he'd become a recluse, terrified of germs, trying to outrun his celebrity, and spooked and disgusted by the tourists he felt were turning the city into Coney Island. His answer was to try to take control of the Las Vegas Strip.

When Lemay arrived, he was initially reluctant to stay out for too long at a stretch, but in the coming weeks and months, he relaxed and spent each evening bouncing among the Sahara, Riviera, Stardust, and Thunderbird on the neon-drenched Strip. He stuck to the bigger casinos where he could fade into the crowd, avoiding Glitter Gulch, the nickname for Fremont Street, where visiting French Canadians spent time at the smaller casinos downtown.

A few days after they'd moved to Vegas, Lemay picked up a 1960 Studebaker, nicely chromed and with elegant tailfins. It was sexy without being flashy and cost six hundred dollars, which he paid for with one-hundred-dollar bills.

Lise would shave Lemay's head about once a week, to the delight of their daughter. His neighbors liked him and knew him as Roberto. He was a gentleman. Roberto didn't bother anyone, was helpful, wasn't a big drinker, and knew his way around a gambling table. When asked, he would tell people he was a casino croupier. He always said he had a system to beat the house, and his neighbors believed him. He was doing well at the tables. Besides gambling and spending time with the family, Lemay was learning Spanish.

His luck, both in gambling and avoiding the law, held steady as spring gave way to summer. He was also back to philandering, stepping out on Lise at least once during the nearly six months they were in Las Vegas.

By that summer, Lemay had won nearly fifty thousand dollars (four hundred thousand dollars today) playing everything from keno to craps. He planned to leave Las Vegas and take his family on an extended holiday. He was working on a deal to buy a large caravan in Los Angeles for nearly twenty thousand dollars—money he'd won gambling at the Stardust—then travel along the Pacific Coast to Mexico.

On July 20, his plan hit a speed bump.

While at a big casino on the Strip, Lemay noticed two straitlaced men who looked as though they worked in law enforcement. One was an FBI agent, the other an IRS agent, and they were there to make sure the casino was taking taxes out of any winnings over one thousand dollars. Lemay had just won big the night before and definitely didn't want to speak to any feds about his finances or anything else. Worse, one man kept staring at him as if he knew him.

Lemay left immediately and went home. In bed he lay awake, unable to sleep. It felt like a close call. He was going to have to make some changes.

Less than two weeks later, on August 1, the family moved to 2752 Hermosa Street in Winchester, an unincorporated town that was a three-minute drive from the Strip. Lemay also changed his name from Robert Bennett to Robert Palmer and forged a matching birth certificate. He maintained a cache of more than sixty blank official U.S. birth certificates for such emergencies. Lemay—Palmer—was now four years younger and born in Plattsburgh, New York.

The new house was furnished and cost $150 a month. He rented it on a month-to-month basis. What Lemay didn't realize when they moved in was that both an FBI agent and a Las Vegas Metropolitan Police Department detective also lived on the same block. Josée soon became friends with Kim Whitney, a neighbor girl who was close in age. Her father, Max, was the police detective. He had no idea his kid was friends with the daughter of the most wanted man in Canada. The FBI agent was also unaware the man the feds had spent thousands of hours searching for was living just a few houses away.

Lemay was soon back to spending his nights at the casinos, only now he resigned himself to the gaming establishments around Fremont Street like the Mint, the Four Queens, the Horseshoe, and the Golden Nugget.

* * *

The FBI continued to track down leads in the Lemay case without much luck. The avenues of investigation were getting more tenuous and far-flung, including investigating a couple living on a boat on Crooked Island in the

Bahamas that a local thought seemed suspicious. It wasn't the Lemays, just a young couple who liked privacy.

Agents also investigated a picture in a bedraggled girlie magazine found on the side of a road in rural Bedford County, Virginia, by a state trooper.

While flipping through the publication, one assumes for investigative purposes, the officer noticed a photograph of a model who closely resembled Lise Lemay. He brought the magazine to the FBI. They agreed the woman looked a lot like Lise and began the arduous process of tracking down the publisher of the magazine, *Satan's Scrapbook*, in North Hollywood.

However, the publisher, American Art Agency, was unenthusiastic about talking to the feds—these types of magazines existed in a legal gray area at a time when the U.S. Supreme Court was refining its views on what constituted obscene material (thus the publisher's use of *art* in its name). The publisher, a woman, pointed the agents to the photography editor who coordinated the collecting of the various photos used in the magazine. He located the model's release (she used a fake name and had an illegible signature), the negatives, and the name of the man who took the pictures in Denmark.

The spread, "Leg Lady of the Night," appeared in the October-November-December 1965 issue. A close inspection revealed that the model was taller than Lise and weighed more, and while they shared some facial characteristics, Lise Lemay definitely wasn't the model.

On June 10, the Dade County Sheriff's Office called the FBI to tell them that a neighboring police department received a misdirected call from a long-distance operator for a Mr. Lemay in Antigua from a Mrs. Lemay in Miami.

Believing they'd stumbled onto the fugitives, the FBI worked in tandem with the sheriff's office to track down the woman in Miami. Agents rushed over to a Coral Gables beauty salon, fully expecting to make an arrest. Upon arrival, however, they discovered that the only resemblance the woman shared with Lise was the last name Lemay.

Special Agent Wendell Hall Jr. summed it up in his report from

July 19, 1966. "Investigation to date by FBI offices, Dade County Sheriff's Office, Miami, Florida, and U.S. INS, Miami, Florida, unproductive as to the current whereabouts of subjects," he wrote. "Individuals thought to be identical to one or both subjects eliminated by investigation. Investigation continuing."

The feds looked north, hoping the RCMP might be having better luck. They weren't.

The Mounties, at the behest of the FBI, made spot checks on Lise's family in Montreal, hoping to locate the Lemays' young daughter. Josée was believed to still be living with the Lemieux family, but she hadn't turned up.

"Lise Lemay allegedly visits the child on a regular basis," the FBI liaison officer, Moss Lee Innes, wrote to the RCMP in July 1966.

Innes also stressed the importance to the Mounties of monitoring Lemay's mother in Montreal and one of his sisters, Carmelle Parent, who still lived in Hull, Quebec.

The RCMP was having a hard time just trying to speak with Carmelle Parent. An investigator finally got her husband, Bernard, a forty-year-old doctor, on the phone, but he was thoroughly unhelpful. He told the officer he didn't recall receiving any phone calls from Lemay since he'd gone on the run and didn't know where Josée could be found.

Lemay's other sister, Suzanne Poisson, and brother-in-law, Guy, lived in New Jersey.

The Ocean Beach Police Department had been secretly keeping tabs on the Poissons for the Montreal Police and had been working with Detective Leblanc for some time, hoping Lemay might try to hide out at his sister's place. Nothing came of their surveillance.

The FBI interviewed Guy Poisson at the electronics manufacturing company in Bridgeport, Pennsylvania, where he was the plant manager. Poisson told the agents he never really had much to do with Lemay, whom he called "a playboy type." The last time they'd spent any time together was nearly five years earlier at Lemay's chalet.

Suzanne had "reluctantly" gone to see her brother after his arrest in Florida, but that was the extent of their contact.

Guy mentioned that he thought he saw Lemay once in Manhattan, a few years back, when Lemay first went on the run. Guy called out to Lemay, who rushed off in the other direction. That was the last time he saw his brother-in-law, he said.

Back in Florida, state attorney Richard Gerstein convened a Dade County grand jury to look into the misdeeds of the sheriff's office. It wasn't just Alger and Jaworski, the two guards that helped Lemay, who had been involved in corruption. The department was long rumored to be in the pocket of vice peddlers who were involved in prostitution and gambling and were even getting payoffs from burglary rings. Lemay's escape was added to the long-reaching probe.

The grand jury questioned Sheriff T. A. Buchanan, who had been in charge of the initial search for Lemay in Miami, about whether Lemay had paid him off. Buchanan repeatedly denied any involvement in the Lemay escape, and no evidence surfaced to disprove his claims.

What the grand jury discovered when it dug deeper into Buchanan's time as sheriff was a twenty-five-thousand-dollar election donation from a Miami gambler that the sheriff didn't disclose in his campaign's finance report. Buchanan, under oath, denied receiving the money. The grand jury promptly indicted him on perjury charges and campaign violations. He denied these charges, but the governor suspended him. The court set a trial date in the case.

The jail guards and Mixon were also headed for trial. It seemed Lemay's escape had kicked open the door to reveal the ugly truth of Dade County's law enforcement, or lack thereof.

The fallout reached the highest levels of Florida politics. Nineteen sixty-six was an election year, and Governor William Haydon Burns was in a runoff against a powerful Miami politician who made a lot of noise about the close relationship between the governor and Sheriff Buchanan.

Politicians weren't the only ones using Lemay for personal gain. Miami tour guide operators had already woven the legend of Lemay into their spiels. One, pointing toward a Miami Beach hotel, told a Montreal reporter on a tour boat with other French Canadians, "This is where the hero Georges Lemay, a Canadian, was arrested last year," even though the arrest had actually taken place thirty miles north in Fort Lauderdale.

* * *

On August 18, 1966, Lemay dropped Lise and Josée off at the movies and headed for the Golden Nugget, one of the busiest casinos in the city. He'd been there enough to feel reasonably safe, even if Fremont Street drew more French Canadians than the glitzier casinos on the Strip.

He walked into the Golden Nugget dressed in a pale-yellow sports shirt and tan trousers. The clinging and clanging of the 1,500 slot machines immediately assailed him as he headed to the craps tables. With its bloodred-and-gold color scheme set off by dark wood paneling, gilded chandeliers, Victorian carved wood, marble imported from Italy, and paintings of reclining nudes, the casino was supposed to have an Old West feel but instead more closely resembled a nineteenth-century New Orleans brothel.

Gangster Guy McAfee built it in 1946 at the beginning of mobster-controlled Las Vegas's golden age. It cost the equivalent of thirteen million dollars today.

McAfee had been an L.A. cop before switching teams and joining the ranks of that city's criminal syndicate. He eventually controlled L.A.'s illegal gambling and prostitution rackets before heading to Nevada along with his former associates, a rogue's gallery that included Bugsy Siegel, whose Flamingo casino would open later the same year.

When it was built, the Golden Nugget was the city's largest casino. It retained cachet well into the 1960s, so much so that *Viva Las Vegas*, the 1964 film starring Elvis Presley, prominently featured the casino.

Sometime after 1:00 a.m. Lemay headed to the bathroom in the Golden Nugget's lower level. He was up eight hundred dollars for the night, playing both craps and blackjack. He felt great.

Lemay hadn't noticed the three FBI agents who had entered the casino and watched him as he gambled. Ten other agents prowled around outside the brilliantly lit casino under the watchful gaze of Vegas Vic, the forty-foot-tall neon-lit cowboy sign for the Pioneer Club, a few doors down. The agents weren't conspicuous among the late-night crowds that streamed down Fremont Street; they could have been a group of Elks Lodge members out on the town.

As Lemay exited the bathroom and headed up the stairs to the main gaming room, the agents approached him. They identified themselves as being with the FBI. One asked him his name, and he answered, "Robert Palmer." They said they didn't believe him, and with a shrug he admitted he was Lemay. The agents cuffed him and hustled him out of the casino so quickly no one noticed.

Lemay told the agents the address of his home and they made the brief journey to Hermosa Street. It was nearly 2:00 a.m. when Lemay came inside with the agents.

Lise had been listening to her favorite singer, Amália Rodrigues—a Portuguese chanteuse known as the Queen of Fado—on their battery-powered portable record player when she fell asleep cuddling Josée.

Harsh noises startled Lise awake. When she realized what was happening, she burst into tears. Lemay, usually so stoic, also began to weep, telling her in French not to worry and that everything would be all right.

The agents told Lise to get dressed and come with them. An officer took Josée to child protective services. The agents searched the house and found nearly ten thousand dollars in cash, mostly in hundred-dollar bills (more than eighty-nine thousand dollars today), and an unloaded .22 pistol, but nothing they could directly tie to the Bank of Nova Scotia bank burglary.

* * *

Joe Bédard, the former Montreal detective involved in the original Dominion Day bank heist investigation, got a phone call early in the morning of August 19, 1966. It was long-distance from Las Vegas. The voice on the other end seemed excited and a little tired. The man spoke quickly in French and told him he'd seen Lemay at the Golden Nugget earlier in the night and had called the FBI as Bédard had instructed. Yes! Finally! The old cop's instincts had paid off.

Even after he retired in 1962, Bédard never gave up hope that he'd catch Lemay. He was no longer a Montreal Police detective, but he kept in touch with his wide network of informants since they still came in handy in his role as the head of security for two large Canadian banks.

One of these men lived in Las Vegas. Bédard had run into him when the informant was visiting family in Montreal a few months earlier. Bédard asked him to keep a lookout for Lemay. He knew Lemay couldn't stay away from Sin City. Bédard provided his informant with a photo of the fugitive and told him to call the FBI if he ever saw Lemay. And now it had come to pass.

During the phone call, the informant said he'd been focused on his cards when he looked up and glanced around at the other players at the various gaming tables near him. One of them looked familiar. It took a minute for him to realize why. It was Lemay, the fugitive Bédard had told him to look out for.

He stepped away from the gaming tables and headed for a nearby pay phone. He called the FBI's Las Vegas bureau and explained the situation. He then returned to gambling but noticed the federal agents when they arrived to arrest Lemay.

While a groundbreaking satellite initially caught Lemay, it took old-fashioned police work and Bédard's correct hunch to recapture the wily thief. Bédard, in order to protect his informant—who has never been publicly named—lied to the press, telling the newspapers it had been a friend of his who was visiting Vegas when he dropped a dime on Lemay.

Later that morning, the police hauled Lemay's Studebaker away from the Golden Nugget's parking lot. It was the first time the staff realized something big had gone down at the casino. The arrest had been so swift, not even the Golden Nugget's staff had been aware of it.

J. Edgar Hoover, the ruthless and despotic head of the FBI, announced Lemay's arrest later the same day, on August 19, in Washington, D.C. That it had taken nearly a year to recapture the now-famous French Canadian had been a continual embarrassment for the FBI, and Hoover wanted to give the country the news himself.

McClellan, the RCMP commissioner, was very pleased to hear the FBI had captured Lemay. It was one less headache to worry about, especially since he again found himself in the spotlight for all the wrong reasons. It seemed like he kept getting dragged into national politics when all he wanted to do was be a cop.

This time, it was what the press was calling the Munsinger Affair, and this one was even more scandalous than the Rivard Affair from a year earlier. It revolved around sex, Russian spies, and Canada's previous Conservative government.

McClellan appeared before a commission concerning Gerda Munsinger, a thirty-six-year-old German. She was allegedly a prostitute spying for the Soviet Union who had an affair with Pierre Sevigny, Canada's associate minister of national defense. The Conservatives accused McClellan of being "political police" in service to the Liberal prime minister Lester Pearson for investigating Sevigny at Pearson's behest.

McClellan was on shaky ground. The news of Lemay's capture might deflect some of the negative publicity the Mounties were then experiencing. McClellan kept close watch on the goings-on in Las Vegas and the coordinated efforts with the U.S. government in Lemay's extradition. He needed to make sure nothing went wrong getting Lemay back to Canada.

* * *

Leslie Hobbs, who was now the Montreal Police chief inspector of detectives, got the call from the Mounties a few hours after Lemay's capture in Las Vegas. The FBI had been going through their Canadian counterpart, the RCMP, rather than speaking directly with the Montreal Police, a sore spot with Hobbs. At least he got the news before having to read about it in the newspapers. Lemay had been captured! Still, Hobbs knew Dade County would likely get first crack at prosecuting Lemay for his jailbreak. Then there were the U.S. federal charges and extradition process. It could still be a long time before Lemay was back in Montreal to face the now five-year-old charges, longer if Lemay pulled another Houdini.

Hobbs looked on the bright side. The delay would give the police time to dust off the evidence and hunt down the various witnesses the prosecution would need for the trial. It would be up to the Montreal Police and the Crown Prosecutor's Office to make sure Lemay paid for his crimes.

21

Extradition

SUMMER–FALL 1966

THE AGENTS TOOK LEMAY AND LISE TO THE THIRD-FLOOR holding cells at the Clark County Courthouse, right around the corner from the Golden Nugget, where they put them into cells next to each other in a section reserved for federal prisoners. Lemay was in a holding cell directly in front of the head jailer.

As the sun rose over Las Vegas, the couple spoke to each other in low tones in French, mostly discussing how much money they could get their hands on in order to secure the best lawyer possible. Guards monitored them over closed-circuit television. Seven cameras covered the cells and hallways. But as the Dade County Sheriff's Office had learned, a modern jail filled with fancy electronics didn't guarantee someone with a quick mind and a fistful of cash couldn't escape from it.

Later that day, U.S. Commissioner A. G. Blad came to their cells to arraign them on the federal charges. The authorities weren't taking any chances with Lemay. Instead of taking the pair to court, the court came to them. The Lemays remained in their adjoining steel- and mesh-covered cells. Blad set their bail at one hundred thousand dollars apiece on the federal charges.

Lemay, sitting in his cell, fidgeted with a matchbook during the proceedings. When he heard the bail amount, he grinned, laughed, and suggested Blad should lower the amount. Blad, stone faced, refused.

It didn't matter since INS filed an immigration hold on the pair for being in the country illegally. Even if they came up with bail, the hold would keep them behind bars. Lemay turned to matters closer at hand.

"My wife wants to comb her hair like a lady," Lemay complained to Blad, saying the jail refused to allow them to wash up or even brush their teeth. "I ordered room service," he said with a rueful smile. Then he told Blad he'd be securing the services of one of the best lawyers around, Harry Claiborne.

A wiry man with a wide mouth and a soft Arkansas accent, Claiborne was flamboyant but smart, dogged in court, and an all-around hard worker. A former Las Vegas cop and assistant DA, he was one of the top defense attorneys in Nevada and counted the likes of Dean Martin and Frank Sinatra among his friends and clients. Claiborne represented Bugsy Siegel, the L.A. gangster who was the driving force behind the creation of the Las Vegas Strip. He also represented Howard Hughes, who had unknowingly set off the events surrounding Lemay when his company hired Harold Rosen a decade earlier.

After the arraignment, the Lemays were transferred from federal custody and turned over to Clark County sheriff Ralph Lamb, the six-foot-two cowboy whose word was law in Las Vegas. He booked them on charges of being fugitives from Florida. Lemay went into the general population of the Clark County Jail and his wife was taken to the women's section. It didn't take them long to make new friends among both the inmates and guards.

The jail allowed the couple to see each other for two hours a day. They would sit together chatting in French, safe in knowing that even if the guards overheard them, they wouldn't understand what was said.

As in the Dade County Jail, Lemay was treated like a celebrity. His jailers found him intelligent, affable, and a great conversationalist. Jack Crisci, a big-time gambler awaiting trial for his involvement in a government food manipulation scam, thought Lemay sociable and whip smart. Lemay sold him his Studebaker for a dollar "and other considerations,"

Lemay's way of making sure he could call on Crisci when and if he needed something from him.

The talk among the inmates in Las Vegas centered on Lemay's great escape, the well-planned bank heist, and where he was hiding all that money. One rumor floating around centered on Patrick Kirkpatrick, an old acquaintance of Lemay's from the Montreal underworld, who was in the Clark County Jail on check fraud charges at the same time as Lemay. Kirkpatrick, several inmates alleged, had his hands on somewhere around two million dollars in stolen bonds from one of Lemay's bank burglaries and was willing to sell them cheap. Kirkpatrick, known as a forger and safecracker in Quebec, could also get his hands on counterfeit hundred-dollar bills, they said.

The FBI looked into these allegations without success.

The stories at the Clark County Jail, true or not, raised Lemay's standing among the inmates. Outside the jail, Lemay remained in the headlines. The Montreal newspaper *La Presse* claimed Lemay had even started a fashion trend in Sin City: shaved heads.

Lise enjoyed special privileges in the jail, including getting to take as many showers as she wished. Her guards comforted Lise when her spirits flagged. The food wasn't bad, either, and her cell was air-conditioned.

Like her husband, Lise became something of a celebrity. She had a growing fan club and received letters of encouragement from both men and women from as far away as Toledo, Ohio, and Tacoma, Washington.

One afternoon, a man in his twenties with curly blond hair appeared at the jail and asked to see Lise. The guards didn't ask who he was, figuring he was the reporter scheduled to interview Mrs. Lemay that day.

Lise came into the jail visitation room. She didn't recognize the man. "What do you want?" she asked in her heavily accented English.

"I wanted to see you," the stranger responded in a Texas drawl. "My wish has been granted. You're so beautiful, even more beautiful than in the newspaper photos." He looked starstruck. He was a fan, not the reporter.

Lise, blindsided, pressed the button for the guard, who shooed the young man away. He apologized for coming unannounced but wasn't sorry. "I'm glad I saw her," he said, a dazed smile on his face.

* * *

Prosecutors back in Florida had the rendition papers on the governor's desk the day after Lemay's arrest. They knew he would fight being returned to Florida. While they waited for the inevitable courtroom tussle between lawyers, they sent two investigators to Las Vegas to interview the Lemays. The Florida authorities hoped the couple would be willing to help them in their cases against Mixon and the two former guards, Alger and Jaworski.

In Quebec, the provincial government kept close tabs on the goings on in Las Vegas and in Miami. Minister of justice Jean-Jacques Bertrand, who had replaced Claude Wagner that June after the conservative Union Nationale once again came into power, was in close contact with the prosecutors in Florida.

The RCMP feared if Lemay made bail, he would again make a run for it. Their apprehension grew when they learned Lemay had secured Claiborne to represent him.

Montreal Police Detective Leblanc couldn't believe the FBI had captured Lemay in Las Vegas. He always considered Lemay a horse racing fanatic and not "a card and dice man." Besides, all the tips they'd gotten indicated Lemay was somewhere in South America, likely in a country without an extradition treaty with Canada. Now, he just hoped the criminal he'd pursued for nearly five years wouldn't escape his jailers in Las Vegas like he did in Miami. Leblanc knew it would take more time and patience before Lemay's return to Montreal, but he'd already waited this long. He was really looking forward to handing Lemay his arrest warrant.

* * *

On Thursday, August 25, Lemay appeared in county court before Judge Delwin Potter, handcuffed to another prisoner. He wore a blue denim jail-issued jumpsuit. Lise, who had been allowed to wear her street clothes, wore a black-and-white dress suit with a similarly colored head scarf, her trademark ponytail hanging out the back. She was also shackled to another inmate. The Lemays were about ten feet apart. It didn't stop them from speaking loudly to one another in French.

"Don't worry. Lise, everything will work out," Lemay told his wife. "Trust me, trust me. Our lawyer is the best in the area. Everything will be all right. I love you."

They also talked of lighter subjects and even laughed a few times as they waited for the judge to set bail. Claiborne was there to represent both of them. Judge Potter got straight to the point, setting their bail at one hundred thousand dollars. The amount stunned the Lemays, especially in Lise's case. Claiborne, visibly upset, angrily rebuked the court's decision.

"Our Supreme Court many times has said that when a court sets bail that is penal in nature, it becomes unconstitutional," he railed, saying any bail over five thousand dollars for Lise would be excessive. "She's being held on a fugitive warrant, and that doesn't involve what her husband is charged with in Canada. This court well knows that Mr. Lemay will be unable to make any of his one-hundred-thousand-dollar bail and if he's unable to, then she most certainly is not." The judge was unmoved.

Even if he made bail, Lemay could still be held on the INS deportation detainer. He wasn't getting another chance to bolt.

Claiborne, frustrated, said, "We wish to tell the court that we will resist extradition and request time. We have the right to a full and complete hearing before the governor before any extradition."

Claiborne and Lemay hoped to drag out proceedings to avoid him being sent to Florida. After that, it would be another fight to keep him from being sent back to Canada.

The judge gave Claiborne sixty days to prepare. The next hearing date was set for late October.

After the hearing, Claiborne told the waiting news reporters he was "damned unhappy" about the judge's decision. He planned to focus on getting Lise's bail reduced. Lemay pushed his attorney on this point. He'd promised to get Lise back to Montreal before Christmas so Josée wouldn't have to celebrate the holiday without her mother.

Back inside the courthouse, a Montreal reporter for *La Presse* arranged an interview with the Lemays in Sheriff Lamb's office. While the jail allowed the couple to be alone with the reporter, there were twenty armed guards in the other rooms and corridors surrounding the office where the interview took place.

Josée, who had been in the custody of child protective services and staying at a county juvenile facility, was also there. She ran into her mother's arms and Lise broke down, crying. Two tears rolled down Lemay's face as he watched the scene.

"You promised not to cry," he told Lise. "You have to be strong."

Lise continued to weep as she held her daughter tightly. This was a farewell for the family. Josée was going back to Montreal, and Lise had no idea when she'd see her daughter again. Even the guards stationed just outside the door were touched.

"A scene like that breaks your heart," one guard said in a choked voice.

One of Lemay's sisters, Rita Lemay-Guimont, flew to Las Vegas on August 26 to retrieve Josée. She also packed up the family's apartment and shipped everything back to Canada.

Saturday, August 27, was Lise's thirtieth birthday. Lemay somehow arranged for an elaborate cake to be sent to his wife in the women's section of the jail on the second floor. It sat in Sheriff Lamb's office until the next day. After the jail checked to make sure there was nothing hidden inside, Lise and four of the other inmates, along with the guards, got to eat it. Lemay wasn't allowed to visit the women's section, but the guards brought him a piece of cake to eat.

The same day, an investigator for the Florida State Attorney's Office and a grand jury investigator arrived from Miami, hoping to interview Lise and Lemay about the Dade County jailbreak. They offered Lise immunity from prosecution if she'd testify against Mixon, Alger, and Jaworski, but the interview didn't go well. Both Lise and her husband refused to answer most of the investigators' questions. The questions Lemay did respond to, he answered with his own questions: "What do you think of it? Do you believe that I could have done that? Do you believe that I had enough money to buy this?"

The circular conversation went nowhere until the investigators stopped bothering to ask questions and instead chatted amiably about topics not related to Lemay's jailbreak.

When the two Florida men left the interview room, Lemay felt secure that they would be returning to Miami knowing no more than they did when they'd arrived in Las Vegas. A magician never reveals his secrets.

As the fight to keep the Lemays out of Florida dragged on, Josée arrived home in Montreal on August 29, flying with her aunt from Las Vegas to New York and finally to Montreal. The press was there to greet her. She looked like a child star. A newspaper photograph shows her on the exit stairs after they arrived at Dorval Airport (now Montréal–Pierre Elliott Trudeau International Airport). She is holding the hand of an Air Canada flight attendant who is helping her down the airstairs. She has an enormous smile on her face and is dressed in shorts and a hooded blouse, with little white Stride Rite boots on her feet.

* * *

FBI agents from the Las Vegas bureau hunted down any local bank accounts the Lemays had used while living in Nevada. After looking into banking records at the state's big banks, they failed to turn up any accounts under the couple's real names or any of Lemay's aliases.

They also spoke with Lemay's neighbors and canvassed the casinos, looking for anyone with information about Lemay's life in Las Vegas. They interviewed one woman who claimed she had gone out with the French Canadian on several occasions. She knew him as Roberto from New Jersey. The FBI learned nothing of importance and spent a lot of time trying to discover the identity of a mysterious young man in his twenties said to have been Roberto's nephew. The trail went cold, and the agents never identified the mystery man. It was just one more of Lemay's secrets they failed to crack.

The agents also hit a wall with the money and pistol they'd found in Lemay's rented home. Neither the cash's serial numbers nor the .22 came up as stolen in the National Stolen Property File, the precursor to the National Crime Information Center, a centralized computer database containing crime information from across the United States.

* * *

Claiborne came to see Lemay most every day to strategize and report on any progress made. In late August, he brought some good news. The district court agreed to hear Claiborne's argument to reduce Lise's bail. On September 1, Claiborne got Lise's bail on the state charge reduced to ten thousand dollars, but a federal agent was at the hearing to take her into custody if she made bail. Claiborne filed a writ of habeas corpus in the immigration case, which the federal court denied. Lise stayed where she was.

Back in Florida, authorities were having second thoughts about bringing the Lemays back to Miami. State Attorney Richard Gerstein found neither the U.S. Attorney's Office nor the FBI seemed interested in pursuing charges, even though Lemay had been in federal custody at the time of his escape. Dade County wasn't interested in the case, either, since Mixon and the two guards wouldn't testify against Lise and Lemay and vice versa. It seemed like everyone on the U.S. side of the border simply wanted to wash their hands of Lemay. He'd caused them all too much embarrassment. Gerstein turned to the Canadians, who promised they had an air-tight case against Lemay. It was easier to send him back where he came from than deal with all the headaches his presence in the United States was causing.

Gerstein contacted Claiborne and discussed cutting a deal. Lemay had a change of heart and was amicable to the proposal. He wanted to keep his promise to Lise to get her back to Montreal and to their child as soon as possible. He also didn't want to go back to Miami and spend more money on lawyers. He'd eventually end up back in Canada no matter the outcome and he was tired of fighting the inevitable.

The plea deal involved Gerstein dropping all the charges in Florida against the couple, if Lemay agreed to immediate deportation to Canada. Gerstein wouldn't budge on one condition: Lise had to accompany Lemay during his deportation. Everyone feared if Lise went free, she'd once again help her husband escape. She would have to fly back to Canada with Lemay and would have to pay her own way. Lemay, on the other hand, would fly home on the Canadian government's dime.

By early October, the plan to get Lemay into the hands of the Montreal Police was in motion, but there were some snags. The U.S. Immigration and Naturalization Service felt regular flights from Las Vegas to Montreal, with stopovers in either New York City or Chicago, could be unsafe if Lemay had confederates ready to help him escape. They decided an international flight that ended in Europe with a stopover in Montreal would be safer. The first available flight that fit the bill was on Lufthansa, which would fly from San Francisco to Frankfurt, Germany, with a refueling stop in Montreal on October 6. The problem came when they discovered the Canadian Transportation Agency's Air Transport Board had to sign off on the plan, as it required special permission to discharge passengers at refueling stops. The board typically levied a five-hundred-dollar fine per passenger, and Lufthansa was unwilling to agree to the plan unless the board waived the fees. The approval came swiftly considering the layers of bureaucracy and international cooperation involved, and on Wednesday, October 5, the first leg of the Lemays' journey home began.

Around four that afternoon, the guards told Lise and Lemay to get ready to leave for Montreal. Fifteen minutes later the couple left the Clark County Jail in the company of two U.S. Immigration officers and headed for the airport. They handcuffed Lemay, but not Lise. The foursome made their first flight with no problems and arrived in San Francisco less than two hours later. The agents took the couple to a holding facility for the night, where they shared a cell.

Neither of them slept well. It was hot and stuffy, and they felt out of place in their new surroundings.

Earlier that day, October 5, the RCMP Criminal Investigation Branch in Ottawa received an urgent phone call from a Lufthansa representative in Montreal. The Lemays' flight might be delayed by two hours. The airline representative wouldn't know for sure until later in the day.

Commissioner McClellan, advised of the possible delay, alerted Mounties in Winnipeg, Ottawa, Toronto, New Brunswick, and Newfoundland. Their orders were to arrest Lemay if the flight was diverted from Montreal. McClellan knew that if that happened, Lemay could easily make a run for it again. The U.S. Immigration agents wouldn't be able to hold the fugitive once the plane landed, since they had no jurisdiction on Canadian soil. McClellan wasn't taking any chances.

The next morning, without getting breakfast, the Lemays and their escorts headed for the San Francisco airport to board a Boeing 707, the company's first jetliner, for the eight-hour flight. The group took up the two back rows of Lufthansa flight 451, which left the runway at 10:30 a.m. on Thursday, October 6. Once they were safely in the air, an immigration officer removed Lemay's handcuffs.

A Lufthansa representative called the RCMP to confirm the Lemays were on the way and would arrive on time. The Mounties contacted the Montreal Police to let them know. Detective Leblanc couldn't wait.

On board, Lemay was his usual gregarious self. When an INS agent dropped his handcuffs, Lemay picked them up and handed them back, telling the flight attendant, "This policeman is my prisoner." He chuckled at his own joke.

At noon they were served a meal, Lemay's first since leaving Las Vegas. He was famished. Afterward, thinking about his homecoming and his life in Montreal, he asked an agent whether he would switch seats with Lise so he could talk with his wife. The agent said no. Lemay bolted up from his seat and turned to the man.

"I don't see why I can't speak with my wife," he said in a harsh tone. "If you want trouble, all you have to do is ask."

The agents gave in and allowed Lise to sit with her husband for the rest of the flight. Lemay got his way, as he often did. By then the agents just wanted to be rid of him. And where could he go, anyway? They were on a plane, after all.

A half hour before the plane landed, Lemay went to the restroom to shave. He would not look like a slob, no matter what the circumstances. He returned to his seat and hugged Lise tightly. The skyline of the city came into view through the window.

"Finally," Lemay said, "Montreal."

Twenty-four hours after leaving Las Vegas, they touched down in Montreal. At the Dorval Airport, an immense crowd jostled for the chance to see Lemay and Lise. A journalist quipped that the throng there for Lemay rivaled the crowd size for the Beatles when they performed in Montreal two years earlier.

Five Montreal Police officers, including Leblanc, met the plane. Leblanc, with a big grin, walked up to Lemay, who was still in his seat, and handed him an arrest warrant. "I've waited five years to hand this to you," he told Lemay.

Lemay stood up and held out his hand, returning the smile.

"Hello, Bob," he said. "How are you? I'm happy to see you."

They shook hands like old friends happily reunited after many years.

"Do you have anything on my wife?" Lemay asked.

"No, we don't. She's completely free," he answered. Lemay was relieved to hear that. He kissed Lise and headed to the front of the airplane with Leblanc. The detective didn't bother to handcuff him.

Besides the large crowd who'd gathered to get a glimpse of the infamous bank burglar and his beautiful wife, there were close to two dozen police officers, from the RCMP, Quebec Provincial Police, and the Montreal Police. They were there to make sure Lemay made it into a jail cell.

Lemay, dressed in a dapper gray suit and a silk repp-stripe tie, his hair already grown back in, stepped off the plane. He descended the stairs with a big smile and a jaunty step. He and Leblanc got into a police cruiser parked at the foot of the ramp and headed into the city.

Lise disembarked like the rest of the passengers and went through Canadian customs. Reporters mobbed her as she made her way through the airport. One journalist asked how Lemay was doing.

"My husband is always in good spirits," Lise answered. "Why wouldn't he be?"

One of Lemay's two attorneys, Guy Guérin, met Lise as she left customs and the two walked to baggage together, discussing what the next days would bring. The lawyer was heading over to the municipal police headquarters on Bonsecours Street to meet with his client to strategize for the coming trial. Lemay would be held in a fifth-floor cell at the police headquarters, at least initially.

Lise left the airport for her reunion with Josée and to prepare for their own kind of long trial.

22

Our World

SUMMER 1967

THE CAMERA SWOOPED PAST TRANSPARENT BALLOONS DECO-
rated to look like the Earth and arced downward toward a crowded Abbey
Road recording studio as the words *London, United Kingdom* appeared
on the screen. The opening strains of the Beatles' "All You Need Is Love"
rose as the camera panned down to the four most famous musicians on
the planet sitting on stools and decked out in full hippie regalia—Nehru
jackets, love beads, flowers in their hair. Before them sat a crowd that
included several nearly equally famous rock stars, like Mick Jagger, Eric
Clapton, and The Who's drummer, Keith Moon. Sitting cross-legged,
they chimed in on the choruses as the Beatles ran through their brand-
new song, freshly penned for "Our World," the first truly international
television broadcast in history, since "This Is Early Bird" and the Tokyo
Olympics broadcasts hadn't encompassed the entire globe.

"This is Steve Race in the Beatles' recording studio in London, where
the latest Beatle record is at this moment being built up," said the disem-
bodied voice of the host of the BBC's music show *My Music*. "Not just a
single performance, but a whole montage of performances. With some
friends in to help the atmosphere, this is quite an occasion." The Beatles,

amid recording the single, had already spent several days working on the composition by the time of the live broadcast on June 25, 1967.

The band had agreed months earlier to be part of "Our World," a seminal two-and-a-half-hour live program, but John Lennon didn't actually get around to writing the song until the last minute.

Its message of peace and understanding worked well with the broadcast's theme of unity. This was, after all, the Summer of Love.

The band released "All You Need Is Love" as a single a month later. The song would eventually find its way onto two albums, *Magical Mystery Tour* and *Yellow Submarine*. It became one of their biggest-selling hits.

Recording this song live before millions of people across the globe fit in perfectly with the Beatles' obsessions at the time: firsts and change. Both George Harrison and Ringo Starr told reporters they were excited about participating in "Our World" because it was the first international television broadcast in history and their musical performance "was part of the change" in the band's direction. It was also their last live performance on television. The band no longer needed to promote themselves, and their rabid fan base made it difficult for them to get around from place to place.

On June 25, two hours before the Beatles' performance, the "Our World" broadcast began with a graphic of a human figure superimposed on a globe that slowly came into focus. Images from around the world followed—sand dunes, tropical flowers, crashing waves, a mountain range—as the angelic and haunting voices of the Vienna Boys' Choir sang the theme song, "Our World," beginning in German and running through twenty-one other languages.

"It's the climax to all man's history of communication," said television host James Dibble during the Australian Broadcasting Corporation's telecast of "Our World."

BBC producer Aubrey Singer, the head of the network's programming, conceived of the broadcast in late 1965. He orchestrated the European Broadcasting Union–produced program that involved forty-five control rooms around the world representing fourteen television broadcasting companies across five continents. The broadcast required nearly ten thousand writers, technicians, producers, interpreters, and others to make it a reality.

The broadcast would not have been possible without Early Bird and her sister satellites: Intelsat II B (later renumbered F-2)—also known as Pacific I—which linked the Pacific and North America in January 1967, and Intelsat II C, dubbed Canary Bird by the press because of its association with the Canary Islands' receiving station. Canary Bird, launched a month after Pacific I, was the second GEO satellite to connect Europe and North America following Early Bird's launch two years earlier. Besides these satellites, the broadcast required hundreds of thousands of miles of electrical cable to get "Our World" to the actual world at nearly instantaneous speed.

One segment from Rome featured the famed film director Federico Fellini shooting a street scene for a short film. The images traveled at 186 miles per second by landline to Milan; through the Albula Pass in Switzerland; on to Lyon and Paris, France; to Brussels, Belgium; then below the English Channel and overland to London and the BBC studios, where the program was master controlled. They then beamed the segment up to Early Bird and down to New York, where, again using landlines, it was sent north to Montreal and south to Mexico City and thence to local stations in Canada and Mexico. From New York, it was also sent via landline to the NASA tracking station in Rosman, North Carolina, and up to NASA's Applications Technology Satellite 1 (ATS-1). ATS-1 was an experimental communications, weather, and scientific GEO satellite launched in December 1966, and the first of five for the program built by Hughes under Rosen's technical direction.

From there they beamed the signal down to the Cooby Creek Tracking Station in Queensland, Australia, and then by landline to Sydney. Yet another path via space, land, and sea got it to Japan. They repeated this process multiple times in alternating variations of landlines and satellites from more than forty different locations around the globe, back to London and on to the world's television screens. And it was all live.

To overcome the language barriers in this broadcast seen in thirty-one different countries, a team of interpreters at the BBC studios translated the remarks by the many international newscasters into various other languages, such as French, English, German, and Japanese. These translations were then sent to the appropriate countries. For instance, in New York, commentator Paul Niven Jr., of National Education Television (the precursor to PBS), received English guide commentary into his headphones—including translations, along with any last-minute or spontaneous changes—which he then related to his U.S. audience as the scenes from around the world played out live on television sets across the United States.

Singer likened the endeavor to the building of the transcontinental railroad in the United States in the nineteenth century. That achievement united a nation, but "Our World" would use television and satellite technology to unite the world when it was deep in the Cold War and a crisis in the Middle East. Just weeks earlier, on June 5, 1967, the Six-Day War between Israel and Egypt, Syria, and Jordan broke out. In less than a week, the small country wrested control of the Sinai Peninsula, the Gaza Strip, East Jerusalem, the West Bank, and the Golan Heights from its larger, more powerful neighbors.

The Soviet Union and its allies—Poland, Hungary, East Germany, and Czechoslovakia—had originally agreed to take part in "Our World," a real coup for Singer, who spent months globe-trotting from government agency to government agency in order to make his dream a reality. The Soviets even offered the use of their Molniya communication satellite network for the event. But just four days before the broadcast, the Soviets and their allies pulled out, citing "Israeli aggression." The Soviets had supported the Arab countries since the mid-1950s in the global chess game between East and West. They claimed "Our World" would be used to smear the Arab states and had "lost its original humanitarian idea." Singer shot back in newspaper interviews, saying, "The show will go on. It will be a damn good program."

Singer's vision was to show the world live as it was at the moment, from a baby being born in Japan to steelworkers in Austria; the problems it faced, from hunger to overcrowding; solutions being sought, like new agricultural advancements and planned housing; humanity's achievements in athletics and the arts; and finally a look at the accomplishments being made in space travel and exploration. It was to be a second-by-second time capsule of what the world was like in 1967.

Even with the Soviet pullout, the global audience for "Our World" was astounding. The number of viewers was about 500 million, around 15 percent of the world population at the time. The cost was the equivalent in today's dollars of about fifteen million, paid for by the various countries involved in the show's production.

"'Our World' is an audacious experiment in international communications," Hugh Greene, BBC director general, said in a 1967 article about the broadcast. "It is nothing less than an attempt to circumnavigate the globe by television. In spite of many satellite broadcasts in recent years 'Our World' is unique and important because it is the first global collaboration in the making of a program instead of in the relaying of an event."

The broadcast was also unusual as much for what it focused on as for what it excluded. There were no politicians, no heads of state.

Besides giving glimpses into the lives of ordinary people, from a cowboy in Alberta, Canada, to two tram conductors in Melbourne, Australia, "Our World" included an A-list of cultural icons, including artists Pablo Picasso, Marc Chagall, Joan Miró, and Alexander Calder; filmmaker Franco Zeffirelli on the set of his film *Romeo and Juliet* with actress Olivia Hussey; and musicians and composers, including Leonard Bernstein, Maria Callas, and, of course, the Beatles.

The broadcast ended with a live shot of Cape Kennedy, where NASA made preparations for the Apollo 4 launch, followed by the CSIRO Parkes Telescope with observatory director John Bolton observing Quasar 0237-23 (at the time it was the most distant object known to humanity).

Space and its role in bringing humanity together was a key idea of the broadcast. The philosopher Marshall McLuhan, dubbed the Prophet of the Electric Age by the press, echoed this idea during an interview by the Canadian Broadcasting Corporation for the "Our World" broadcast. He described how the use of satellite technology for the program was helping build the "global village" and changing how humans saw themselves and others. He compared the "Our World" telecast to Expo 67, an extravagant World's Fair then going on in Montreal:

What is happening around the world today is what has happened with the Expo: a huge mosaic has been created in which, in effect, is a kind of X-ray of world cultures, not a storyline, not a perspective, not a point of view, but a kind of X-ray through this mosaic is created in which everybody can participate . . . People will be drawn in as participants, whereas they're only viewing themselves as spectators at the moment. . . X-ray means depth, participation in depth no matter what they're doing.

While Lemay had been on the run, Expo 67 had reshaped Montreal's Saint Lawrence River, where twenty-five million tons of fill, some from the excavation for the city's brand-new metro, created Notre Dame Island and enlarged a second island, Saint Helen's. By the fair's opening day on April 27, while Lemay sat in Bordeaux Prison awaiting trial, the fair's designers had transformed the islands into a glittering showpiece of late-1960s design. Like Disney's Tomorrowland, the architecture had a decidedly Hollywood sci-fi aesthetic. From the massive geodesic dome of the U.S. pavilion, designed by the genius R. Buckminster Fuller—architect, author, inventor, and thinker—to the futuristic spires of the U.K. pavilion, right down to the sculptures and kids' rides inspired by atoms and outer space.

The minirail that snaked through the vast World's Fair, the largest in history at the time, drove straight into the U.S. pavilion, where millions of visitors glided past physical manifestations of the nation's global supremacy in space. Among these objects was one of the crew capsules (officially called a reentry module) from Project Gemini, in which sixteen astronauts flew low-Earth-orbit missions over five years. The beaker-shaped capsule hung from the dome's ceiling as if floating in space.

Also on display was a life-sized model of the Lunar Orbiter sitting on a simulated moonscape, two years before the actual mission to the moon; Surveyor, a robotic spacecraft that had actually been on the moon; and the Apollo Command Module suspended from parachutes.

Tucked amid these grand and popular exhibits was a small case labeled "Satellite Communications" that displayed information about Early

Bird, Pacific I, Canary Bird, and Lani Bird, the first of the Intelsat II satellite series launched in October 1966.

The display was nearly lost amid the others celebrating manned space exploration, even though the satellites were an integral part of their success. Early Bird provided live coverage of the splashdown of Gemini VI-A—the first mission in which two manned spacecraft rendezvoused—in December 1965 and would go on to provide vital communication for NASA after the failure of another satellite during the Apollo 11 mission that landed the first men on the moon. These Hughes-built satellites allowed 500 million viewers to witness the historic moment when astronaut Neil Armstrong set his foot on the lunar surface.

The same summer as "Our World" and Expo 67, Hughes Aircraft invited Arthur C. Clarke, the author who first envisioned GEO satellites, to its Culver City plant to meet Harold Rosen, the man who made them a reality.

On August 25, 1967, the men spent the afternoon together touring the Space Systems Division and chatting amiably about everything from outer space to ground stations, the linchpins in the communication system that made the dissemination of information from continent to continent possible. By this time, Rosen had begun to be lauded for his work. The National Space Club, a D.C.-based organization devoted to fostering excellence in space activity through the interaction between industry and government, was one of the first to honor Rosen's achievements in 1963. The organization awarded him its top prize for scientific achievement that year. In 1965, the American Academy of Achievement—a nonprofit educational organization—awarded Rosen the Golden Plate Award. Rosen also now had a second son, Rocky, born the year before.

But there was something missing from all the laurels surrounding the acclaim of the synchronous satellite. Rosen couldn't help but recall the last day he saw Don Williams. It was Monday, February 21, 1966. Williams had come into Rosen's office. He seemed troubled. Williams apologized for not including his old friend on the patent for the Syncom control system. Rosen insisted it was fine, and his friend had no reason to apologize. Later that day, just before noon, Williams went back to his apartment in

Inglewood, California. He loaded a Colt Frontier model revolver while his wife, Gloria, a former police officer, tried desperately to stop him. "Think of all the blood," she cried, grasping for any reason she could to keep him from killing himself. He'd already written a note leaving everything to her. Williams locked himself in the bathroom, got into his bathtub fully clothed, and shot himself in the head. Williams, just thirty-four, was under psychiatric care at the time of his death.

The news shocked Rosen, along with the rest of Hughes Aircraft. No one could believe it. Afterward, several other Hughes employees recalled Williams coming into their offices to say goodbye. To one, he commented about what a beautiful morning it was. While they thought it was odd, they had no idea their colleague, whom they all considered a genius, was suicidal.

"The important contributions of Don Williams to the synchronous communication satellite are already of historical record," Pat Hyland, the company's head, told them later that week. "Millions of people in the far corners of the world have and will continue to benefit from his scientific genius that helped give birth to practical space communications. Let us remember in our shock at his loss, he pioneered the way and that his brilliant work contributed in major degree to the nation's leadership in space."

Rosen believed all the attention given to Williams, Tom Hudspeth, and himself for Syncom and Early Bird had just been too much for Williams to handle. He was a very private person who shunned the limelight. A month earlier, the Junior Chamber of Commerce of the United States had awarded Williams as one of the "Ten Outstanding Young Men of 1965," along with two astronauts, Charles Conrad and Edward White; Bill Moyers, then White House press secretary; and six others. The news of the award received national attention.

Additionally, the patent for the control system had become embroiled in a well-publicized lawsuit filed by Hughes Aircraft against NASA. The company alleged the government had stolen their control system and incorporated it into other satellites without paying Hughes any royalties.

While Rosen received his accolades, Lemay awaited his fate.

PART 4

A Changing Landscape

(Fall 1966–1984)

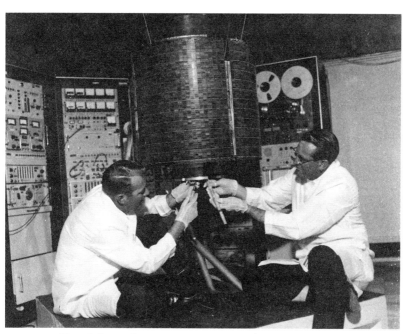

From left to right: NASA engineers Stanley R. Peterson and Ray Bowerman working on Early Bird, which was launched on April 6, 1965. NASA/Wikimedia Commons.

23

Waiting

FALL 1966—FALL 1967

ON OCTOBER 7, 1966, THE DAY AFTER LEMAY'S RETURN TO Montreal, he was finally in front of a judge for the bank heist that now seemed as if it happened a million years ago. Still wearing the suit he flew home in, but with a more conservative tie, he stood with one of his lawyers, Guy Guérin, as Judge Armand Sylvestre read the conspiracy and burglary charges the Crown had filed against him so long ago. He was in a courtroom in the Palais de Justice, the neoclassical courthouse where his former lieutenant, Primeau, had his trial four years earlier.

Slim and classically good looking, Jean Bruneau had become the chief Crown prosecutor for the Montreal district only two months earlier. He addressed the court, saying that he and Lemay's attorney had agreed on a date for a preliminary hearing a month hence. Guérin didn't enter a plea or even bother to ask for bail until after the preliminary hearing. The entire arraignment took less than a minute. Lemay returned to his cell to await his next court date in what would end up being one of the longest criminal trials in Montreal up to that time.

While Lemay faced Canadian justice, back in Miami, the men who helped him escape from the Dade County Jail were dealing with their own tribulations. Jaworski, the jail guard who provided Lemay with a rope, hacksaw blades, knife, and gloves, was the first to go to trial.

His lawyer told the jury his client "has a big heart and feels sorry for people behind bars." The defense alleged Lemay duped Jaworski into helping him. They claimed that the guard smuggled in some magazines and when he handed them to Lemay, the French Canadian revealed they contained hacksaw blades. Supposedly, he told Jaworski he would expose him if he didn't continue to aid in his escape. Whether or not the jury believed this story, they found him not guilty because of a Phoenix, Arizona, man charged with rape, kidnapping, and robbery whose case had recently helped change U.S. policing.

A jury found Ernesto Miranda guilty of kidnapping and raping an eighteen-year-old girl back in 1963. He'd confessed to the crimes during a two-hour-long police interrogation. No lawyer was present and none of the detectives explained to Miranda his rights against self-incrimination. Miranda had mental health issues and a ninth-grade education, and his confession was the entire basis for the prosecution's case. After being convicted and sentenced to twenty years in prison, his case went all the way to the U.S. Supreme Court. On June 13, 1966, the justices decided in favor of the defendant in *Miranda v. Arizona* in a five-to-four decision, written by Chief Justice Earl Warren. The groundbreaking decision affected numerous cases and changed the way police handled interrogations. Most cops today carry a Miranda warning card with them, but all of them know the words by heart: "You have the right to remain silent . . ."

Like Miranda, no one had told Jaworski of his rights before he confessed. The judge directed the jury to acquit him, but he was still out of a job as a jailer.

Mixon, the bail bondsman, and Alger, the jail guard who'd been instrumental in Lemay's escape, went to trial together in November 1966. A jury also found them not guilty because of the Supreme Court's Miranda ruling. Lemay may have cheated them out of their thirty-five thousand dollars, but at least they were free, while Lemay was now behind bars.

The Dade County grand jury looking into police misconduct released its findings that month and castigated both the Dade County Sheriff's

Office and Miami Police Department. The grand jury determined that "for the past ten or fifteen years, gambling, prostitution, and other forms of vice have flourished in Dade County with the obvious knowledge and active cooperation or tacit acquiescence of many local law enforcement agencies." They recommended a complete "overhaul" of the sheriff's office and the firing of any untrustworthy deputies.

The grand jurors also indicted Dade County sheriff T. A. Buchanan of conspiracy to commit bribery, accusing him of taking money from gamblers and pimps to allow them to operate in the county. Buchanan had beaten the earlier charge of perjury and kept his job. These new charges didn't stick either. A Dade County jury acquitted him on technicalities. The county again suspended Buchanan, and he lost his job when the voters made the sheriff an appointed position rather than elective. He then became a practicing lawyer. He was struck and killed by a car while crossing a busy Miami street in 1976.

Lemay's escape helped tear the lid off the pervasive corruption of Miami law enforcement and got two guards on the take and a powerful sheriff out of policing.

* * *

Following a delay by the prosecutor, who required more time to prepare, Lemay's preliminary hearing began on November 16 before Judge Emile Trottier. This constituted a dry run for the coming trial, giving Lemay's defense attorneys, Guy Guérin and Léo-René Maranda, a chance to see what they were up against and refine their plan of attack before facing a jury.

The day began with the testimony of a bank employee who gave a final tally from the heist, which was $633,605 ($5.8 million today). Twelve customers had refused to tell the bank what they kept in their safe-deposit boxes. Lemay knew the figure was closer to $2 million ($19 million today), but he certainly wasn't going to share that with the court. Instead, he insisted that the prosecution provide every one of the 365 written declarations in court that day. The bank eventually produced two massive boxes filled with the paperwork.

Guérin provided the hearing with a bit of levity when he produced the remains of an anemic-looking ham sandwich. The lawyer may have looked conservative with his penchant for sober suits—when not in his barrister's trappings of dark pants, white wing tip–collared shirt, black vest, long black robe—and horn-rimmed glasses, but he had a flair for the dramatic.

"This was all that my client was offered for lunch, along with a half cup of coffee," he told the court. "This morning he was served only one bowl of cereal and another half cup."

Judge Trottier asked Guérin what he considered a proper meal for his client. "There has already been a famous ruling by a higher court that a glass of freshly served milk could actually be a complete meal," the judge continued with a smile.

"What I want for my client, so that he can defend himself properly in court, are proteins, vegetables, all that is needed for a human organism to keep a man in physical and mental health."

The lawyer then pulled out a slice of fruitcake, which he had just bought in the courthouse cafeteria, and asked the judge to allow him to give it to Lemay to sustain him through the afternoon. The unique request flummoxed Trottier but he eventually agreed. Lemay sat back in his chair and ate his treat with a knowing smile.

The testimony on the first day included that of Detective Plouffe, who brought out dozens of items Lemay and his gang left behind at the scene of the crime. He did well under questioning by Chief Crown Attorney Bruneau, explaining how he located the tunnel used by the thieves as well as the various tools and how they were used in the break-in.

Then it was Maranda's turn to question the witness. The attorney was a master of cross-examination and was unrelenting in his attacks. He got Plouffe to admit that five years on from the crime, his memory of the details of his investigation was a bit hazy. It didn't help when the defense attorney began parsing out the slight differences in the officer's testimony from when he took the stand in Roland Primeau's trial in the spring of 1962. The prosecution compounded the problem by misplacing the copy of Plouffe's earlier testimony, preventing the detective from refreshing his memory.

Missing items and faulty memories would plague the prosecution throughout the length of the court case. When the judge suggested Maranda share his copy of Plouffe's previous testimony, the lawyer blurted out that he had no more questions for the witness and sat down.

The pretrial hearing dragged on for two weeks—abnormally long for this type of case—with the testimony of Jacques Lajoie, the man who'd landed Lemay in court, taking up a good part of the time.

Rumors circulated for months that Lajoie had gone missing. Before the hearing, the defense, in a somewhat unprecedented move, sent Detective Leblanc a subpoena to have Lajoie brought to court. They couldn't send it to the witness because the Montreal Police had been keeping Lajoie's whereabouts secret.

On the witness stand, Guérin wore down Lajoie, now forty-five years old, until he was visibly weary. He sagged in his seat as the attorney peppered him with questions about his criminal history and the favors he received from the Montreal Police while in jail. The witness frequently couldn't recall many of the details, especially as they related to his past crimes. Lajoie finally cracked. "All you want to do is get on my nerves," he shouted. "I know your tactics." The judge reprimanded him for his outburst. Lajoie apologized, and the questioning continued unabated.

Guérin's tactic of trying to show that Lajoie had a faulty memory and had become a prosecution witness to save his own neck didn't work. On November 29, Judge Trottier said he had no hesitation in reaching the conclusion that a properly instructed jury could render a guilty verdict based on the evidence presented by the Crown over the past two weeks.

Guérin and Maranda said they planned to exercise their client's right to a voluntary statement hearing, the stage in Quebec legal proceedings in which a defendant can present evidence to forestall a trial. Lemay spent his first Christmas back in Montreal in the somber confines of the ancient Bordeaux Prison as his case dragged on. His voluntary statement hearing on December 30 was short. His attorneys called only one witness, Detective Leblanc. Maranda questioned the officer on everything from the search warrants used to search Lemay's chalet to the special favors the police gave Lajoie. Leblanc denied making any promises to the prosecution's star witness.

Lemay claimed that he was at his Laurentian chalet the entire Dominion Day weekend and therefore couldn't have pulled off the burglary, but the defense didn't present any witnesses who could back up Lemay's alibi. The statement, given by Guérin to the court, caused a heated discussion between the lawyers on either side of the case.

Crown Prosecutor Bruneau argued that the defense couldn't just "declare" Lemay's alibi without either having Lemay testify or presenting witnesses who could prove Lemay hadn't left Mont-Rolland that weekend. Guérin and Maranda countered that the law in no way obliged a defendant to reveal his entire defense strategy during the voluntary examination. The judge agreed with the defense, but it didn't matter.

"I find the proof prima facie amply sufficient to send the defendant to trial," he said, ending the discussion. Lemay now had an important decision to make. He could have his trial either before a jury or a single judge.

Lemay opted for a jury trial with a tentative March trial date. Meanwhile, he remained in custody. On March 7, Lemay appeared in the Court of Queen's Bench under heavy guard with his arms and legs shackled. Nearly a dozen alleged murderers appeared in court that day, but it was Lemay who everyone wanted to see. He'd become a star even as his case continued to drag on, seemingly without end. Lemay had been back in Montreal for five months already. He assumed his trial would begin that day, but the prosecution asked for another delay, which pushed the trial to May. Lemay, angered over yet another delay in his case, sent a terse letter to see if he couldn't get things to move along a little faster. While Lemay's game plan before being deported had been to stall his return to Canada, now that he was sitting in jail in Montreal, he just wanted to get it all over with. As he'd soon learn, his wishes wouldn't necessarily jibe with his lawyers' strategy.

He sent the telegram straight to the top, to the Quebec minister of justice Jean-Jacques Bertrand, asking him to intervene. Lemay also complained that the administration of Bordeaux Prison twice prevented his attorneys from seeing him.

"In October 1966, I agreed not to fight a deportation order from the

United States on the promise of the Canadian authorities in reflection that I would stand trial upon my return to Canada," the note began. "But now I have already been detained for almost six months in the prison of Montréal, despite the requests and the work of my lawyers, Mr. Guérin and Mr. Maranda. I learned from them yesterday that the Crown did not seem disposed to me undergoing my trial in the shortest time possible without delay."

Lemay pointed out that the Crown had had five years to prepare for trial (leaving out the reason they had so long to prepare) and that he was being held without bail (not mentioning that his lawyers had yet to request bail).

"So, I have only you to whom I can turn as Minister of Justice in order that my rights are respected," the letter ends. "Hoping that you will pay special attention to me. Pending your response I remain, your very grateful, Georges Lemay."

To make sure the letter would make an impression on the justice minister, Lise went to the *La Presse* office with a photostatted copy of Lemay's letter and a lot to say about how the jail was treating her husband. She alleged the guards were preventing Lemay's lawyers from seeing him.

Lise got the media to do her work for her. The newspaper reporter who interviewed her attempted to speak with Bordeaux's warden, Albert Tanguay, for comment on Lemay's allegations, without success. But it was enough to guarantee Lemay's lawyers could see him when they needed.

During her interview, when the newspaper reporter mentioned to Lise that her husband might rightly be considered a flight risk given his history, she brushed the idea aside as being ridiculous.

"Never, not this time," she said, an edge of annoyance in her voice. "On the contrary, he cannot wait for this story to be over."

Lemay's telegram didn't have its intended effect. Bertrand didn't step in to hurry the trial along, but it did become political fodder. The former Liberal Quebec minister of justice Claude Wagner, who prosecuted Lemay's gang three years earlier when still a Crown attorney, blasted his Conservative replacement, suggesting he was soft on crime. He pointed to Lemay's letter as evidence.

A week later, Lemay's lawyers requested bail for their client. They could go as high as fifty thousand dollars. Their request included more than forty reasons the court should give Lemay bail, chief among them that the prosecution pushed the trial back another month. "As a result of this prolonged and indefinite detention, the physical and moral state of the applicant suffers considerably," the lawyers claimed.

Other reasons included a prosecution case "based solely on the testimony" of alleged accomplices who were known criminals without "incriminating circumstance to corroborate or confirm this evidence."

The lawyers argued that Harry Post and Oscar Gelfand, then on trial for a $1.5 million arson scheme in which they burned down a massive furniture manufacturing plant for the insurance money, got bail, and so should Lemay.

Finally, they suggested Lemay should be given bail since "in accordance with the provisions of the penal code, the declaration of human rights and common law and the spirit of these laws," Lemay was cloaked with "a presumption of innocence and has the right to freedom."

Maranda and Guérin's arguments were all for naught. Lemay's daring escape from the Dade County Jail remained fixed in the mind of Judge Peter Shorteno, who heard Lemay's bail request. He quickly determined the prisoner would remain one.

When May arrived, it was the defense's turn to ask for a postponement. Guérin told the court he was too busy acting as a special prosecutor in the sensational Sicotte Affair, a police brutality case in which Jean-Louis Sicotte, an insurance adjuster involved in an alleged arson-murder plot, claimed he'd had his confession beaten out of him by the Quebec Provincial Police. The provincial government tasked Guérin with looking into the allegations. A preliminary hearing had already dragged on for fourteen weeks by that point and didn't look like it would end anytime soon.

Maranda said he needed more time as well after coming off the trial of James Coe, a twenty-eight-year-old acquitted of conspiracy and armed robbery for his alleged role in a cigarette truck heist.

Lemay wasn't pleased that his own lawyers were now dragging the case out, especially since only two months earlier he'd made such a stink about the prosecution's delay, but he didn't want to lose either of his talented attorneys and so reluctantly agreed to the postponement.

In August, Lemay changed his mind on how he wanted to proceed with his case. In a surprising move, Lemay asked for a trial before a single judge, rather than the jury trial already scheduled for September. Why Lemay made this choice remains a mystery.

For his attorneys, it meant a change of tactics. Unlike in a jury trial, where emotionality and theatrics could sway a jury, a judge was more likely to base his decision on the strict merits of the case.

The court pushed back the trial until the end of October 1967. Lemay had already been waiting for nearly a year. He couldn't have known just how long he would be forced to wait for his trial to end.

24

Trial

FALL 1967–WINTER 1969

BY THE TIME THE CASE CAME TO TRIAL ON OCTOBER 30, 1967, more than a year after Lemay's return to Montreal from Las Vegas, he was down to one lawyer. Minister of justice Jean-Jacques Bertrand had named Guy Guérin a sessions court judge for Montreal the previous month, which meant he could no longer represent Lemay. Léo-René Maranda would have to push on alone.

The trial got off to a rocky start. They had to wait an hour for a court-room to open up in the busy Palais de Justice. The mass of journalists there to cover the first day of the trial milled around along with the merely curious and those actually involved in the case. Lemay, who had lost weight during his time in jail but remained a bit paunchy, wore a dapper blue suit. He was handcuffed to a guard and closely watched by three others.

Once the proceedings got underway, Maranda wasted no time objecting to everything from how Judge Jacques Trahan came to oversee the case to the wording of the charging document. He also presented a motion to quash the indictment on technical grounds. Maranda's fireworks shocked the Crown attorneys prosecuting the case, Pierre Sauvé and Stephen Cuddihy. Both men were relatively new. Cuddihy had been a prosecutor for only a few months. It didn't bode well for a quick end to the trial.

Judge Trahan put an end to it.

"Do we really want to proceed, in this case, or do we want to make mountains with little piles of sand?" he asked Maranda.

"I just want the law to be followed," Maranda answered.

The judge rejected the motion to quash the case and hurried it along.

Lise sat in the gallery as close to Lemay as allowed, watching the scene. The Crown had subpoenaed her as a witness, a strange move since burglary wasn't a crime for which the prosecution could force her to testify against her husband. Canadian law specified that the prosecution could compel a spouse to testify only in cases where there is a potential for violence against the spouse or their child or a violent or sexual offense against a child. Perhaps the Crown believed they would somehow still be able to flip her, or it could have simply been a tactic meant to inflict emotional pain on Lemay.

Before the trial had really even gotten started the judge made Lise leave the courtroom, on a request from the Crown prosecutors that any subpoenaed witnesses not be in court until called to testify.

It would be up to the prosecution to prove that the surreptitious thirty-second wedding ceremony in Miami wasn't legal and then convince Lise to testify against Lemay. They didn't know her. She was unhappy that she wouldn't be by Lemay's side during the trial, but she wasn't about to roll over on her husband.

That morning, Maranda convinced the judge to let Lise remain at home until they needed her in court. It was a small victory.

The trial's first week centered on Leo Plouffe's testimony. He had been promoted to detective captain in January 1967. He was as busy as ever with forensics and the bomb squad yet found time to build one of the world's first bomb-disposal robots. He nicknamed it Leo Jr. Plouffe also developed the first CCTV system in North America. It linked all the Montreal Police stations. But Plouffe wasn't on the witness stand for any of his accomplishments.

Maranda spent hours asking Plouffe complex scientific questions on explosives and how sound travels, to which Plouffe, exasperated, finally declared, "I didn't spring from the thigh of Jupiter and I'm not a living encyclopedia."

Plouffe explained he was "in possession of certain precise data and had made certain studies in several fields. Having been in daily contact, for years, with the acts and methods of criminals, I could say that I have acquired a certain 'criminalistic' science, which, on occasion, allows me to be of service to the police officers who are pursuing an investigation." Beyond that, he couldn't say one way or another the precise means by which sound traveled inside the tunnel without performing complex scientific tests.

Maranda's questions weren't pointless; he was hoping to use Plouffe's testimony to show that Jacques Lajoie had lied about conversations he overheard while in the tunnel between gang members inside the vault during the heist.

The detective surmised Lajoie could have heard Lemay's conversations inside the vault, but it would require tests either way, since there were "a large number of contingencies which could even vary to infinity." Science, Plouffe knew, couldn't easily be bent to a lawyer's desires.

On Friday, November 3, 1967, Lemay had a terrible day. It began with a surprise witness and ended with Lemay's personal life on public display. The Crown called to the stand Marek Vonchovsky, a silversmith and victim of the bank burglary.

Maranda turned to Lemay, confused. His client looked equally befuddled. Maranda bolted from his seat and exclaimed this was the first he'd heard of this witness and asked for time to discuss strategy. Trahan granted the defense a short recess. The prosecution had a few surprises that day.

When court resumed, Vonchovsky, a Jewish man in his seventies, openly wept as he told the story of how he'd come to be in court. He had had a successful silversmith company in Prague, Czechoslovakia, before the war. Following Hitler's invasion of Prague in 1939, Vonchovsky buried a trove of jewelry he'd made himself. The Nazis deported him and his family to Theresienstadt, a "camp-ghetto" north of Prague, which served as both a transit camp and forced labor camp. A year later, the Germans sent them to the Auschwitz concentration camp, in Nazi-occupied Poland.

Once there, his captors brutally tortured him, including shooting him in the foot, attempting to extract where he'd hidden his treasure. He never revealed his secret, knowing that as long as he was alive, the guards believed they'd eventually learn where it was hidden. The jeweler survived the war, recovered his fortune, and immigrated to Montreal in 1948.

After several burglaries of his home, the elderly man put his jewelry in a safe-deposit box at the Bank of Nova Scotia. He couldn't get a life insurance policy due to his wrecked health from his time at Auschwitz, and he considered the jewelry, worth more than a quarter of a million dollars today, as his legacy. Then, three years later, Lemay and his gang broke into the bank and stole it all. Vonchovsky thankfully recovered the bulk of his stolen jewelry.

During cross-examination, Maranda tried to shake Vonchovsky's story that he'd designed the jewelry recovered by the police. The old man, looking the defense attorney in the eyes, angrily repeated over and over, "They are mine. I made them with my hands. I know. I'm sure." It wasn't a good look for Maranda, especially as the witness had to take several pills for his heart during the intensive cross-examination.

Judge Trahan finally broke in. "What's the point of this line of questioning?" he demanded. "After all, you've been harping on the same thing for the last half hour."

"I'm here all day," the defense attorney retorted. "I'm in no hurry."

The next witness was more damaging to both the case and Lemay's personal life. Lise Vaudry, the young woman Lemay spent time with before the heist and showered with stolen jewelry, took the stand for the prosecution after Vonchovsky shakily left. At least one reporter remarked on her resemblance to the first Mrs. Lemay, Huguette, who had disappeared in the Keys back in 1952.

Judge Trahan ordered the reporters present not to reveal the names of either witness, but he didn't explain why.

Now in her early twenties, Vaudry nervously revealed that she had met Lemay in Montreal a few months before the Dominion Day burglary. She'd visited him at his chalet. After a pause that lasted nearly a minute, she identified the jewelry he'd given her—some of which Vonchovsky had made—which she turned over to the police back in 1962. The judge had been forced to order her to answer the question posed by the prosecutor about whether she had recognized the jewelry. Vaudry looked uncomfortable as she answered the questions. So did Lemay, who knew her testimony was damning as it directly connected him to the burglary. She also identified photographs of the Lemieux brothers, Primeau, and Lajoie. Vaudry had met them all. The prosecution then put the postcards Lemay sent her from his trip to Cuba into evidence.

Vaudry also revealed that she was the mother of Lemay's illegitimate child. She said Lemay knew he was the five-year-old's father and had never denied the fact. Lemay squirmed in his seat a bit during this portion of the testimony, as much for himself as for Vaudry, who was embarrassed about making these revelations in open court. It only got worse for the woman as the questioning continued. At the end of her direct examination, Lemay pushed his lawyer to ask the court for a ten-minute recess so Vaudry could calm down before what he knew would be a brutal cross-examination by his bulldog defense attorney.

She became testy with Maranda's questioning on the first day, but by day three she was in tears, physically exhausted, pale, her eyes red-rimmed, and sagging in her seat as she told the court that she'd had to confess to her fiancé about Lemay fathering one of her children. Maranda also forced her to reveal that she had another child out of wedlock, a fact her fiancé was unaware of until then.

She obfuscated a bit, initially telling the court her affair with Lemay ended in 1961, when in truth it continued into 1962. She'd met up with Lemay in New York City after he'd fled from Canada in the fall of 1962. Vaudry later shamefacedly admitted this to the judge.

"Yesterday, my future husband was in court," she said hoarsely, bursting into tears. "I didn't want him to know that I had two children. I wanted to save my marriage." She added, "I was told that I shouldn't have to lay out my private life. And you see what happens. For three days now,

I have been asked questions, questions, questions. I have had enough. I can't take it anymore."

Maranda asked for a brief recess, but Vaudry said she didn't need a break.

"No, I want to stay here. I want to continue. I want to end it."

Maranda sarcastically asked whether it was because the witness wanted everyone to see her tears. Judge Trahan cut him off.

"Enough. We are not at the circus. And we are not presenting a play. Let the witness be questioned, but stop making comments and remarks about her behavior."

The attorney then asked her if she'd seen Lemay around Easter 1963. "Maybe," she answered. As the questions dragged on, "maybe" became her go-to answer.

Lemay didn't enjoy seeing Vaudry suffer, but Maranda was trying to show her bias against his client to mitigate her damning testimony. The defense attorney asked her whether it upset her to learn Lemay had married another woman, the other Lise. The Crown prosecutors both stood up and objected, not to the question, but to Maranda's reference to Lemay and Lise being married, as they still planned to pursue putting Mrs. Lemay on the stand.

Vaudry said she felt no animosity toward Lemay. The questioning finally ended, and she was allowed to step down.

Among the other witnesses who took the stand in the coming weeks was René Morin, the Miami mechanic and school friend of Lemay. In the intervening years, he'd moved back to Quebec and become a firefighter. He tearfully described how he did his friend's bidding and tossed most of the stolen jewelry he'd removed from the *Anou* in January 1962. He later admitted to selling a ring to a mutual friend of theirs from Montreal.

The most Maranda got out of Morin during the cross-examination was that he failed to identify the walkie-talkies in evidence, and he had conflicted feelings about his old friend.

"He was always good to me," Morin said, choking up.

On Friday, November 10, Lajoie took the stand. He and Lemay ignored one another. The prosecution was protective of him, so much so that they asked the judge to order the press not to photograph the witness. The Crown prosecutors even fought the defense on revealing Lajoie's address or where he was working to the defense.

Lajoie's direct examination by Cuddihy went smoothly. Lajoie seemed at ease and even got a few chuckles from the gallery as he described the bank heist in great detail. When it was Maranda's turn, he forced Lajoie to recount his long criminal career, beginning with his first conviction when he was just a teenager in 1938, for the crime of robbing his employer.

"I think [the conviction] was for a burglary," Lajoie told the court.

"And what did you take?" Maranda asked.

"Many articles. Among others, a horse, a cart, and a dog."

"Did you leave him *anything?*" Maranda asked, acting shocked.

"His home," the witness answered to a peal of laughter from the gallery.

As the questions continued, Lajoie's demeanor soured and at several points, he lost his temper, as did the prosecutors. Cuddihy and Sauvé argued that the defense lawyer's questioning of Lajoie was becoming "abusive" since he was asking the witness the same questions over and over. While the judge found that some of Maranda's questions were "useless," he refused to restrict the rights of the defendant, even if it would prolong the trial. Lemay, as well, didn't want to have his rights restricted, but he also didn't want the trial dragged out forever.

The biggest inconsistency in Lajoie's testimony was his exact age. He gave a different birth date practically every time he appeared on the stand. Lajoie blamed the court reporters for the inconsistencies, a tactic he often resorted to during the marathon of questioning. His other go-to responses included "perhaps," "I don't remember," and "that could very well be." Lajoie's memory for names and dates also wasn't the best. He couldn't recall the birthday of his girlfriend or of their youngest child. The exceptions to his faulty memory were the names of the judges who'd sentenced him over the years. "You never forget the name of a sentencing judge," he explained.

At one point during questioning, Maranda noticed Lajoie looking over at Detective Leblanc. The officer seemed to be signaling to the witness. Maranda stopped his cross-examination to complain to the judge and asked him to remove Leblanc from the courtroom.

Cuddihy and Sauvé exploded. Both stood up to defend Leblanc, calling it an "unjustified" accusation. Judge Trahan agreed.

"I've seen nothing untoward in the officer's conduct," he said, ordering the case to continue.

Maranda hounded Lajoie on the many favors he had received while in jail, such as having his cell unlocked, getting takeout delivered, receiving conjugal visits, and having a television and radio in his cell. The favors continued even after his release. Lajoie admitted Detectives St. Pierre and Leblanc acted as references for him when he wanted to buy a car.

Maranda also thoroughly questioned him on every job he'd held down in his life, along with many questions that seemed superfluous, like his shoe size. It was all part of Maranda's strategy to discredit the Crown's star witness. Lajoie had taken the stand on multiple occasions in the long history associated with the bank heist. The defense attorney ruthlessly and exhaustingly mined his previous statements for contradictions to show Lajoie was a career criminal and a liar with a bad memory to boot.

A few days into Maranda's cross-examination of Lajoie, the attorney began feeling ill. A virulent case of the flu laid him out. The trial was postponed several times as Maranda attempted to shake it off, but it migrated to his chest. He was weak and had a persistent fever. Maranda finally returned on the morning of November 22 after a week away and continued his cross-examination of Lajoie, only to bow out from the afternoon session and head back to bed. His doctor appeared before the court to explain that the defense attorney had undergone two chest X-rays as they tried to figure out his illness.

By November 27, Maranda was back and ready with more questions for Lajoie. Cross-examination stretched into December and became so tedious that even the hardcore court watchers grew bored. The courtroom was nearly empty, except for the reporters, who were being paid to suffer through the mind-numbing proceedings. Judge Trahan broke up the monotony on December 5 when he insisted on seeing the scene of the crime.

The newspaper articles about the trial, which had migrated deeper into the back pages of the Montreal papers, were back on the front pages.

The event had the same carnival-like atmosphere as that of the court's visit to the same crime scene during Roland Primeau's trial five years earlier.

Passersby stopped and stared at the strange scene as Judge Trahan, both prosecutors, and Lemay, his handcuffs removed, dressed in khaki-colored overalls, all crowded into the foyer of the building used to access the tunnel to the bank. Maranda wore a black one-piece sportswear outfit. Lajoie sat on the stairs while the court stenographer used an overturned wastebasket as a desk to take his notes. Two police officers kept a close eye on Lemay and would move closer to him every time he got too close to the doorway. Reporters and photographers also crammed into the space.

Maranda asked Lemay to try to remove the heavy cover to the old well. He struggled with it, perhaps a little too dramatically, for several minutes before getting it off. Trahan, the lawyers, and Lemay then descended into the tunnel. Maranda was trying to prove that the tunnel narrowed too much to allow a person through, but both Cuddihy and himself, who were thin, made it through. The judge, who was heavier, couldn't get past the gap and abandoned the attempt. Lemay, paunchier than he'd been in the summer of 1961, six years earlier, when he was younger and in better shape, didn't even try.

Maranda wanted to test out another claim made by Lajoie that he could clearly hear coins being dumped into a bag during the heist. But because the hole the burglars blew open in the vault floor had since been resealed, the judge nixed Maranda's plan, saying it would be impossible to recreate the exact circumstances.

They returned to the foyer, where Maranda questioned Lajoie some more. They then headed across the street to have a look at the office that Lajoie had rented as the heist's command center.

They looked out the windows at the building that once housed the bank. The branch had closed not long after the 1961 robbery and now stood empty. There was a single fading sign left in the window. It advertised all of the bank's services and included a blurb about one of its

offerings. DO NOT TAKE CHANCES WITH YOUR IMPORTANT DOC-
UMENTS AND YOUR PRECIOUS JEWELS, the sign read. PROTECT
THEM FROM THEFT WITH A SAFE-DEPOSIT BOX.

By December 11, after spending fourteen days—stretched over a
month—on the witness stand, the judge allowed Lajoie to step down.

"Thank you very much for your cooperation," Maranda told Lajoie
with a straight face.

"You are quite welcome, Mr. Maranda," he responded in the same
deadpan manner. He left the stand with a palpable sense of relief. The
reporters covering the case felt the same way.

The prosecution recalled Detective Plouffe on December 14. He was
there to discuss the walkie-talkies used in the heist.

As he took the stand, however, he noticed that a jar of blasting caps
sat near the judge's bench. They were evidence. Another officer had earlier
testified he'd found the explosives in a hollow tree on Lemay's island. No
one had considered that the candy jar full of volatile explosives might pose
a danger, but Plouffe knew better.

"Hold everything," he told the court. "I'm not going to fool around
with these walkie-talkies in the presence of these detonators."

Plouffe explained they needed to be stored properly and
could explode in their current state. The judge cleared the courtroom, and Plouffe removed the explosives and dealt with them.
The next important prosecution witness in the trial, which had stretched
to seven weeks, was Primeau's brother-in-law, Yvon Bélanger. Maranda
objected to the witness because Bélanger's testimony "did not concern
the accused, Lemay." The lawyer explained that "the words of the so-
called accomplices cannot bind the accused or be presented as evidence
against him." Trahan took the motion under advisement but still allowed
Bélanger to take the stand.

Bélanger described how Lemay and Primeau had him purchase a drill
and other equipment. He watched the entire gang testing out drills and
saws in his brother-in-law's basement, he said. Primeau made him repair
the floor with cement Lemay had purchased, he told the court.

Under Maranda's questioning, Bélanger admitted he didn't know

there was going to be a burglary. The defense attorney had the witness re-
cite all his convictions. He then tried to impeach the witness through his
previous testimony. But Bélanger, unlike Lajoie, had been so vague in his
responses during his previous court appearances that there was little for
Maranda to work with. Bélanger's testimony backed up some of Lajoie's
statements, which wasn't good for Lemay.

The defense attorney got Bélanger to admit former Quebec minister of justice Claude Wagner wrote him a job recommendation in 1963.
Maranda made this out as some sort of bribe to secure Bélanger as a
prosecution witness. Wagner, before his tenure as justice minister, had
prosecuted Primeau's case in which Bélanger testified. The attempt to discredit Bélanger, along with Wagner, went nowhere.

The cross-examination dragged on for a week, and Maranda's health
again faltered. On December 21, Trahan decided to halt the proceedings
until after the holidays. Lemay spent another Christmas behind bars in
the drab Bordeaux Prison in a cell typically reserved for inmates on death
row. Lemay didn't know how many more holidays he might have to spend
behind bars.

The New Year saw Lemay's defense gain some momentum. Throughout the trial the prosecution referred to the Laurentian chalet as being
Lemay's, with Maranda objecting to these references. A prosecution
witness, a notary, provided proof that Lemay wasn't the chalet's owner.
Lemay had sold the island to his brother-in-law, Bernard Parent, in 1958
for one dollar and "other good and valuable considerations." Parent believed the property had been given as a sort of gift and the considerations
included medical care for Lemay, and the understanding he would take
care of Lemay's mother if she ever needed a place to live.

Maranda focused on the fact that Lemay didn't own the chalet. It
weakened the evidence the police uncovered at the property.

The Crown scrambled and brought in J. Roger Bernier, who lived
next door to the island property. He testified that he'd seen only Lemay
at the chalet and never Bernard Parent. Maranda took the opportunity
during cross-examination to lay the groundwork for his client's alibi. He
asked Bernier if he recalled Lemay being at his annual garden party on

Dominion Day weekend in 1961, the same weekend as the bank burglary. Bernier couldn't recall if Lemay attended that year. The lawyer tried to refresh his memory by recounting some specifics about the event, but the man just shrugged his shoulders. The attorney suggested the witness might have photos of the annual event.

"I may," the man answered, "but they won't be very useful. They're not dated."

Maranda's attempt to place Lemay at the party was a bust.

The Crown ended its case in mid-January after a fruitless search for the scrap of cardboard the police had found at the island chalet with figures related to the payoffs from the heist. Lajoie testified to seeing Lemay write the figures out and the prosecution had a photograph of the cardboard, but the actual item had disappeared from the case files sometime during the previous six and a half years. Several court clerks testified to their intensive search for the elusive piece of evidence, and Inspector Morin, the police handwriting expert, testified he'd seen the paper back in 1962 but couldn't say whether it had been in Lemay's handwriting.

The Crown had long ago given up their attempt to force Lise to testify, feeling they had a strong enough case without her. She was free to once again attend the trial.

It was now the defense's turn. Maranda immediately moved to have Lemay acquitted of the charges. On Tuesday, January 16, 1968, he spent four hours arguing his case to a courtroom packed full of entranced spectators. He told the court most of the Crown's evidence came from "unreliable thugs or liars," and that Lajoie's and Bélanger's testimony was "so full of contradictions and lies" that it should be inadmissible. He pointed to all the favors the Montreal Police did for Lajoie. Detective Leblanc, ordinarily an honest man, had aided and abetted Lajoie's escape from legal custody, while the Crown gave the criminal a sweetheart deal for his role in the heist—one day in jail—the defense attorney asserted.

As for Bélanger, Maranda mentioned Wagner's job recommendation and a short jail sentence for an unrelated crime. He'd already subpoenaed Wagner, who was expected to be the first witness when Maranda presented Lemay's defense.

"Both these men were clearly bought and their testimony is not therefore that of free men providing honest evidence," Maranda said. "The Crown was forced through pressure from the public to provide some sort of evidence against Lemay, so it gave us the testimony of two bandits whose accounts were rank with perjury."

Judge Trahan, in his response, said there was enough evidence to continue with the trial.

The next day, Maranda called for a mistrial. He claimed that the court had denied Lemay the right to a "complete and entire defense" because of several missing pieces of evidence, including fifteen of Lemay's suits; the crystal from one of the walkie-talkies, which prevented the defense attorney from determining whether the device worked; and the scrap of cardboard alleged to have been written on by Lemay.

Because of the missing evidence, Maranda said he wouldn't even attempt to present "a mere part of a defense." He wanted the current proceedings annulled and a new trial scheduled, with all the evidence available for his inspection.

Crown Prosecutor Cuddihy pointed out it had been several years since the crime and that it surprised him there weren't more missing items. The prosecution presented photographs of Lemay's suits and the piece of cardboard.

"As for those that are not there or that have suffered some damage," he said, "they are not so essential to the evidence that the defense wants to believe, and it is certainly not in bad faith on the part of the prosecution because they are missing or have been slightly modified."

Before Trahan ruled on this motion, Maranda shocked the courtroom, and especially the judge, whose face visibly paled, by declaring he would seek to have Trahan removed from the case.

Maranda claimed the judge had overstepped his jurisdiction the day before when the defense asked for an acquittal. "The court shifted the burden of proof and put the accused in a position where he should not normally be placed," he said.

Maranda read aloud from the trial transcript in which Trahan discussed evidence related to the gang's testing of the drills and saws at Primeau's house.

"The marks are there, therefore there isn't total absence of evidence," the judge had said. "Give me proof now as to who made them. If the accused is not mixed up with all this, so much the better for him; I shall acquit him."

Trahan defended his statements, saying that he based his rejection of the motion to acquit on the total "non-absence" of evidence, and that he did not shift the burden of proof onto the defendant. He then declared, "I have no objections that you resort to procedures made available to you by the law."

Trahan adjourned the trial to give the defense time to pursue the motion in Superior Court. The Superior Court rejected Maranda's first attempt on technical issues. He succeeded on his second attempt in getting the Superior Court to look at the case. Besides Maranda's accusation that Trahan overstepped his jurisdiction, he also alleged the judge was biased against Lemay. A Superior Court judge threw out the case, but the defense attorney kept pursuing the issue all the way to the Quebec Court of Appeal.

Maranda's crusade delayed the rest of Lemay's trial for eight more months, angering Lemay, who just wanted the trial to be over.

During a hearing before Judge Trahan in June, Lemay told him he wasn't happy with Maranda's pursuit to remove the judge. Trahan told him that it was something he should be taking up with his lawyer and not with the court. Trahan said he was being generous by continuing to grant postponements in the case.

Lemay smiled and said, "I would find you really generous if you would agree to grant me a bond."

The judge said it wasn't up to him.

On September 18, 1968, the Court of Appeal rejected Maranda's appeal in a unanimous decision, finding "nothing in the record before us that would indicate that, by allusions, comments or interventions, Judge Trahan disclosed a prejudicial opinion to the accused." Maranda could, if his client was convicted, raise these issues on appeal. The defense attorney planned to, if it came to that.

On October 8, Lemay's trial resumed. In a surprising move, Maranda announced he wouldn't be calling any witnesses.

"It has been our position right along that the Crown has failed to make any valid proof against my client, so why should we attempt to refute it?" the defense attorney said in court. "The loss of certain exhibits by the Crown has deprived us a full and entire defense."

A week later, Crown prosecutors Cuddihy and Maranda gave their closing arguments.

The prosecutor told the court that the defense couldn't refute any of the evidence the Crown presented, and that Lajoie's testimony—corroborated by Bélanger—pointed directly to Lemay being the mastermind behind the bank heist.

Maranda said it would be a dangerous precedent for the court to find Lemay guilty based on the contradictory testimony of a career criminal.

Judge Trahan gave his verdict on the morning of January 17, 1969, concluding the trial, which had dragged on for nearly a year and a half, making it one of the longest criminal trials in Montreal's history, according to a report of the time by the Canadian Press.

Police—including Detectives Leblanc and St. Pierre, who'd spent so much time and energy hunting down Lemay—reporters, and the public, who'd been following the elusive thief's many adventures for more than eight years, packed the Montreal courtroom for the verdict.

Lemay was still a celebrity, especially in Quebec and Florida, where the big Miami newspapers carried coverage of the trial. All the press reports touched on Early Bird's role in Lemay's initial capture in 1965. While there is no direct evidence, Rosen would likely have been aware of his creation's use in capturing Lemay.

Lise wasn't able to make it to the sentencing, as she was at home taking care of Josée, who was sick in bed. The other Lise in Lemay's life, Lise Vaudry, was on hand, sitting in the second row of the gallery.

Lemay, looking rather nervous and irritable, a frown replacing the trademark smirk he'd worn through the bulk of the trial, stole glances in Vaudry's direction from time to time, but mostly focused on the judge.

Trahan referred to his 274-page decision during a ninety-minute explanation of his conclusions in the case. He gave a lot of credence to Lajoie's testimony, even if it contained some errors and contradictions.

"That he made a few errors on the dates, or that one can find certain contradictions between his various statements, should not, however, move us unduly," the judge said. "And, on this subject, the court believes it necessary to declare that too often we ask a lot more of our witnesses than we can give ourselves."

He said that while rereading the case file, he found that the Crown prosecutors, Maranda, and he himself had all made factual errors during the trial.

"This proves that it is very easy to make mistakes on dates, days, times, the places and even the people present, at certain times, and that without a second thought," he went on.

The defense cross-examined Lajoie for fourteen days, the judge said, under "unfavorable circumstances" for the witness, yet he remained calm, dignified, and reserved. Lajoie's testimony, he said, was backed up by physical evidence the police found at the scene of the crime and at Lemay's chalet.

Trahan also gave a lot of weight to Bélanger's testimony. The judge remarked that Bélanger wasn't involved in the heist, but had witnessed some of its preparations, which correlated with Lajoie's version of events. The judge also put a lot of stock in the prosecution's other witnesses, including Vaudry and the jeweler, Vonchovsky, who directly tied Lemay to items stolen during the heist. Trahan stated that his decision was not based solely on the testimony of one person but on his careful study of the case in its entirety.

Of the missing exhibits Maranda had made such a show over, the judge said that while it showed the Crown needed to improve its evidence handling, it didn't prevent the defendant from presenting a complete defense. Trahan then declared that at no time did he act prejudicially against Lemay, as Maranda had alleged.

"The court finds the accused guilty on both counts against him," he said.

Lemay's expression didn't change when he heard the verdict. He looked resigned, if none too happy. The court took a break until the afternoon to give the lawyers a chance to weigh in on Lemay's sentencing.

Maranda may have been disappointed by the verdict, but he knew he still had a chance to mitigate the damage by getting Lemay the least amount of prison time possible. To do that the lawyer had some verbal gymnastics planned for the judge.

Once court resumed, Maranda pointed to Lemay's minimal criminal record, especially when compared to Primeau, who was then serving a thirteen-year sentence for the same crime, and pointedly, to Lajoie, who as a career criminal received only one day in jail for his part in the heist.

"What the defense suggests is that the court finds a middle ground between the penalties that have been imposed on its various associates, and that penalty should be set at no more than two years' imprisonment," Maranda told the court.

The defense attorney also pointed out that during the entire time Lemay was on the run, he didn't commit any other crimes, so he was, in a sense, "rehabilitating himself without being under sentence," he explained with a straight face. Maranda glossed over the fact that breaking out of jail in Miami, bribing the guards, and using false identity papers while on the run were all crimes.

Crown Prosecutor Cuddihy viewed Lemay's record differently than Maranda. The courts had gone easy on Lemay over the years, he said. Lemay was the undisputed leader of the gang involved in the burglary, who made all the decisions but didn't do any of the hard work, like the chairman of a board of directors, he said.

Cuddihy then launched into a series of rhetorical questions. "Has the defense lawyer told us where his client has been working in recent years? Did he tell us what his job was? Did he tell us that Lemay would reimburse, even in part, the half a million stolen from 377 different people?" He ended by asking for the maximum sentence of fourteen years.

Trahan, in determining the amount of time Lemay should remain behind bars, relied on three pillars: the seriousness of the offense and the maximum sentence; "the immense harm done to the holders of the 377 disemboweled security coffers"; and the "particularly prolonged preventive imprisonment incurred by the accused for the most diverse reasons, in recent years." Lemay had already been in jail, held without bail, for two years and nine months. He'd also spent months incarcerated in both Florida and Nevada awaiting deportation back to Canada.

Trahan sentenced Lemay to eight years in prison. As Lemay was led off to serve his time, Maranda made plans to appeal the sentence.

The bulk of the money from the bank heist was never recovered. But Lemay's lawyer was likely one of its biggest beneficiaries, as he racked up untold billable hours.

25

Out but Not Down

1974–1984

GEORGES LEMAY WALKED OUT OF PRISON IN JULY 1974 AFTER serving five years and five months of his eight-year sentence. His appeals all failed, but between the credit for the time he sat in jail awaiting trial and what he knocked off for good behavior, he was out early. He'd been a model prisoner and had become so trustworthy by the end of his prison stretch that the warden granted him more than a dozen passes. It began with day passes, and as his release day drew closer, the prison allowed him to leave for up to two weeks at a time. He always returned. Lemay had grown tired of running. He had been in one jail or another since his capture in Las Vegas back in 1966, and Montreal, the city he'd once known so intimately, had changed dramatically during his incarceration.

The city now had a metro and a professional baseball team, the Expos. The World's Fair, Expo 67, had come and gone, but left an indelible mark on the city with F. Buckminster Fuller's geodesic dome and the many other futuristic pavilion buildings remaining on Saint Helen's Island and neighboring Notre Dame Island. The glittering city skyline was filled with more and more glass-and-steel skyscrapers that joined those Lemay recalled from back in 1961. Montreal was also gearing up to host the 1976 Summer Olympics, creating even more construction. The Olympic Stadium, French architect Roger Taillibert's modernist centerpiece of Olympic Village, was going up in Viau Park. Crews ripped out ancient elms and displaced millions of feet of earth to make way for the dream of mayor Jean Drapeau, the driving force behind much of this change, and, perhaps, the only constant in Montreal. He had been in power since before Lemay pulled his dramatic bank heist.

While Lemay served his time, the FLQ, the paramilitary French Canadian separatist group, continued its violent bid for Quebec sovereignty. The unrest reached its zenith in 1970, during the October Crisis, when members of the FLQ kidnapped the provincial deputy premier Pierre Laporte and British trade commissioner James Cross. In response, Prime Minister Pierre Trudeau invoked the War Measures Act, which sent troops into Montreal and curtailed citizens' rights, including habeas corpus. The FLQ murdered Laporte and negotiated for the release of Cross, destroying themselves in the process as they lost popular support for their objectives.

Policing had also changed. In 1970, Montreal and the surrounding suburban communities formed the Communauté Urbaine de Montréal (CUM)—Montreal Urban Community in English—a regional government entity. It created an integrated police force five thousand strong with a centralized communication system that meant it would be harder for criminals to slip in and out between city and suburb as they once had.

The underworld had changed as well. Outlaw biker gangs were ascending, especially in the illegal narcotics business, while Montreal's Mafia, headed for decades by Vincenzo Cotroni, was in the midst of a violent power struggle. The Dubois Brothers, a gang of French Canadians whose nucleus comprised nine brothers, took over the city's downtown drug, loan-sharking, and prostitution businesses by brute force. On the other side of the city, the West End Gang, an independent association of criminals mainly of Irish descent, led by Frank "Dunie" Ryan, was growing more powerful and flagrant as they hijacked trucks and robbed banks. As a sole practitioner, Lemay would have to walk a tightrope if he hoped to return to his trade.

With his release, he avoided the press he once courted and returned to the bosom of his tight-knit family, who hadn't abandoned him during his long incarceration. He was forty-nine and once again single. Lise had divorced him during his first year in prison. In the petition from March 1970, Lise alleged that her husband no longer loved her and would no longer wish to live with her if released from prison.

Lise had had some legal troubles of her own prior to the divorce. The Montreal Police had charged her with possession of a sawed-off rifle that they'd found in her car. Maranda had represented her in the case. The wily lawyer was able to get Lise acquitted of the charge.

Lise was living in Montreal North and working under an assumed name, managing go-go dancers at a downtown Montreal club.

Lemay tried several legitimate ways of making a living, from designing kitchen cabinets to real estate to rare stamp trading to joining in a venture to build inexpensive housing using materials imported from South America. None succeeded. His name had become synonymous with his criminal escapades. He was just too infamous for the square world to embrace. What choice did he have but to return to what he knew best?

* * *

In April 1975, Lemay was busy hatching another caper when two police officers looking for a murder suspect crashed through the door of a North Montreal apartment and discovered Lemay and three others inside. The investigators didn't locate their suspect but arrested Lemay, Yves Audette, Yvon Derepentigny, and Marc Beaulne after finding what appeared to be a well-stocked arsenal of burglary equipment. The cache included walkie-talkies, an illegal police scanner, a blowtorch, high-powered binoculars, a revolver disguised as a pen, a shotgun, a flare gun, blank birth certificates and driver's licenses, police badges, press cards, and various saws, drills, and picks.

Near the apartment, police found a van equipped for surveillance, similar to one used by the infamous Red Hood Gang that Joe Bédard had busted back in 1960.

The police arrested the men and charged them with possession of burglary tools, the only charge they could come up with after consulting with Crown prosecutors. The Montreal Police believed Lemay and his new crew had been planning what appeared to be a big heist, but the cops couldn't prove it.

Lemay and the others appeared in court on May 3 represented by attorney Frank Shoofey, who worked for many underworld clients. He had recently made international headlines for helping recover the (actual) heart—an icon—of Brother André Bessette, a beloved Catholic priest who died in 1937 and was later canonized.

Lemay pleaded not guilty to the charge and the judge released him and the others after they promised they wouldn't move from their present abodes, leave town, or hang out together while the case remained open.

The press anxiously waited on the courthouse steps for Lemay, but he continued to shy away from the media. While his codefendants walked into the crowd of waiting photographers, Lemay slipped out a back door.

A month after Lemay's court appearance, during the weekend of June 7–8, 1975, burglars used a stolen key to slip into a branch of the Bank of Montreal in the suburb of Lachine. They disabled the alarm system and went to work on the vault. The burglars spent the weekend leisurely drilling through the massive door and bypassing the lock before smashing open three hundred safe-deposit boxes, removing more than one million dollars' worth of loot, cleaning up, and making their getaway.

Police and the press bandied Lemay's name about in connection with the burglary since it fit his MO. Even fourteen years later, the Bank of Nova Scotia heist remained in the city's collective memory. Lemay steadfastly denied any involvement in the newest burglary, telling a young crime reporter, Michel Auger, that he'd been at home playing the lotto that weekend and even won a thousand dollars.

"I won this money quite easily," he said, then chuckled, "I would rather be the million-dollar winner, but I'll be happy with what I got." Auger believed Lemay had become a little annoyed by the publicity that continued to surround him.

The police never solved the June 1975 Bank of Montreal break-in.

They did, however, recover nearly one million dollars in stolen bonds the following October, but made no arrests.

Lemay and the other men's case finally went to court more than two years after their arrests, on May 24, 1977, before Judge John O'Meara, who promptly dismissed the charges, citing reasonable doubt.

At the time, Lemay was living in La Petite-Patrie, a working-class neighborhood in east central Montreal, and dating yet another woman with the first name of Lise. This one was named Lise Labbé. She was twenty years younger than Lemay and ran an escort business under the guise of a dating service, according to the police.

By the late 1970s, Lemay, now in his early fifties, realized that the world was changing and so must he. Over his criminal career, Lemay had mostly been a bank burglar, but it was time to expand his repertoire. He chose the lucrative drug business, focusing on a new hallucinogen, Eticyclidine (PCE), a more potent cousin to PCP that had its heyday as a recreational drug during that decade.

Lemay began working with André-Pierre Quintal, a small-time operator a decade his junior. They set up a state-of-the-art drug lab in Rivière-des-Prairies, a neighborhood in northwest Montreal. The lab was in a building in an industrial area along the river on Fourth Avenue, which Quintal rented under an assumed name.

Lemay, as was his style, dove into the project with aplomb, doing extensive research—even getting Quintal to seek advice from a university chemistry professor—and designing some of the machinery needed to manufacture the drug himself. It took months and cost thousands of dollars to set up, but once it was operational, it would make money hand over fist.

On the evening of January 26, 1979, around 6:30 p.m., Lemay and Quintal left the lab, secured the massive padlock that required a specially modified key to unlock, and headed for their cars. Lemay was happy with their progress. They'd produced thirty grams of PCE so far and were about to start manufacturing on an industrial scale.

Suddenly the world erupted with movement, lights, and noise. Dozens of cops swarmed the street, coming from everywhere at once. Neither man had time to make a break for it. Lemay didn't even bother. He just threw up his hands and proclaimed his innocence, telling the arresting officers that this was a mistake and that he was not involved. He was carrying a garbage bag filled with lactose, which can be used in PCE production. In his pocket, he also carried two pieces of paper with chemical formulas written on them.

Lemay and Quintal had unknowingly built their clandestine drug lab near Viol Importing, a company tied to the Italian mob that the RCMP had been watching when officers noticed Lemay and Quintal bringing large amounts of chemicals and heavy equipment into a nearby warehouse. Investigators, armed with a search warrant, had already snuck into the lab through a window left open for ventilation to identify what Lemay and Quintal were making inside the space. Manufacturing was underway, but they hadn't yet started selling their product. An RCMP narcotics squad had been surveilling them for ten months when Sergeant-Major André Rhéaume decided it was time to shut down the operation and arrest the pair.

Once again it was modern policing methods that tripped up Lemay. The RCMP used electronic surveillance, including wiretapping, to record conversations between Lemay and his partner, along with taking hundreds of photographs and tailing the men as they went about getting what they needed for the lab. Law enforcement's use of wiretapping had become legal in Canada only a few years earlier, though the RCMP had been doing it illegally for two decades in the name of national security, spying on Communists, Quebec separatists, and even gay rights groups.

When *La Presse* reporter Michel Auger shot some quick questions to Lemay as he was being led away by officers, his only reply was, "It's all a big mistake." Auger noticed Lemay didn't have his signature smirk as the police cruiser drove off with him in the back seat.

The officers initially couldn't get into the warehouse. They made Quintal draw them a diagram of how the special key worked and finally got inside. It took twelve hours for the police to dismantle the laboratory and transport all the material in a truck to police headquarters.

The cops also searched Lemay's and Quintal's homes but didn't turn up much in the way of incriminating evidence. The lab provided all the evidence they would need when combined with the surveillance photos and recordings. Investigators found 38.5 grams of the finished product and enough chemicals to produce about twenty-five thousand pills, valued at $88,000 (about $350,000 today), along with distillation apparatus, chemicals, and metal barrels of various sizes.

The RCMP charged Lemay and Quintal with conspiracy and drug trafficking under the Food and Drugs Act, since PCE didn't fall under the same category as heroin or cocaine. The crimes still carried a stiff penalty of up to ten years in prison.

Four days later, during a bail hearing, the prosecutor dredged up Lemay's past, specifically his dramatic escape from the Dade County Jail in Miami in 1965, as the reason he shouldn't be given bail. Crown attorney Ronald Picard noted the defendant's notoriety, the romanticization of his crimes, and the public's sympathy toward Lemay. He asked the court not to fall into the same trap. Picard also argued that Lemay had become more dangerous since his 1961 bank burglary because he had switched to drug manufacturing. "In this case, it was not a violent climax, but here, with the manufacture of an LSD-like drug that he was making, these are hundreds of individuals of all ages who could have been in danger," Picard told the court.

Frank Shoofey, who had represented Lemay back in 1977, appeared for both defendants and argued against holding them. He said that Lemay's bank heist and jailbreak happened nearly twenty years earlier and that if it was anyone other than Lemay before the court, there wouldn't be any question about giving him bail. "There are many other defendants who, before this court, in recent years, have obtained their provisional release for far more serious crimes," Shoofey said, mentioning a recent political kidnapping case and even an accused murderer who received bail.

Judge Joseph Tarasofsky refused to give bail to either man, lumping Quintal in with Lemay. He ordered them held until trial.

Lemay asked Shoofey to look into a plea deal with the Crown. He was willing to do a year in prison for a guilty plea, which would save the prosecution the time and expense of a trial, but the Crown wanted five years and wasn't willing to budge. They were at an impasse.

In April, Lemay was still being held without bail. His codefendant, Quintal, was luckier. The court released him on a ten-thousand-dollar bond after Shoofey argued Quintal had suffered unjustly because of his association with Lemay.

A month later, Quintal's lucky streak ended.

On the evening of Tuesday, May 8, 1979, Quintal went to dinner with his friend Joe Lefebvre, who had put up his bail, at a restaurant on Cherrier Street in the Le Plateau-Mont-Royal area of Montreal. The restaurant was in the same building as attorney Frank Shoofey's office. Quintal ran into the lawyer, who no longer represented him in the case, on his way to his dinner date. He stopped to say hello.

Around 9:00 p.m., Quintal excused himself from the table and headed for the bathroom. A few minutes later, shots rang out from somewhere in the building, shattering the relaxed atmosphere of quiet conversation and cutlery scraping against plates.

They found Quintal on the fifth floor near Shoofey's law office. He had gone there to photocopy court documents. Quintal lay dead from six gunshots to the head. Next to the body, the police found a Colt .45 pistol left by the killer. A secretary in Shoofey's office witnessed the murder, but it happened so quickly she couldn't identify the shooter.

Michael Vleminckx, who had agreed to take over representing Lemay and Quintal from Shoofey before the murder due to the defendants not being able to afford their former lawyer, quickly responded to reports of Quintal's shooting, telling reporters, "We cannot link Quintal's death to Georges Lemay. He was an essential element in Lemay's defense, and I believe his death has nothing to do with Lemay's case."

The court refused to delay Lemay's trial, which began on May 22. Quintal, who was also supposed to go to trial that day, haunted the proceedings. Since he obviously couldn't be there in person, the lawyers and witnesses in the case identified him by photographs. No one told the jury what had befallen Quintal. Lemay's lawyer didn't hesitate to shift the blame of alleged drug manufacturing onto the dead defendant.

Lemay was older and heavier with thinning hair, but he still looked stylish in his dark-blue suit, a lightly patterned dress shirt, and thick striped tie. He sat with his attorney, actively involved in his defense, including jury selection.

The Crown, led by Jacques Letellier, a tough-minded rising judicial star, believed they had an airtight case. They had photographs and audio evidence, all corroborated by each of the seventy-two RCMP officers who participated in the long-term surveillance of Lemay and Quintal.

The most Vleminckx could do was get one of the RCMP officers to admit he hadn't personally seen Lemay nor Quintal go in or out of the warehouse while on surveillance duty.

Among the prosecution's witnesses was Professor Jacques Lenoir, a Concordia University chemist who had unknowingly helped Lemay perfect his product.

The year before, Quintal had approached Lenoir about carrying out some mysterious research and experiments for him. The professor believed Quintal was developing a new type of plastic, but he soon suspected things weren't aboveboard. He brought his suspicions to the RCMP, which had already begun their surveillance on the pair.

Unlike his previous trials, Lemay took the stand in his own defense, a risky move, as it meant a drawn-out cross-examination by the prosecution.

From the stand, Lemay proclaimed his innocence, telling the jury he had only been helping Quintal with the machinery and it wasn't drugs they were making but a chemical base that could be used in dry-cleaning, in stripping furniture, or as peat fertilizer. Quintal would have been much better able to explain the chemistry aspect, he claimed.

Under cross-examination by Letellier, Lemay became visibly angry when the prosecutor brought up his "past mistakes," as the defendant called the 1961 bank burglary and subsequent jailbreak. Lemay told the jury he'd spent all the money from the heist. Whether true or not, he had a court-appointed lawyer, meaning he could prove he was indigent. When the prosecutor asked him to recount the crime, he snapped at him. "Why are you asking me this question? It's been twenty years since that happened, and it has nothing to do with this case. Besides, everyone knows the story."

He denied committing any crimes while hiding out in the United

States and claimed that he never made a dramatic breakout from the Dade County Jail.

"I didn't escape, I went out the front door," he told the jury.

"With a guard?" Letellier asked.

"No, with the connivance of two, if you want to know," Lemay answered.

Letellier went over the transcripts from the hundreds of hours of wiretapped recordings with Lemay, who reinterpreted them for the jury in a way that made them seem innocuous.

"The pity is that the police chose only what could help their case in these conversations," Lemay said. "And while they were watching me closely enough to know exactly what time I was going to the toilet at night, there are many other incidents which relate to the words that have been typed, but obviously, I can't remember them, because they only produced a small part of this wiretapping."

Letellier mentioned recorded calls between Lemay and one of his girlfriends, to which Lemay remarked that he didn't want her parents to know she was seeing him. He faced the jury and asked them, "What would you guys have thought if your daughter had told you like that, that she was dating Georges Lemay?"

Lemay made it through his testimony with his usual charm and wit, but the prosecution's evidence against him was very strong.

Vleminckx, in his closing argument, maintained that the Crown had provided no proof that his client was aware of what Quintal was producing in the lab he helped set up.

It took two days for the jury of five men and seven women to decide on the verdict. This was the first time Lemay was before women jurors, who were only allowed to begin serving on juries in Quebec in 1971. The jurors discussed the case for five hours, then spent the night in a nearby hotel—watched over by guards, their room telephones disconnected and televisions removed—before rendering the verdict the next day.

Lemay's explanation wasn't convincing enough. The jury found him guilty on the two main charges, conspiracy and drug distribution, but not guilty on a lesser charge of drug possession. Lemay's neutral expression didn't change when he heard the verdict.

On July 13, the judge sentenced him to eight years in prison. He was fifty-four. As at his earlier trial, when he learned of his fate, he remained calm. "He looks as dignified as he did when he was a gentleman burglar," one reporter noted.

* * *

For nearly four years, the police investigation into Quintal's murder went nowhere. Then a hitman came forward, claiming to know who killed Quintal, who ordered it done, and why.

By 1983, Donald Lavoie was a star. He helped peel back the steel veil of the notoriously tight-lipped Montreal underworld, aiding the police with not only the twenty-seven murders he copped to—fifteen in which he'd pulled the trigger himself—but seventy-six others he said he knew about. He was a media darling, having appeared on the hugely popular CBC show *The Fifth Estate* in April 1983 after helping put away several gangsters, including Claude Dubois and his brother, Adrien.

He had turned police informer out of necessity. For more than ten years he worked for the Dubois gang as their number one enforcer, but after refusing two hits from his boss, Claude Dubois, feeling they were unnecessary, he nearly became a victim himself.

In November 1980, at the wedding of an underworld friend at a Montreal hotel, Lavoie overheard Claude and another gang member discussing his execution when they thought he was dead drunk. He wasn't and he slipped out of the room, hurled himself three floors down a laundry chute, landed heavily on the concrete of the building's underground garage, and hid out for two hours before making his escape from the gang into the arms of the police. The former hitman provided so much information to the police, its anti-gang squad dedicated nine officers to work on cases only involving Lavoie. They had plenty of work, several years' worth.

By 1983, the former choirboy, who, like Lemay, had once dreamed of becoming a Catholic priest, was living in a roomy jail cell with a phone and television in a special wing of the Montreal Urban Community Police

Service headquarters in Montreal. Lavoie spent his time studying philosophy. He had a particular fondness for Descartes.

In early November 1983, Lemay was fifty-eight years old and over the hump of his sentence, already receiving day passes as his conditional release day drew nearer. Then the police charged him and three other men—Frank Laennens and brothers Alain and Serge Charron—with Quintal's murder. Like Lemay, Alain Charron and Laennens were already incarcerated on unrelated charges. Laennens was serving a life sentence for murder and Alain Charron was awaiting trial on two other killings.

On November 6, 1984, their trial began in Montreal Superior Court before Judge Jean-Guy Boilard, a tough jurist known for dressing down lawyers who appeared before him.

Vleminckx once again represented Lemay while Lemay's former attorney, Léo-Réne Maranda, appeared for Alain Charron. The two other defendants had equally tough lawyers. The four high-powered defense attorneys faced off against Crown Prosecutor François Doyon. The motley-looking crew of defendants—Alain Charron, thirty-eight, short and sporting a shaggy beard; thirty-five-year-old Laennens with a walrus mustache; Lemay wearing glasses and a fashionable blue suit; and Serge Charron, thirty-five and already getting pudgy—sat behind this phalanx of defenders during the trial. Doyon told the jury of five women and seven men that Lemay had ordered the killing of Quintal because he believed his partner would turn state's evidence against him. The other defendants helped pull it off, the prosecutor alleged.

"All four obviously did not physically participate in the assassination," the prosecutor said. "But each of these men had a specific role to play in the death of Pierre Quintal."

Doyon said Lemay had been in Parthenais Detention Center awaiting trial on drug charges at the same time as Alain Charron, who contacted his brother, Serge, on the outside. Serge then contracted Laennens for the hit. Lemay had spoken by phone nearly every day with Quintal at Shoofey's office, so he knew when to send the killer, Doyon said.

The Crown's star witness was Lavoie. Lavoie wasn't directly involved in the Quintal murder, but he was willing to testify to what he knew of the crime. Lemay must have found it strange that the name of the man trying to put him away sounded eerily similar to that of his former nemesis, Jacques Lajoie.

As the Crown had done with Lajoie, the court took special precautions to guarantee Lavoie's safety. The hitman-turned-informant had a huge price on his head. Anyone coming into court that day, besides having to go through a metal detector, was also frisked. When it was time for the star witness to testify, a signal was given and Lavoie, who was in his early forties, short and lithe, swaggered in and took the stand. He wore a corduroy jacket paired with a tie. He had sharp, but not unhandsome features, and dark, dark eyes.

He told the jury he was friends with Alain Charron, with whom he'd worked in the Dubois gang, and had become acquainted with Lemay while the three were at Parthenais. Lavoie testified that Lemay told him of the plan to take out Quintal; that he saw Alain Charron flash a written message ordering the killing to his brother, Serge, through a window of the visiting room; and that he'd seen Laennens, whom he also knew, handle a Colt .45 similar to the pistol used in the murder.

Under cross-examination, he told the jury he'd testified in order to "clean up my life. I had decided to speak to the police, but not to come and testify. I'm just forced to do it like any other citizen."

The four defense attorneys each took turns working on Lavoie, relishing in having him reveal the shocking details of the long list of murders he'd admitted pulling off. The most gruesome of these was the brutal stabbing of Linda Majore, the girlfriend of another of his victims. Before murdering Majore, Lavoie shot the boyfriend to death in front of her. The attack on Majore was so frenzied that the blade of the knife Lavoie used had broken into three pieces.

The attorneys also focused on the facts that the police had provided the witness with special favors, that he hadn't been charged with any of the murders he'd confessed to committing, and that he was yet to serve a day of the eight-year sentence for the kidnapping and extortion for which he'd originally been convicted.

The trial lasted six weeks and also saw testimony from Claude Jodoin, a disgraced journalist who, like Lavoie, worked for the Dubois gang before turning police informant. He was also facing an underworld death sentence. Paul Pomerleau, a small-time extortionist also tied to the Dubois gang, and André Grisé, a drug trafficker and repeat offender, rounded out the main witnesses.

Jodoin testified that he'd become friends with Serge Charron, who confessed his role as go-between in setting up the murder. Serge told the ex-reporter he had been in the building when Laennens shot Quintal, he testified.

Pomerleau, a soft-spoken extortionist who always gave precise answers, told the jury he'd been in the Parthenais Detention Center with Lemay, who he said confided in him about Quintal's murder. Lemay had been angry that the hitman killed Quintal so close to his lawyer's office, instead of outside the building as planned, Pomerleau alleged.

The defense spent a lot of time questioning Pomerleau on the sweet deal the Montreal authorities gave him. They paid the informant eighteen thousand dollars a year while he attended classes and lived rent free.

Grisé, a forty-year-old who'd been in and out of prison for years, told the jury of learning about Quintal's murder from Lemay as they played bridge in the jail where they both awaited trial. Grisé also alleged that he helped block off a hallway so Lemay and Alain Charron could discuss the murder plot in private.

Other prosecution witnesses included a jail guard who alleged Lemay seemed pleased when he heard of Quintal's murder, and the secretary who witnessed the shooting. She recalled seeing "a big hand holding a big gun" appear as Quintal was about to press the elevator button. Loud gunshots followed, and Quintal stumbled back and crumpled at her feet. She looked down the hall but only saw the back of a fleeing man who weighed between 180 and 200 pounds, perhaps five foot eleven, "and having . . . big hands."

None of the defendants testified nor called defense witnesses during the trial. Their attorneys relied on the tactic of trying to destroy the credibility of the prosecution's four main criminal underworld witnesses. It would come down to whether the jury believed a hitman, an ex-journalist with gangland ties, an extortionist, and a recidivist drug trafficker.

Crown Attorney Doyon addressed this issue during his final summation on Thursday, December 6, 1984. He urged the jurors not to forget it was the four defendants on trial and not the four police informants who had testified against Lemay and the others.

The prosecutor admitted one of the witnesses had committed more than a dozen murders, another kidnapped women and children, and a third trafficked drugs, but it didn't mean they weren't telling the truth about what they knew concerning Quintal's murder.

After three full days of deliberations, at a little after 4:00 p.m. on Saturday, December 14, 1984, the jury foreperson stood up and in a clear, loud voice, without perceptible hesitation, repeated for each of the defendants the same sentence: "Not guilty."

For Lemay, who was nearly sixty, a guilty verdict was akin to a death sentence, since he would have spent his remaining years moldering behind bars. He smiled slightly when he heard the jury's decision. For a man who smiled easily, even in the harshest of circumstances, he had been unusually solemn throughout the long trial. Now, his trademark smile returned.

Three days later Lemay was released on parole. He was free and intended to stay that way. He retired and returned to philately—stamp collecting and sales—a pursuit he had become interested in around the time of his drug arrest.

The End of the Line

ON SEPTEMBER 27, 1995, HAROLD ROSEN AND JOHN PIERCE shared the stage at the National Academy of Engineering in Washington, D.C., to receive the Charles Stark Draper Prize, one of the world's most prestigious engineering awards. The honor included a four-hundred-thousand-dollar prize. Hailed by Arthur C. Clarke as the fathers of the communication satellite, the two men had come a long way from an encounter in the early 1960s where they allegedly nearly came to blows over their differing stances on GEO satellites. "How wrong I was," Pierce told a reporter from *The New York Times* during a 1973 interview. "Dr. Rosen turned out to be a very good engineer."

The prize was the latest in an impressive line of accolades for Rosen, who by this time had already received nearly a dozen awards for his work, including the National Medal of Technology and Innovation and the L. M. Ericsson International Prize for Communications, presented by Carl XVI Gustaf, the king of Sweden. No doubt, the event provided an aging Rosen an opportunity to reflect on a remarkable life and career. Following the passing of his first wife, Rosetta, in 1969, Rosen married a fellow Hughes engineer, Deborah Castleman, in 1984. Early Bird proved to be a springboard for Rosen, who continued at Hughes until his retirement in 1993, having attained the level of vice president of engineering for the space and communications group. Over the course of his nearly forty-year tenure at the company, Rosen developed more than 150 satellites, dreamed up DirecTV—the direct satellite broadcast service, an idea he was promoting as far back as 1965—and helped build Hughes into the largest communication satellite business in the world.

Retirement didn't suit Rosen, however. After leaving Hughes, he turned his attention to automobiles, founding Rosen Motors with his brother Benjamin and Castleman, who served as vice president. The start-up was developing a hybrid-electric power train for automobiles before it shuttered in 1997. But Rosen wasn't finished with aerospace. Along with Castleman and J. B. Straubel, he started another company, Volacom, to develop his idea of providing internet service via unmanned aircraft. While his vision never came to fruition, Rosen and Straubel did patent a long-endurance hybrid propulsion system that they licensed to Boeing. When Boeing acquired Hughes's Space and Communications Group, Rosen came onboard as a consultant.

Rosen, perhaps inadvertently, also helped facilitate the creation of Tesla Motors. In the fall of 2003, he and Straubel met Elon Musk for lunch at a seafood restaurant in Los Angeles to try to get Musk interested in a Volacom project. Instead, the conversation turned to electric cars, and helped propel the idea for the groundbreaking electric vehicle company. While Rosen did not participate in Tesla, Straubel became part of the founding team as chief technical officer.

Rosen continued to make waves and headlines to the end, particularly regarding his views on climate change, namely that it wasn't as severe as others believed and that climate engineering or a space-based solution, not cutting greenhouse gas emissions, could solve the problem. He died on January 30, 2017, at his home in Santa Monica. He was ninety and had more than eighty patents to his name, the last awarded just days before he passed away. Pierce died in 2002, at ninety-two, in Sunnyvale, California, 350 miles north of Rosen's home.

* * *

Tom Hudspeth died on May 27, 2008. Until his death at age eighty-nine, he continued to work two days a week at Hughes Space and Communications. In addition to satellites, he worked on projects including an electronic low-noise amplifier for MRI machines, a "solder jockey" until the end.

* * *

On April 5, 1976, a disheveled seventy-year-old Howard Hughes, badly suffering from malnutrition and barely recognizable, died on a plane en route from Mexico to Texas. It was perhaps a fitting end for a man known for both his eccentricities and his contributions to the aerospace industry. The cause of death was later determined to be kidney failure, perhaps due in part to complications stemming from injuries he suffered in a near-fatal plane crash years earlier. He left no will. It would take decades to unravel his finances and business holdings, including the much-debated question of who controlled the Howard Hughes Medical Institute and its subsidiary Hughes Aircraft. After a court-ordered shake-up at the medical institute, Hughes Aircraft was sold to General Motors in 1985 for $5.2 billion. Growing from a de facto tax shelter in its early days, the institute would become the second largest medical research foundation in the world.

The fight between NASA and Hughes Aircraft over the patent for the Syncom control system that Don Williams discussed with Rosen the day Williams took his own life would drag on for more than thirty years. Hughes eventually won the case in 1994.

* * *

Georges Lemay died in 2006, just before his eighty-second birthday, after a long decline. He spent his last few years living quietly at his Montreal South Shore home, avidly collecting and selling rare stamps. He outlived both George B. McClellan and Joe Bédard. At Lemay's request, news of his death wasn't reported for nearly two years until his daughter, Josée, announced it in September 2008 on a Canadian radio program. Lise Lemieux Lemay died in 2005.

Bédard retired as head of security for the Bank of Montreal in 1972 and died peacefully in bed at age ninety-two on December 29, 1992.

McClellan, after retiring from the RCMP, became Canada's first ombudsman, serving the province of Alberta investigating citizens' complaints against the government. He died on July 19, 1982, in Edmonton, Alberta.

Leo Plouffe, who was thrice decorated for bravery by the Montreal Police and had defused more bombs than any other Canadian police officer, retired in 1978 as deputy director of criminal investigations. Subsequently, Plouffe left Canada for the Gulf Coast city of Dunedin, Florida, approximately 260 miles from the Fort Lauderdale marina where Lemay hid out following the infamous heist. Plouffe died in 1996. He was seventy-four.

The former Bank of Nova Scotia branch that Lemay and his gang looted is now an A&W restaurant.

* * *

The more than 4,500 active satellites circling the globe and impacting our daily lives in a variety of ways all rely on many of the design elements Rosen and his team came up with more than sixty years ago. Geostationary satellites like the Hughes-built Westar 1, launched in 1974, and RCA's Satcom 1, put into space in 1975, transformed television by beaming programming down to ground stations that were then sent via cable to customers across the United States. It's thanks to them that we have not just DirecTV but also Home Box Office (HBO) and other similar cable television services. Today's satellites also track the weather, help us get from point A to point B via the Global Positioning System (GPS), and are becoming more popular as an internet provider. They help scientists monitor environmental changes here on Earth and better understand the origins of our universe through space-based telescopes like the James Webb Space Telescope that's helping us peer back in time to study the first stars and galaxies to emerge following the Big Bang. They provide farmers with tools to better manage their crops, help in search and rescue operations, and allow governments to gather intelligence on foreign adversaries.

After traditional methods failed, Law enforcement's use of Early Bird to blanket the planet with Lemay's likeness helped kick off a revolution in policing. Using technology to disseminate information to the public about fugitives and to track escapees has become an everyday occurrence. Amber Alerts can simultaneously reach millions of people with up-to-the-second information on child abductions, and real-time crime centers can access CCTV cameras that blanket most major cities to track wanted individuals. The world we now live in is a boon for law enforcement but raises all kinds of issues concerning our personal privacy and civil rights that will continue to be litigated well into the future. The world is getting smaller and smaller. Lemay wouldn't have stood a chance against today's technology-laden law enforcement, but he would have enjoyed the challenge.

While the satellites Rosen helped dream up are no longer functioning, they still orbit the Earth, now quiet and lifeless, an epitaph for the ground-breaking technology that continues to play an important role in our day-to-day lives. They remain a testament to the steadfast determination and unbending will of engineers like Rosen; bureaucrats such as John Rubel, who had the foresight to see past the easy answers and throw their full support into geosynchronous satellite systems; and television producers like Av Weston, who saw Early Bird's potential to not just entertain viewers but to show what humanity was capable of, given the opportunity.

Early Bird represented the best aspects of the 1960s, a decade that strove for justice and opportunity and attempted to throw off the shackles of a past steeped in the opposite of those virtues. In our current times, when it sometimes feels as if those same forces have returned a hundredfold to drag the world back into darkness, look up into the sky at dusk some summer evening. Perhaps you'll see the faint flicker of a satellite as it passes and marvel at the idea that given the right set of circumstances, humanity can achieve the seemingly impossible.

Acknowledgments

THIS BOOK WOULDN'T HAVE BEEN POSSIBLE WITHOUT THE love, support, and gentle nudging of my wife, Kara Thurmond.

My agent, Jeff Ourvan of the Jennifer Lyons Literary Agency, has been a wonderful advocate, teacher, and guide.

Dan López and Dan Smetanka, my editors at Counterpoint Press, were instrumental in helping to create a coherent narrative out of a hydra-like story. Their suggestions were always on point.

A big thanks also to Counterpoint's Laura Berry, the production editor; Elana Rosenthal, my sharp copy editor; and the rest of the team that helped make this dream a reality.

My early readers, including Kara Thurmond, Niva Dorell, Annick de Bellefeuille, and Morris Ardoin, provided insight and guidance during the beginning stages of the writing process.

Michel Auger, an author and former crime reporter who passed away in October 2020, gave me a lens into the world of the Montreal underbelly of the 1960s that helped provide vivid color to cold facts. He was a great guy and a tough-minded journalist who is sorely missed.

Deborah Castleman gave me valuable insight into Harold Rosen, which helped give a fuller picture of this amazing man. I can't thank her enough for all she provided me for this book.

I was helped along in my research by a long list of folks, including Minni Ang; Eric Beaudin of the Bibliothèque et Archives nationales du Québec; Benoit Robitaille of the Archives for the Service de police de la Ville de Montreal; Gilles Lafontaine of the Service de référence for the Archives de la Ville de Montréal; my aunt Georgie Champion; and Sarah H. Jenkins, archivist for NASA's History Program Office.

Thanks also to Beth Schneck for the amazing author photo.

A big thanks to my extended family for always being supportive of my endeavors.

Finally, I have to thank my dog, Bingo, who sat next to me during the entire process of writing this book. He was good boy. RIP.

A Note on Sources

MOST OF THE PEOPLE I WROTE ABOUT IN THIS BOOK DIED before I started this project, so I had to rely on secondary sources for *Satellite Boy*. These included declassified government reports, first-person interviews from the time, court records, and various contemporary media reports, among other sources. For more information see the bibliography on page 283.

For Lemay's story I relied on a 1,200-page Royal Canadian Mounted Police file; thousands of pages of court records related to Lemay's trial; extant interviews; various contemporary newspaper reports (he was a favorite of the Quebec press); several genealogical sites, including Ancestry. com and GenealogieQuebec.com; and conversations with Michel Auger recorded before his death in October 2020. Auger was a Montreal-based crime reporter and author who knew Lemay.

For the story on Harold Rosen and Early Bird, I relied on conversations with Rosen's widow, Deborah Castleman, who was also a Hughes Satellite Systems engineer, as well as unpublished recordings of conversations between Castleman and Rosen, unpublished recollections from John Rubel, reports from NASA and other U.S. government agencies, newspaper accounts, and various other sources. Two of special note are the wonderfully detailed *Something New Under the Sun: Satellites and the Beginning of the Space Age* by Helen Gavaghan and the *Our Space Heritage 1960–2000* website dedicated to the aerospace history of Hughes Aircraft. The site, overseen by Jack Fisher, before his death in November 2020, and Steven Dorfman, contains a wealth of information on the inner workings of Hughes Aircraft through the written recollections of former employees, reprints of stories from the company's internal publication *Hughes News*, and other ephemera.

Bibliography

"1965- Hurricane Betsy." Hurricanes: Science and Society. HurricaneScience .org. www.hurricanescience.org/history/storms/1960s/betsy/.

Abuelsamid, Sam. "AutoblogGreen Q&A: Tesla Motors Chairman Elon Musk Pt. 1 - In the Beginning." *Autoblog*, June 23, 2008. www.autoblog.com/2008 /06/23/autobloggreen-qanda-tesla-motors-chairman-elon-musk-pt-1-in-th/.

Adams, Val. "35 Features Due on Early Bird TV." *New York Times*, April 21, 1965. timesmachine.nytimes.com/timesmachine/1965/04/21/106991038. html?pageNumber=91.

———. "2 Continents See Global TV Today." *New York Times*, May 2, 1965. timesmachine.nytimes.com/timesmachine/1965/05/02/97196197 .html?pageNumber=35.

The Age (Melbourne, Australia). "Inquiry Told Canadian PM Knew." April 30, 1966. www.newspapers.com/newspage/122121638/.

Alonso, José F., and Armando M. Lago. "A First Approximation Model of Money, Prices and Exchange Rates in Revolutionary Cuba." *The Association for the Study of the Cuban Economy* 5 (1995). www.ascecuba.org/c/wp -content/uploads/2014/09/v05-FILE11.pdf.

American Astronautical Society. *Space Exploration and Humanity: A Historical Encyclopedia*, vol. 1. Edited by Stephen B. Johnson. Santa Barbara: ABC-CLIO, 2010, 416.

Arkell, Debby. "A Proud Founding Father." *Boeing Frontiers*, April 2008. www .boeing.com/news/frontiers/archive/2008/april/cover.pdf.

Associated Press. "Cuban Projects." *Honolulu Star*, July 25, 1961. www.news papers.com/newspage/269803409/.

———. "Pick Builder of Space Station." *Kansas City Times*, August 12, 1961. www.newspapers.com/newspage/658870227/.

———. "Bank Theft Hunt Turns to Florida." *Fort Lauderdale News*, January 9, 1962. www.newspapers.com/newspage/271681491/.

———. "Suspect Freed in Error." *Oneonta Star* (Oneonta, New York), May 31, 1962. www.newspapers.com/image/47259925/.

———. "Kennedy Hails Space Bill as World Benefit." *Tallahassee*

Democrat (Tallahassee, Florida). August 31, 1962. www.newspapers.com
/newspage/244159592/.

——. "President Kennedy Signs New Satellite Measure." *Times Argus* (Barre, Vermont), August 31, 1962. www.newspapers.com/newspage/660049264/.

——. "Lost Syncom Satellite Found." *Rapid City Journal* (Rapid City, South Dakota), March 3, 1963. www.newspapers.com/newspage/350886909/.

——. "Bomb Found on Bridge Over Seaway." *Palladium-Item* (Richmond, Indiana), May 19, 1964. www.newspapers.com/newspage/246926202/.

——. "News, Photos Bounce Off Syncom 2." *Times* (Munster, Indiana), August 5, 1964. www.newspapers.com/newspage/308148049/.

——. "Early Bird Returns Excellent Pictures." *Journal and Courier* (Lafayette, Indiana), April 8, 1965. www.newspapers.com/newspage/261925324/.

——. "TV Satellite Achieves Near Perfect Orbit." *Chicago Tribune*, April 10, 1965. www.newspapers.com/newspage/376345531/.

——. "Pope Speaks to Americans Directly for 1st Time on Early Bird Telecast." *Sacramento Bee*, May 3, 1965. www.newspapers.comnewspage/618587586/.

——. "Canadian Is Arrested in Florida Through Photo Sent by Satellite." *New York Times*. May 7, 1965. timesmachine.nytimes.com/timesmachine /1965/05/07/issue.html.

——. "Police Technique of Satellite TV Brings About Canadian's Arrest." *El Dorado Times* (El Dorado, Arkansas), May 7, 1965. www.newspapers .com/newspage/31452518/.

——. "Two Men Held as Police Press Hunt for Lemay." *Gazette* (Montreal, Canada), September 23, 1965. www.newspapers.com/image/421030189/.

——. "Probe Finds Collusion in Lemay Break." *Brandon Sun* (Brandon, Canada), October 15, 1965. www.newspapers.com/image/68575853/.

——. "Jaycees Honor Crippled Author, Two Astronauts." *Los Angeles Times*, January 10, 1966. www.newspapers.com/newspage/382391591/.

——. "Top Space Scientist A Suicide." *Miami News*, February 22, 1966. www.newspapers.com/newspage/302079093/.

——. "FBI Nabs Georges Lemay in Vegas." *Brandon Sun* (Brandon, Canada), August 19, 1966. www.newspapers.com/image/67089255/.

——. "Lemay Flown to Montreal." *Fort Lauderdale News*, October 6, 1966. www.newspapers.com/newspage/272051129/.

——. "Miami Jail Guard Accused of Helping Georges Lemay." *Star-Phoenix* (Saskatoon, Canada), October 18, 1966. www.newspapers.com /newspage/508679231/.

————. "Ex-Jail Guard Acquitted." *Ottawa Journal*, October 19, 1966. www .newspapers.com/newspage/42604345/.

————. "Theft Of Gem Collection from Bank Described." *Miami Herald*, November 4, 1967. www.newspapers.com/image/621599734/.

————. "Harry Claiborne, 86, Is Dead; Was Removed as U.S. Judge." *New York Times*, January 22, 2004. www.nytimes.com/2004/01/22/us/harry -claiborne-86-is-dead-was-removed-as-us-judge.html.

Astronautics and Aeronautics, 1965: Chronology on Science, Technology, and Policy. Washington, D.C.: National Aeronautics and Space Administration, 1966, 101, 122, 128, 136, 147,173, 313 319. history.nasa.gov/AA chronologies/1965.pdf.

L'Avenir du Nord (Saint Jérôme, Canada). "Prélude d'une série de comparutions à St-Jérôme de membres éminents de la bande de Georges Lemay." May 9, 1962. numerique.banq.qc.ca/patrimoine/details/52327/2512002.

————. "Chronique Judiciaire." May 23, 1962. numerique.banq.qc.ca /patrimoine/details/52327/2512004.

Auger, Michel. "Georges Lemay arrête." *La Presse* (Montreal, Canada), January 27, 1979. numerique.banq.qc.ca/patrimoine/details/52327/2409484.

Baker, Ryan. "Our World 1967 Full Broadcast (First Worldwide Television Broadcast) (Super Rare) (BBC1 Version)." 1:34:04. January 2, 2020. youtu .be/s3LmQFt4pQc.

Baltimore Sun. "Comsat Asks Design Bids on Satellite." December 30, 1965. www.newspapers.com/image/377650094/.

Bantley, Bill. "Lemay House Set Afire as Decoy?" *Gazette* (Montreal, Canada), March 20, 1962. www.newspapers.com/image/421008909/.

Barbour, John. "Those Satellites." *Logansport Pharos*. December 5, 1990. www .newspapers.com/image/31635460/.

Bedard, Joseph and Ken Johnstone. "How I Captured the Red Hood Gang." *Maclean's* (Toronto, Canada), August 22, 1960. archive.macleans.ca /article/1960/8/22/how-i-captured-the-red-hood-gang.

Benedict, Howard. "'Early Bird' Launch Set for April 6." *Daily Press* (Newpoert News, Virginia), March 29, 1965. www.newspapers.com /image/232713783/.

Bloomfield, Larry. "Hughes, Me and the 'Birds.'" Tech-notes.tv. Accessed on March 23, 2019. www.tech-notes.tv/History&Trivia/Sattelite%20 Communications/satellite_communications.htm.

Bourdon, Guy. "Une éclipse de huit ans pour Georges Lemay." *Le*

Devoir (Montreal, Canada), July 14, 1979. numerique.banq.qc.ca/patrimoine /details/52327/2776340.

Brimmel, George. "Deputy Commissioner Rocks Dorion Inquiry." *Calgary Herald*, February 27, 1965. www.newspapers.com/image/481221335/.

———. "Who Directed RCMP in Dorion Inquiry?" *Ottawa Citizen*, February 25, 1965. www.newspapers.com/image/459215822/.

Briskman, Robert D. "Memories of Discussions In 'The Garret.'" *Communications Satellite Corporation Magazine*, 1983. www.iothistory.org/COMSAT %20Magazine/COMSAT%20Magazine,%2012,.PDF.

Broadcasting: The Businessweekly of Television and Radio. "Big Plans Made for Early Bird's TV debut." April 26, 1965, 62. worldradiohistory.com /Archive-BC/BC-1965/1965-04-26-BC.pdf.

———. "Early Bird Is Off and Winging." May 10, 1965, 68–69. worldradio history.com/Archive-BC/BC-1965/1965-05-10-BC.pdf.

———. "NET to Carry Ball for Global Show." February 13, 1967, 72–73. worldradiohistory.com/Archive-BC/BC-1967/1967-02-13-BC.pdf.

Bruemmer, René. "Toy Drive Brought Fidel Castro to Montreal in 1959." *Gazette* (Montreal, Canada), November 27, 2016. montrealgazette.com/news /local-news/toy-drive-brought-fidel-castro-to-montreal-in-1959.

Brun, Claude. "André Lemieux se rendrait bientôt." *La Presse* (Montréal, Canada), June 5, 1962. numerique.banq.qc.ca/patrimoine/details/52327/2757194.

Buchanon, Jim. "Lemay Probe Stood Up by Cellmates." *Miami Herald*, October 5, 1965. www.newspapers.com/image/620727041/.

———. "Charges on Lemay Dropped." *Miami Herald*, October 4, 1966. www .newspapers.com/image/621409745/.

Burke, Tim. "Sgt. Plouffe and the FLQ: A Long, Hot Spring for a Man Who Dismantles Bombs." *Maclean's* (Toronto, Canada), July 6, 1963. archive .macleans.ca/article/1963/7/6/macleans-reports.

Butts, Edward. *Wrong Side of the Law: True Stories of Crime.* Ontario: Dundurn, 2013, 173–177, 182–185, 195.

Canadian House of Commons Debates, 26th Parliament, 3rd Session, vol. 1., 1027; 1099. Ottawa: Library of Parliament, 1965. parl.canadiana.ca/view/oop .debates_HOC2603_01/1029.

Canadian House of Commons Debates, 26th Parliament, 3rd Session, vol. 2., 1888. Ottawa: Library of Parliament, 1965. parl.canadiana.ca/view/oop .debates_HOC2603_02/804.

Canadian Press. "Crime Laboratory Head Is Montreal's Sherlock Holmes." *Star-Phoenix* (Saskatoon, Canada), May 16, 1957. www.newspapers.com /image/509896371/.

———. "'Missing Petrov Slain, Body Hidden, Says Detective as 3 Forces Search." *Ottawa Citizen*, July 16, 1957. www.newspapers.com/image/456886087/.

———. "'Unafraid' Lemay Fined, Released." *Gazette* (Montreal. Canada), July 19, 1957. www.newspapers.com/image/421001367/.

———. "Police Raid Homes." *Edmonton Journal* (Edmonton, Canada), January 5, 1962. www.newspapers.com/image/470285865/.

———. "Police Raid Private Residences." *Windsor Star* (Windsor, Canada), January 6, 1962. www.newspapers.com/image/506433648/.

———. "Police Seek Playboy." *Windsor Star* (Windsor, Canada), January 17, 1962. www.newspapers.com/image/506436197/.

———. "Shillings Identified as Loot." *Windsor Star* (Windsor, Canada), January 18, 1962. www.newspapers.com/image/506436590/.

———. "Underworld Nemesis Just Changed Offices." *Brandon Sun* (Brandon, Canada), July 11, 1962. www.newspapers.com/image/66572195/.

———. "RCMP Manhunt in Central B.C. Centred on Georges Lemay." *Nanaimo Daily News*, August 14, 1964. www.newspapers.com/image/324705078/.

———. "7 Suspended as Manhunt for Rivard Grows." *Times Colonist* (Victoria, Canada), March 3, 1965. www.newspapers.com/image/506518499/.

———. "Dorion Inquiry Stalled by Shouting Match." *Gazette* (Montreal, Canada), March 5, 1965. www.newspapers.com/image/423611082/.

———. "Lemay Movements in B.C. Traced." *Nanaimo Daily News*, May 12, 1965. www.newspapers.com/image/324708245/.

———. "'Sinister Forces' Attack Mounties." *Vancouver Sun*, May 29, 1965. www.newspapers.com/image/492407622/.

———. "Politicians, Aides, Lawyer, Criminals Star in Dorion Cast." *Gazette* (Montreal, Canada), June 30, 1965. www.newspapers.com/image/421202497/.

———. "Prison Escape Brings Call for Troops to Aid in Hunt." *Star-Phoenix* (Saskatoon, Canada), July 10, 1965. www.newspapers.com/image/508606791/.

———. "'Bebe' Rivard." *Ottawa Journal*, June 4, 1966. www.newspapers.com /image/42973416/.

———. "Lemay Goes into Hole During Burglary Trial." *Calgary Herald*, December 6, 1967. www.newspapers.com/image/481242582/.

———. "Electrical Inspector Tells Lemay Court of Detonating Device."

Windsor Star (Windsor, Canada), December 14, 1967. www.newspapers
.com/image/501821613/.

———. "Lemay Pal Tells Jewel Dumping." *Windsor Star* (Windsor, Canada),
November 9, 1967. www.newspapers.com/image/502167439/.

———. "Told to Dump Jewelry into Ocean, Says Witness." *Ottawa Journal*, November 9, 1967 www.newspapers.com/image/44405938/.

———. "Lemay Robbery Trial Now in Third Week." *Nanaimo Daily News*, November 15, 1967. www.newspapers.com/image/324872730/.

———. "Just Answered an Ad –McClellan." *Ottawa Citizen*, May 10, 1967.
www.newspapers.com/image/459237131/.

———. "Lemay to Face Judge." *Ottawa Citizen*, August 23, 1967. www.news
papers.com/image/457233634/.

———. "Lemay Chalet Quiet Place, Says Next-Door Neighbor." *Calgary Herald*, January 11, 1968. www.newspapers.com/image/481210010/.

———. "Lemay Prosecution Ends: Defense Prepares Motion." *Windsor Star* (Windsor, Canada), January 16, 1968. www.newspapers.com/
image/502177250/.

———. "Press Charge Dismissed." *Leader-Post* (Regina, Canada), March 27,
1968. www.newspapers.com/image/494605054/.

———. "Lemay Appeal Charges Judge Biased." *Ottawa Journal*, February 1,
1969. www.newspapers.com/image/44458721/.

———. "Acquittés du meurtre de Pierre Quintal. *La Tribune* (Montreal, Canada), December 15, 1984. numerique.banq.qc.ca/patrimoine/details/52327
/3697586.

———. "Decorated Hero, '60s Bomb Expert Dies in Florida." *Edmonton Journal*, October 9, 1996. www.newspapers.com/image/473096951/.

———. "Police Bomb Expert Foiled FLQ." *Vancouver Sun*, October 10, 1996.
www.newspapers.com/image/496267176/.

Champeau, Lucien. "La police perce peu à peu le mystère de l'île Lemay." *La
Presse* (Montreal, Canada), May 26, 1962. numerique.banq.qc.ca/patri
moine/details/52327/2757177.

Chandler, David L. "Two Get Draper Prize." *Boston Globe*, October 2, 1995.
www.newspapers.com/image/441106399/.

Charbonneau, Jean-Pierre. "Rivard Affair: Scandal Rocks House of Commons,
as Douglas Claims Bribery Attempt." *Star-Phoenix* (Saskatoon, Canada),
August 27, 1976. www.newspapers.com/image/509500988/.

Charyk, Joseph V. "Comsat History Project Interview with Joseph V. Charyk,

Vol. 1." By Nina Gilden Seavey. Comsat Legacy Project. April 1, 1986. www.comsatlegacy.com/COMSATOralHistory/ComsatHistory-Joseph_ V_Charyk_Vol_1.pdf.

Chicago Tribune. "Early Bird in Orbit." May 2, 1965. www.newspapers.com /image/376508730/.

CIA. "Intelligence Memorandum: Soviet Comsat Program: Status and Prospects." June 1968. fas.org/irp/cia/product/sovcom68.pdf.

"Claims Resolution Tribunal." Holocaust Victim Assets Litagation, January 23, 2003. www.crt-ii.org/_awards/_apdfs/Stein_Otto.pdf.

Clarke, Arthur C. "The Space-Station: Its Radio Applications" and "Extra-Terrestrial Relays: Can Rocket Stations Give World-Wide Radio Coverage?" In Using Space. Vol. 3 of Exploring the Unknown: Selected Documents in the History of the U.S. Civil Space Program, edited by James M. Logsdon. NASA SP-4407 (1995): 11–21.

Collister, Eddie. "Police Merger Takes Time: Saulnier." Gazette (Montreal, Canada), December 24, 1971. www.newspapers.com/image/421146438/.

"The Communications Satellite Act of 1962." Harvard Law Review 76, no. 2 (December 1962): 388–400.

"Communications Satellite Legislation: Hearings Before the Committee on Commerce, United States Senate, Eighty-seventh Congress, Second Session, on S. 2814 . . . and S. 2814, Amendment . . ." Washington, D.C.: U.S. Government Printing Office, 1962.

COMSAT. "Comsat Building Application for National Register of Historic Places." COMSAT-History.com. January 31, 2005. www.comsat-history. com/COMSATLabsBuilding/COMSATBuildingApp.pdf.

———. Transcript of "This Is Early Bird." MediaBurn.org. Accessed February 1, 2019. mediaburn.org/video/the-hypercube-projections-slicing-others/.

"Comsat Corporation History." FundingUniverse.com. Accessed April 3, 2019. www.fundinguniverse.com/company-histories/comsat-corporation-history/.

Copley News Service. "Early Bird Launching Set for '65." Orlando Sentinel, July 5, 1964. www.newspapers.com/image/223822453/.

Côté, Robert. "Léo Plouffe, héros et homme-orchestre." Service de Police de la Ville de Montréal, 1996. spvm.qc.ca/upload/capsules_historiques /2010/NMC_mai2010_En%20hommage%20%C3%A0%20notre%20coll %C3%A8gue%20policier,%20d%C3%A9c%C3%A9d%C3%A9%20 dans%20l%E2%80%99exercice%20de%20ses%20fonctions%20le%20 7%20juin%201973.pdf.

CQ Almanac. "Congress Enacts Communications Satellite Bill." 1962. CQPress
.com. library.cqpress.com/cqalmanac/document.php?id=cqal62-1325059.

David, Edward E., Jr., Max V. Mathews, and A. Michael Noll. "John Robinson
Pierce." Biographical Memoirs, vol. 85. Washington, D.C.: National Academies Press, 2004, 233–45. www.nap.edu/read/11172/chapter/15#233.

Davis, Miller. "Fired Guard Was Too Late to Save Job, He Says." Miami Herald,
October 4, 1965. www.newspapers.com/image/620722944/.

Dawe, John, Michael deCourcy, and Gavin Walker. "The Original Cellar Jazz
Club." TheOriginalCellarJazzClub.blogspot.com. December 7, 2010.
theoriginalcellarjazzclub.blogspot.com/2010/11/story-by-john-dawe.html.

Dorion, Frederic. Special Public Inquiry 1964: Report of the Commissioner, the
Honorable Frederic Dorion, Chief Justice of the Superior Court for the Province
of Quebec. Ottawa: R. Duhamel, 1965. epe.lac-bac.gc.ca/100/200/301/pco
-bcp/commissions-ef/dorion1965-eng/dorion1965-eng.pdf.

"Dr. John Thomas Mendel." February 8, 2014. Dignitymemorial.com. www
.dignitymemorial.com/obituaries/placerville-ca/dr-john-mendel-5860168.

Du Brow, Rick. "Early Bird Satellite Opens New Era With 1-Hour Telecast."
Shreveport Journal, May 3, 1965. www.newspapers.com/image/601288406/.

Dubois, Paul. "Cmdr. Way Nears End of Work in City, Press Conference Today Last Function." Gazette (Montreal, Canada), March 22, 1962. www
.newspapers.com/image/421009980/.

———. "Coiffeur Buys Lemay Isle." Gazette (Montreal, Canada), June 2, 1962.
www.newspapers.com/image/420803364/.

———. "Andre Durocher Found Hanged." Gazette (Montreal, Canada), June 6,
1966. www.newspapers.com/image/421236410/.

Duhaime, Lloyd. "Montreal Lawyer Léo-René Maranda, R.I.P. - An Extraor-
dinary Legacy." lawMAG, February 12, 2012. www.duhaime.org/LawMag
/LawArticle-1388/Montreal-Lawyer-Leo-Rene-Maranda-RIP--An
-Extraordinary-Legacy.aspx.

Durand, Jacques. "Georges Lemay vu à Québec et à Nominingue?" La Presse
(Montreal, Canada), April 2, 1962. numerique.banq.qc.ca/patrimoine/details
/52327/2757071.

Dwiggins, Don. "Dr. Harold Rosen—Edison of Space." Shreveport Journal,
April 14, 1965. www.newspapers.com/image/601295333/.

Elbert, Bruce R. Introduction to Satellite Communication. 3rd ed. Boston: Artech
House, 2008, 40–41.

Emme, Eugene M., comp. "Aeronautical and Astronautical Events of 1961,

Report of the National Aeronautics and Space Administration to the Committee on Science and Astronautics, U.S. House of Representatives, 87th Cong., 2d. Sess. Washington, D.C.: National Aeronautics and Space Administration, 1962, 14–30. www.hq.nasa.gov/office/pao/History/Timeline /1961-2.html.

Ezell, Linda N. "Relay." In *Programs and Projects 1958–1968*. Vol. 2 of *NASA Historical Data Book*. Washington, D.C.: NASA Scientific and Technical Information Division, 1988. www.nasa.gov/centers/goddard/missions/relay .html.

Federal Bureau of Investigation. "Ten Most Wanted Fugitives FAQ." FBI.gov. www.fbi.gov/wanted/topten/ten-most-wanted-fugitives-faq.

Finn, Shaun, and Mathieu Beauregard. "It Pleases the Court. The Ernest Cormier Building Rededicated a Hall of Justice." *Revue générale de droit* 35, no. 3 (2005): 441–49. www.erudit.org/fr/revues/rgd/2005-v35-n3-rgd 01583/1027263ar.pdf.

Finney, John W. "Kennedy's Satellite Bill Fought by Industry and Congressmen." *New York Times*, March 4, 1962. timesmachine.nytimes.com/times machine/1962/03/04/83486125.html?pageNumber=44.

———. "Compromise Near on Space Radio Bill." *New York Times*, March 20, 1962. timesmachine.nytimes.com/timesmachine/1962/03/20/82040807 .html?pageNumber=18.

Fisher, Jack. "Hughes Aircraft History, 1932–1986." HughesSCGHeritage .com, May 8, 2015. www.hughesscgheritage.com/hughes-aircraft-history -1932-1986-transcribed-by-faith-macpherson/.

Fort Lauderdale News. "Canadian Police Have Little Hope of Getting Lemay."September 23, 1965. www.newspapers.com/image/272504525/.

Gagnon, Yves. "L'Ânou' revient . . . sans Lemay." *La Presse* (Montreal, Canada), June 7, 1962. numerique.banq.qc.ca/patrimoine/details/52327/2757198.

Galloway, Jonathan F. "Originating Communications Satellite Systems: The Interactions of Technological Change, Domestic Politics, and Foreign Policy." In *Beyond the Ionosphere: Fifty Years of Satellite Communication*, edited by Andrew J. Butrica, 186–92. Washington, D.C.: National Aeronautics and Space Administration, 1997. history.nasa.gov/SP-4217/ch13.htm.

Games of the XVIII Olympiad, Tokyo 1964: The Official Report of the Organizing Committee, vol. 1. Tokyo: Organizing Committee of the Games of the XVIII Olympiad, 1964, 389–96. digital.la84.org/digital/collection/p17103coll8 /id/27658/rec/29.

Gardner, Paul. "Today: Early Bird." *New York Times*, May 2, 1965. times machine.nytimes.com/timesmachine/1965/05/02/97196630.html?page Number=501.

Gartner, Hana. "Hitman." The Fifth Estate. *Canadian Broadcasting Corporation*. Air date: April 27, 1983. www.cbc.ca/fifth/episodes/40-years-of -the-fifth-estate/hitman.

Gavaghan, Helen. *Something New Under the Sun: Satellites and the Beginning of the Space Age*, 199–222. New York: Springer, 2012.

Gaver, Jack (United Press International). "Satellite TV to Bind the Globe With News." *Atlanta Constitution*, April 26, 1965. www.newspapers.com /image/398441001/.

Gazette (Montreal, Canada). "City Constable Selected for FBI Course." August 16, 1952. www.newspapers.com/image/419529935/.

———. "HQ Shakeup 'Sets Up Skeletons, Meat to Come Later.'" July 4, 1961. www.newspapers.com/image/420709828/.

———. "Vault Blasted: 373 Boxes Looted." July 4, 1961. www.newspapers.com /image/420709828.

———. "Four Arraigned in Bank Theft." January 10, 1962. www.newspapers .com/image/421026798/.

———. "Police Search for Evidence at Chomedey." January 11, 1962. www .newspapers.com/image/421028825/.

———. "Two Heading Here, Miami Inquiry Off." March 22, 1962. www.news papers.com/image/421009789/.

———. "Judge Sets Bail at $25,000 for Singer, But She Can't Get It." April 12, 1962. www.newspapers.com/image/420981044/.

———. "Witness Says Accused Was at Funeral During Robbery." April 12, 1962. www.newspapers.com/image/420981044/.

———. "Witness Says $7,000 Spent Within Month of Bank Robbery." April 14, 1962. www.newspapers.com/image/420982734/.

———. "Man Convicted of Bank Burglary." April 25, 1962. www.newspapers .com/image/420991089/.

———. "Robbery Suspect Charged." May 30, 1962. www.newspapers.com /image/420836903/.

———. "Was Georges Lemay Here? Detectives Checking Clues." July 23, 1962. www.newspapers.com/image/420773421/.

———. "Georges Lemay Found in Town But Goes Free." July 28, 1962. www .newspapers.com/image/420776593/.

———. "Crown Witness in $500,000 Theft Gets One Day, Plus Time in Jail." September 21, 1963. www.newspapers.com/image/423795131/.

———. "Separatist Group Hits at Army." March 9, 1963. news.google.com /newspapers?nid=Fr8DH2VBP9sC&dat=19630309&printsec=frontpage &hl=en.

———. "N.D.G. Resident Accused in Bond Conspiracy Case." April 20, 1963. www.newspapers.com/image/420782101/.

———. "'Lemay Aide' Due Back." May 4, 1964. www.newspapers.com /image/423622519/.

———. "No.1 Spot Now Goes to Lemay." August 27, 1964. www.newspapers .com/image/423818012/.

———. "Lise Lemay Has Bail Reduced." September 2, 1966. www.newspapers .com/image/421409700/.

———. "Threw Jewelry into Sea Says Witness." November 9, 1967. www .newspapers.com/image/421449572/.

———. "Minister Names New Judges." September 1, 1967. www.newspapers .com/image/421228981/.

———. "Lawyer Wants Detective Out." November 16, 1967. www.newspapers .com/image/421454978/.

———. "Bid to Remove Judge by Lemay Is Denied." September 19, 1968. www .newspapers.com/image/421478536/.

———. "Eva Roden." May 9, 2020. montrealgazette.remembering.ca/obituary /eva-roden-1079153740.

Gendron, Hubert. "'Leo Junior' Tank Unit Teleguided To 'Plant.'" *Gazette* (Montreal, Canada), September 2, 1965. www.newspapers.com /image/421014450/.

Gertner, John. *The Idea Factory: Bell Labs and the Great Age of American Innovation*, 184–97, 339. New York: Penguin Press, 2012. s3.amazonaws .com/arena-attachments/1606731/a41cb3f6903d5ace340477d62a8bbf73 .pdf?1516213556.

Gilliece, Russell. "4 Years for Raid on Bank." *Gazette* (Montreal, Canada), October 27, 1962 www.newspapers.com/image/420990915/.

———. "Six-Year Term for Share in Bank Burglary." *Gazette* (Montreal, Canada), October 15, 1964. www.newspapers.com/image/423847254/.

———. "Lemay Pulls Surprise Asking Adjournment." *Gazette* (Montreal, Canada), May 2, 1967. www.newspapers.com/image/421173044/.

Gooden, Joe. "The Beatles on Our World: All You Need Is Love." *The*

Beatles Bible, December 7, 2021. www.beatlesbible.com/1967/06/25/the
-beatles-on-our-world-all-you-need-is-love/.

Gould, Jack. "When TV Lost the Olympics." *New York Times*, October 18,
1964. timesmachine.nytimes.com/timesmachine/1964/10/18/118931649.
pdf?pdf_redirect=true&ip=0.

———. "The Early Bird Is Ready for Its Public Debut." *New York Times*, April 28,
1965. timesmachine.nytimes.com/timesmachine/1965/04/28/97195352.
html?pageNumber=49.

———. "Early Bird Relay Links 2 Continents with Live TV Show." *New York
Times*, May 3, 1965. timesmachine.nytimes.com/timesmachine/1965/05
/03/issue.html.

Greenberg, Herb. "$5.7 Billion GM Bid Wins Hughes Aircraft." *Chicago Tri-
bune*, June 6, 1985. www.chicagotribune.com/news/ct-xpm-1985-06-06
-8502050453-story.html.

Gross, Ben. "Early Bird Makes Great Catch." *Daily News* (New York), May 3,
1965. www.newspapers.com/image/459660808.

Gugliotta, Guy. "Spin Doctors" *Air & Space Magazine*, September 2009. www
.airspacemag.com/space/spin-doctors-38952524/?page=2.

Handman, Stanley. "Canada's 5 Most-Wanted Men." *Ottawa Citizen*, December
13, 1958. www.newspapers.com/image/469747850/.

"Harold A. Rosen." *Engineering and Technology History Wiki*, October 1, 2018.
ethw.org/Harold_A._Rosen.

Harrington, Jack. "Comsat History Project Interview with Jack Harrington."
By Nina Gilden Seavey. Comsat Legacy Project. January 6, 1988. www
.comsat-history.com/COMSATOralHistory/ComsatHistory-Jack_
Harrington.pdf.

Harris, Louis. "Bomb Surgeon Hangs Up His Coathanger." *Gazette* (Montreal,
Canada), March 1, 1978. www.newspapers.com/image/421437855/.

Hayes, Bob. "Bedard Goes Back to Old Life, But in New Setting." *Gazette* (Montreal, Canada), June 29, 1962. www.newspapers.com/image/420811996/.

Helder, George K. "Customer Evaluation of Telephone Circuits with Delay."
Bell System Technical Journal 45, no. 7 (September 1966): 1157–91.

———. "Subjective Evaluation of Telephone Communications Via Early Bird
Satellite and Cable Circuits." *Progress in Astronautics and Rocketry* 19
(1966): 85–93.

Heller, Robert. "An Early Bird Sure of the Worm." *Observer* (London), March
14, 1965. www.newspapers.com/image/257983991/.

Henry, Varice F., and Michael E. McDonald. *Television Tests with the Syncom II Synchronous Communications Satellite July 1, 1965.* Washington, D.C.: National Aeronautics and Space Administration, 1965. ntrs.nasa.gov /citations/19650019255.

Higgins, Jonathan. *Satellite Newsgathering,* 294. New York: Taylor & Francis, 2012.

Historic American Engineering Record Southeast Regional Office. "Historic American Engineering Record: Cape Canaveral Air Force Station, Missile Assembly Building AE (Hangar AE)." Atlanta. lcweb2.loc.gov/master /pnp/habshaer/fl/fl0700/fl0785/data/fl0785data.pdf.

Hoig, Robert. "Doors And More Doors Make New Jail 'Tight.'" *Miami News,* June 5, 1960. www.newspapers.com/image/299251096/.

Howard Hughes Medical Institute. "History of the Howard Hughes Medical Institute." HHMI.org. Accessed January 23, 2019. www.hhmi.org/about /history.

Hughes News. "Improved Syncom C Set for May Launch." April 10, 1964. HughesSCGHeritage.com. www.hughesscgheritage.com/improved-syncom -c-set-for-may-launch-hughes-news-april-10-1964/.

———. "Early Bird Ready for April Launch." March 26, 1965. HughesSCG Heritage.com. www.hughesscgheritage.com/early-bird-ready-for-april-launch -hughes-news-march-26-1965-transcribed-by-faith-macpherson/.

———. "Hughes Wins New Satellite Contract." December 3, 1965. HughesSCGHeritage.com. www.hughesscgheritage.com/hughes-wins-new -satellite-contract-hughes-news-december-3-1965/.

———. "Death Ends Work of Satellite Star Donald Williams." February 25, 1966. HughesSCGHeritage.com. www.hughesscgheritage.com/death -ends-work-of-satellite-star-donald-williams-hughes-news-february -25-1966/.

———. "Spin Stabilization 'Simple, Elegant, Brilliant.'" June 28, 1985. HughesSCGHeritage.com.www.hughesscgheritage.com/spin-stabilization -simple-elegant-brilliant-hughes-news-june-28-1985-transcribed-by-faith -macpherson/.

Hurley, Neil P. "Satellite Communications: A Case Study of Technology's Impact on Politics." *The Review of Politics* 30, no. 2 (1968): 170–90. www.jstor .org/stable/1405412.

Hyland, L. A. *Call Me Pat: The Autobiography of the Man Howard Hughes Chose to Lead Hughes Aircraft,* 313–19, 322. Marceline: Walsworth, 1994.

Jaffe, Leonard. "Comsat History Project Interview with Leonard Jaffe." By Nina Gilden Seavey. Comsat Legacy Project. September 23, 1985. www.com satlegacy.com/COMSATOralHistory/ComsatHistory-Leonard_Jaffe.pdf.

Johnson, Lyndon B. "Evaluation of Space Program." Memorandum to President John F. Kennedy, April 28, 1961. In Roger D. Launius, *Apollo: A Retrospective Analysis*, 35. Washington, D.C.: National Aeronautics and Space Administration, 1994. history.nasa.gov/Apollomon/apollo2.pdf.

Johnston, Grant. "Canada's Most Wanted Man Captured Here Without Struggle." *Gazette* (Montreal, Canada), August 27, 1964. www.newspapers.com /image/423818012/.

Le Journal de Montreal. "Voleur célèbre décédé." September 24, 2008. www .pressreader.com/canada/le-journal-de-montreal/20080924/281767035 034626.

Kennedy, John F. "President John F. Kennedy's Speech Announcing the Quarantine Against Cuba, October 22, 1962." MtHolyoke.edu. Accessed March 20, 2019. www.mtholyoke.edu/acad/intrel/kencuba.htm#:~:text=Kennedy's% 20Speech%20Announcing%20the%20Quarantine%20Against%20Cuba%2 C%20October%2022%2C%201962,-WASHINGTON%2C%20October %2022&text=Good%20evening%20my%20fellow%20citizens,on%20 the%20island%20of%20Cuba.

Kennedy, John F., and Abubaker Tafawa Balewa. "Conversation with the Prime Minister of Nigeria by means of the Syncom Communications Satellite, 23 August 1963." John F. Kennedy Presidential Library. www.jfk library.org/asset-viewer/archives/JFKWHA/1963/JFKWHA-211-003/JFK WHA-211-003.

Kerner, Jordan R. "The Communications Satellite Corporation: Toward A Workable Telecommunications Policy." *Hastings Law Journal* 27, no. 3 (1976): 721–52. core.ac.uk/download/pdf/230139197.pdf.

Klooster, John W. *Icons of Invention: The Makers of the Modern World from Gutenberg to Gates*, vol. 1, 565–68. Santa Barbara: Greenwood Press, 2009. www.google.com/books/edition/Icons_of_Invention/WKuG-VIwID8C ?q=%22Harold+Rosen%22+%22Intelsat+1%22&gbpv=1#f=false.

LaFlash, Jud. "A Part of History." *Hughes News*, April 9, 1965. HughesSCG Heritage.com. www.hughesscgheritage.com/a-part-of-history-hughes-news -april-9-1965-by-jud-laflash-technical-information-officer-early-bird-launch -transcribed-by-faith-macpherson/.

Lapierre, Lise. "Georges Lemay." *Photo-Journal* (Montreal, Canada), August 14, 1968. numerique.banq.qc.ca/patrimoine/details/52327/3543214.

———. "Lise Lemieux-Lemay: 'Je n'ai pas honte d'être la femme de ce Georges Lemay!'" *Photo-Journal* (Montreal, Canada), June, 26 1968. numerique .banq.qc.ca/patrimoine/details/52327/3543207.

LaVergne, Claude. "Un enfant nous est né: celui de GEORGES Lemay." *La Patrie* (Montréal, Canada), October 4, 1962. numerique.banq.qc.ca /patrimoine/details/52327/4062514.

Leogrande, Ernest. "'Most Wanted' Man with the Most Gall." *Daily News* (New York), September 18, 1966. www.newspapers.com/image/462049921/.

Levine, Arnold S. *Managing NASA in the Apollo Era*, 214–29. Washington, D.C.: National Aeronautics and Space Administration, 1982. history .nasa.gov/SP-4102/ch8.htm#:~:text=Writing%20to%20Webb%20in%20 June,DOD%20furnishing%20the%20ground%20support.

Levinson, Leon. "Art Slashing Suspect to Trial." *Gazette* (Montreal, Canada), October 27, 1961. www.newspapers.com/image/420558988/.

———. "Pair Of Warrants Are Issued by Police for Georges Lemay." *Gazette* (Montreal, Canada), January 9, 1962. www.newspapers.com/image /421026328/.

———. "Mystery Man Lemay Plotted Robbery." *Gazette* (Montreal, Canada), January 18, 1962. www.newspapers.com/image/421033147/.

———. "Lise Lemieux Loses Freedom Bid." *Gazette* (Montreal, Canada), March 30, 1962. www.newspapers.com/image/421015244/.

———. "Singer Pleas Again for Bail in Court." *Gazette* (Montreal, Canada), April 4, 1962. www.newspapers.com/image/420976242/.

———. "Separate Trials for 3 in $500,000 Robbery." *Gazette* (Montreal, Canada), April 10, 1962. www.newspapers.com/image/420979948/.

———. "Array of Tools Produced in Vault Robbery Trial." *Gazette* (Montreal, Canada), April 11, 1962. www.newspapers.com/image/420980596/.

———. "Blasting 'Expert' Was Paid $65,000 for Bank Job." *Gazette* (Montreal, Canada), April 17, 1962. www.newspapers.com/image/420984566/.

———. "Bank Janitor Thought Blasting Just 'Noises.'" *Gazette* (Montreal, Canada), April 18, 1962. www.newspapers.com/image/420985633/.

———. "Judge, Jury Visit Crime Scene." *Gazette* (Montreal, Canada), April 18, 1962. www.newspapers.com/image/420985633/.

———. "Only Connection with Lemay Was Peso Deal, Says Accused."

Gazette (Montreal, Canada), April 19, 1962. www.newspapers.com /image/420986221/.

———. "Suspect 'Missing' During Robbery." *Gazette* (Montreal, Canada), April 20, 1962. www.newspapers.com/image/420988305/.

———. "Did Primeau, Lemay Plan Bank Burglary?" *Gazette* (Montreal, Canada), April 24, 1962. www.newspapers.com/image/420990414/.

———. "$25,000 Bail Set for Lise Lemieux." *Gazette* (Montreal, Canada), May 31, 1962. www.newspapers.com/image/420837218/.

———. "Chanteuse Given Time in Jail on Conspiracy Count." *Gazette* (Montreal, Canada), June 14, 1962. www.newspapers.com/image/420806557/.

———. "Witness Details Role as Lemay Aide." *Gazette* (Montreal, Canada), November 11, 1967. www.newspapers.com/image/421451305/.

———. "Fingerprints Used to Corroborate Crown Evidence in Lemay Trial." *Gazette* (Montreal, Canada), December 13, 1967. www.newspapers.com/ image/421471522/.

Levitt, I. M. "Enjoys Rapid Advances." *Orlando Sentinel*, April 4, 1965. www .newspapers.com/image/223830590/.

Leung, Rebecca. "Howard Hughes: Patron of Science?" *CBS/60 Minutes* online. November 21, 2003. www.cbsnews.com/news/howard-hughes-patron -of-science-21-11-2003/.

Lippman, Thomas W. "Hughes' Legacy: Struggle for Power." *Washington Post*, July 17, 1983. www.washingtonpost.com/archive/business/1983/07/17/ hughes-legacy-struggle-for-power/3247d75b-80c3-4b86-9f38-f1c08ac 62d4e/.

Lizotte, Léopold. "En ouvrant son 'lunch', Lajoie ne retrouve pas les $10,000 promis." *La Presse* (Montreal, Canada), April 14, 1962. numerique.banq .qc.ca/patrimoine/details/52327/2757094.

———. "Lise Lemieux coupable, mais libre." *La Presse* (Montréal, Canada), June 13, 1962. numerique.banq.qc.ca/patrimoine/details/52327/2757210.

———. "Lajoie incrimine, avec le sourire, un Lemay beaucoup moins souriant!" *La Presse* (Montreal, Canada), November 22, 1966. numerique.banq.qc.ca /patrimoine/details/52327/2698285.

———. "Primeau en avait assez, mais Lemay, lui, voulait vider jusqu'au dernier coffret." *La Presse* (Montreal, Canada), November 29, 1966. numerique .banq.qc.ca/patrimoine/details/52327/2698298.

———. "Lemay subira probablement son procès au mois de mars et présentera une preuve d'alibi." *La Presse* (Montréal, Canada), December 31, 1966. numerique.banq.qc.ca/patrimoine/details/52327/2698352.

———. "La première tâche de Lajoie chez Lemay: 'épousseter' les pelouses." *La Presse* (Montreal, Canada). November 10, 1967. numerique.banq.qc.ca /patrimoine/details/52327/2698973.

———. "Georges Lemay aurait lui-même fabriqué les explosifs et inventé un détonateur à relais très astucieux." *La Presse* (Montreal, Canada), November 11, 1967. numerique.banq.qc.ca/patrimoine/details/52327/2698974.

———. "Lemay remis en liberté." *La Presse* (Montreal, Canada), April 23, 1975. numerique.banq.qc.ca/patrimoine/details/52327/2604205.

———. "Lemay: une décision sur le cautionnement vendredi." *La Presse* (Montreal, Canada), January 31, 1979. numerique.banq.qc.ca/patrimoine/details /52327/2409510.

———. "Lemay aurait eu un sourire inhabituel en apprenant la mort de son copain Quintal." *La Presse* (Montreal, Canada), November 21, 1984. numerique.banq.qc.ca/patrimoine/details/52327/2288187.

Los Angeles Times (Washington Post News Service). "Hughes Readies Plan for Employees' Buy of Half of Stock." *Tucson Citizen*, March 14, 1984. www .newspapers.com/image/578557216/.

Lowry, Cynthia (Associated Press). "Communication Landmark." *Courier-News* (Bridgewater, New Jersey), May 3, 1965. www.newspapers.com /image/221855181/.

Mahon, Jack. "The Space Age's Richest Feat." *Daily News* (New York), April 9, 1967. www.newspapers.com/image/463731908/.

Maksian, George. "Surgery Via Early Bird." *Daily News* (New York, New York), April 21, 1965. www.newspapers.com/image/460063439/.

Manning, Mary. "Howard Hughes: A revolutionary recluse." *Las Vegas Sun*, May 15, 2008. lasvegassun.com/news/2008/may/15/how-vegas-went-mob -corporate/.

Martin, Edward J. "The Evolution of Mobile Satellite Communications." In *Beyond the Ionosphere: Fifty Years of Satellite Communication*, edited by Andrew J. Butrica, 269–70. Washington, D.C.: National Aeronautics and Space Administration, 1997. history.nasa.gov/SP-4217/ch21.htm.

McClintock, Jack. "Communications: Harold Rosen." *Discover Magazine*, November 9, 2003. www.discovermagazine.com/the-sciences/communications -harold-rosen.

McElheny, Victor K. "Communication Satellite Ages." *New York Times*, August 27, 1973. www.nytimes.com/1973/08/27/archives/communication-satellite -ages-communications-satellite-has-grown.html.

McLuhan, Marshall. "Transcript of Marshall McLuhan on 'Our World' (Global Satellite Broadcast on June 24th, 1967)." Transcribed by Manuel Correa and Olivia Leiter. *Triple Ampersand Journal*, May 29, 2015. tripleampersand .org/transcript-of-marshall-mcluhan-on-our-world-global-satellite-broad cast-on-june-24th-1967/.

"Memorandum from S. G. Lutz to A.V. Haeff: Commercial Satellite Commu-nication Project; Preliminary Report of Study Task Force." October 22, 1959. In *Using Space*. Vol. 3 of *Exploring the Unknown: Selected Documents in the History of the U.S. Civil Space Program*, edited by James M. Logsdon. NASA SP-4407 (1995): 31–34.

Metzger, David, Philip Metzger, and Sally Fasman. "Sidney Metzger." In *National Academy of Engineering Memorial Tributes*, vol. 17, 213–15. Wash-ington, D.C.: National Academies Press, 2013. www.nap.edu/read/18477 /chapter/36#214.

Metzger, Sidney. "Geosynchronous Vs. Low Orbit, The First Big Technical De-cision." *Comsat Magazine*, 1983. www.iothistory.org/COMSAT%20Magazine /COMSAT%20Magazine,%2012,.PDF.

———. "COMSAT History Project: Interview with Sidney Metzger." By Thomas M. Safely. Comsat Legacy Project. July 11, 1984. www.comsatlegacy .com/COMSATOralHistory/ComsatHistory-Sid_Metzger.pdf.

Miall, Leonard. "Obituaries: Derek Burrell-Davis." *Independent*, January 2, 1995. www.independent.co.uk/news/people/obituaries-derek-burrelldavis -1566385.html.

Miami Herald. "Lemay Bank Box Empty." January 13, 1962. www.newspapers .com/image/620527757/.

Miami News. "$4 Million Bank Loot Believed on Yacht." January 11, 1962. www .newspapers.com/image/301250089/.

———. "2 Ex-Deputies Acquitted of Aiding Lemay Escape." November 30, 1966. www.newspapers.com/image/301988741/.

"Miami-Dade County Spring 1966 Grand Jury Final Report." November 8, 1966, 1–8. miamisao.com/wp-content/uploads/2021/02/gj1966s4.pdf.

"Michael DeBakey with the Duke and Duchess of Windsor." Michael E. DeBakey Papers. U.S. National Library of Medicine. profiles.nlm.nih.gov /spotlight/fj/catalog/nlm:nlmuid-101743405X29-img.

Miller, Gene. "Coast Guard Hunts Robbery Suspect." *Miami Herald*, January 10, 1962. www.newspapers.com/image/620286532/.

Minenna, Damien, Frédéric André, Yves Elskens, Jean-François Auboin, Fabrice Doveil, et al. "The Traveling-Wave Tube in the History of Telecommunication." *European Physical Journal H*, EDP Sciences, 2019. hal.archives -ouvertes.fr/hal-01754885/document.

Moorcraft, Bethan. "Satellite insurance – a brief introductory guide." *Insurance Business America*, August 5, 2019. www.insurancebusinessmag.com/us/guides /satellite-insurance--a-brief-introductory-guide-174465.aspx.

Moore, William. "Incredible Story of Crime Ending." *Fort Lauderdale News*, January 18, 1969. www.newspapers.com/image/272262979/.

Morin, Maurice. "Escortés, Lajoie et Primeau revoient des lieux familiers." *La Presse* (Montreal, Canada), April 13, 1962. numerique.banq.qc.ca /patrimoine/details/52327/2757093.

———. "$65,000 en billets de banque comptés et placés dans un 'thermos'; le voleur A. Lemieux, volé de $7,900 par un cousin." *La Presse* (Montreal, Canada), April 17, 1962. numerique.banq.qc.ca/patrimoine/details/52327/2757101.

———. "Roland Primeau nie avoir participé au vol de banque." *La Presse* (Montreal, Canada), April 19, 1962. numerique.banq.qc.ca/patrimoine /details/52327/2757105.

———. "André Lemieux brille toujours par son absence; les quatre ex-policiers de la PP subiront leur procès deux par deux." *La Presse* (Montréal, Canada), September 11, 1962. numerique.banq.qc.ca/patrimoine /details/52327/2757389.

———. "Le témoin-vedette Jacques Lajoie est libre après 21 mois en cellule." *La Presse* (Montreal, Canada), September 21, 1963. numerique.banq.qc.ca /patrimoine/details/52327/2758128.

———. "Yvon Lemieux écope de 4 ans de pénitencier." *La Presse* (Montréal, Canada), October 27, 1962. numerique.banq.qc.ca/patrimoine /details/52327/2757483.

NASA. "NASA's Syncom C Satellite Is Set for Launching." NASA Press Kit. August 13, 1964. www.scribd.com/document/49069214/Syncom-C -Press-Kit#download.

———. "Project Echo." NASA.gov, August 13, 2011. www.nasa.gov/centers /langley/about/project-echo.html.

———. "July 12, 1962: The Day Information Went Global." NASA.gov, July 9, 2012. www.nasa.gov/topics/technology/features/telstar.html.

New York Times. "Ocean Space Link Now Set for 1965; F.C.C. Is Asked to Approve Atlantic Satellite." March 5, 1964. www.nytimes.com/1964/03/05 /archives/ocean-space-link-now-set-for-1965-fcc-is-asked-to-approve-atlantic .html.

———. "Siegfried H. Reiger, Officer of COMSAT." July 16, 1970. www .nytimes.com/1970/07/16/archives/siegfried-h-reiger-officer-of-comsat .html.

Newman, Georges. "Canadian Hunt Revives Mystery of Keys." *Miami News,* September 2, 1962. www.newspapers.com/image/300993376/.

Newton, Dwight. "It's Early Bird Watchers' Day." *San Francisco Examiner,* May 2, 1965. www.newspapers.com/image/458835365/.

"Nuclear Test Ban Treaty." John F. Kennedy Presidential Library. Accessed May 2, 2019. www.jfklibrary.org/learn/about-jfk/jfk-in-history/nuclear-test -ban-treaty#:~:text=The%20Treaty&text=Kennedy%20signed%20the%20 ratified%20treaty,the%20nation%20conducting%20the%20test.

"Ocean Ranch Hotel Pool in 1960s." *Miami History,* February 25, 2021. miami -history.com/photos/ocean-ranch-hotel-pool-in-1960s/.

O'Connor, D'Arcy, with Miranda O'Connor. *Montreal's Irish Mafia: The True Story of the Infamous West End Gang.* Mississauga: Wiley, 2011, 77–80.

Office of U.S. Commission General. "Expo'67 United States Pavilion Press Kit." WorldsFairPhotos.com. www.worldsfairphotos.com/expo67/united _states_pavilion_press_kit.htm.

Oneonta Star. "Early Bird Won't Pay Dividends for Awhile." April 26, 1965. www.newspapers.com/image/48128239/.

Orlando Sentinel. "Lemay Hopes for Haiti." May 22, 1965. www.newspapers .com/image/223789517/.

Ostapiuk, Peter. "The Beatles Said, 'It's Easy,' But the 50th Anniversary of the 'Our World' Broadcast Reminds Us That It Wasn't." Intelsat.com, June 20, 2017. www.intelsat.com/news/blog/beatles-said -its-easy-but-50th-anniversary-of-our-world-broadcast-wasnt/.

Ott, Andy. "The DirecTV Story." HughesSCGHeritage.com, July 23, 2015. www.hughesscgheritage.com/the-directv-story-space-segment-andy-ott/.

Ottawa Citizen. "Out of the Frying Pan." May 26, 1962. www.newspapers.com /image/459063261/.

———. "McClellan Describes Bilingualism Problem." March 5, 1965. www .newspapers.com/image/459171424/.

Ottawa Journal. "Batista's Cuba a Haven for Rivard Operations." July 6, 1976. www.newspapers.com/image/49288166/.

Palmer, Al. "Behind Prison Walls: Experiment in Rehabilitation." *Gazette* (Montreal, Canada), March 3, 1960. www.newspapers.com/image/419331123/.

———. "1960—Worst Year Ever for Montreal as Crime and Violence Hit New Peak." *Gazette* (Montreal, Canada), January 11, 1961. www.newspapers.com/image/420554809/.

———. "'Suspicious' Fire Levels Lemay North Retreat." *Gazette* (Montreal, Canada), March 12, 1962. www.newspapers.com/image/421004572/.

———. "Major Robbery Was One Year Ago; Police Wonder—Where's Georges?" *Gazette* (Montreal, Canada), July 2, 1962. www.newspapers.com/image/420766749/.

Palmer, Al, and Paul Dubois. "Eight Suspected Terrorists Held, Bombs Seized in Anti-FLQ Raid." *Gazette* (Montreal, Canada), June 3, 1963. www.newspapers.com/image/420770432/.

———. "'Escape-Proof' Jail Beaten by Thorough Planning." *Gazette* (Montreal, Canada), September 22, 1965. www.newspapers.com/image/421028928/.

Past In The Present. "Habana Libre and the Story of Modern Cuba." January 28, 2015. pastinthepresent.net/2015/01/28/cuba-on-the-cusp-part-one-habana-libre-and-the-story-of-modern-cuba/.

La Patrie (Montreal, Canada). "George Lemay en liberté." May 4, 1975. numerique.banq.qc.ca/patrimoine/details/52327/4063937.

Pelton, Joseph N. "The Start of Commercial Satellite Communications." *IEEE Communications Magazine* 48, no. 3(March 2010): 24–31. www.researchgate.net/profile/Joseph_Pelton/publication/224126023_The_start_of_commercial_satellite_communications_History_of_communications/links/55b6452308ae092e9655d391/The-start-of-commercial-satellite-communications-History-of-communications.pdf.

Peltz, James F. "End of an Era: Closure of Building 15 Shuts Book on Hughes Aircraft Complex." *Los Angeles Times*, May 26, 1994. www.latimes.com/archives/la-xpm-1994-05-26-fi-62373-story.html.

Perkins, Robert. "Harold Rosen, 1926–2017." Caltech.edu, January 31, 2017. www.caltech.edu/about/news/harold-rosen-1926-2017-53790.

Phillips, Alan. "The Inner Workings of the Crime Cartel." *Maclean's* (Toronto, Canada), October 5, 1963. archive.macleans.ca/article/1963/10/5/the-inner-workings-of-the-crime-cartel.

Pierce, John R. "Telstar, A History." Southwest Museum of Engineering, Communications and Computation Vintage Electrics, 1990. SMECC.org. www.smecc.org/john_pierce1.htm.

———. "Oral-History: John Pierce." By Andy Goldstein. Center for the History of Electrical Engineering, August 1992. ethw.org/Oral-History:John_Pierce.

Piket, Casey. "Brickell Bay Drive in 1950s." *Miami History*, November 30, 2016. miami-history.com/brickell-bay-drive-in-1950s/.

The Porticus Centre. "Bell System Memorial — Telstar." February 25, 2021. www.beatriceco.com/bti/porticus/bell/telstar.html.

Potts, James B. "Early Bird as Seen from Andover." *Comsat Magazine*, 1983. www.iothistory.org/COMSAT%20Magazine/COMSAT%20Magazine ,%2012,.PDF.

La Presse (Montreal, Canada). "Georges Lemay serait revenu à Montréal?" January 11, 1962. numerique.banq.qc.ca/patrimoine/details/52327/2756913.

———. "Lemieux a été vu à Ste-Adèle." May 31, 1962. numerique.banq.qc.ca /patrimoine/details/52327/2757184.

———. "L'île de Lemay est vendue à un coiffeur." June 1, 1962. numerique.banq .qc.ca/patrimoine/details/52327/2757186.

———. "Lise Lemieux passe la nuit à St-Jérôme." June 15, 1962. numerique .banq.qc.ca/patrimoine/details/52327/2757214.

———. "Maintien de la sentence contre Primeau, lieutenant de Lemay." February 13, 1963. numerique.banq.qc.ca/patrimoine/details/52327/2757690.

———. "Jacques Lajoie fait une courte réapparition." March 18, 1963. numer ique.banq.qc.ca/patrimoine/details/52327/2757757.

———. "André Lemieux est arrêté à Hamilton." April 23, 1964. numerique .banq.qc.ca/patrimoine/details/52327/2758580.

———. "André Lemieux comparaît aux Assises." May 9, 1964. numerique.banq .qc.ca/patrimoine/details/52327/2758615.

———. "Lemay ne dit rien à la police." May 13, 1965. numerique.banq.qc.ca /patrimoine/details/52327/2758926.

———. "Capture de Lemay." August 19, 1966. numerique.banq.qc.ca /patrimoine/details/52327/2698115.

———. "Georges Lemay est arrêté dans un appartement de la rue Jarry." April 21, 1975. numerique.banq.qc.ca/patrimoine/details/52327/2604194.

———. "Un professeur de chimie a fait des travaux pour Quintal et Lemay." June 9, 1979. numerique.banq.qc.ca/patrimoine/details/52327/2410365.

———. "Un quatrième délateur au procès de Lemay." December 1, 1984. numerique.banq.qc.ca/patrimoine/details/52327/2288281.

———. "Georges Lemay saura mardi s'il subira son procès pour meurtre." May 4, 1984. numerique.banq.qc.ca/patrimoine/details/52327/2286669.

Pronovost, Martin. "Lise Lemieux est arrêtée puis libérée sous caution." *La Presse* (Montreal, Canada), May 13, 1965. numerique.banq.qc.ca/patrimoine /details/52327/2758926.

———. "Georges Lemay comparaît devant l'enquêteur spécial du département de l'Immigration américaine, à Miami." *La Presse* (Montreal, Canada), May 14, 1965. numerique.banq.qc.ca/patrimoine/details/52327/2758928.

———. "Je suis allé à Montréal quelques fois depuis 1961." *La Presse* (Montreal, Canada), May 15, 1965. numerique.banq.qc.ca/patrimoine/details /52327/2758933.

———. "'Je ne donnerais pas $100,000 pour une liberté provisoire', affirme Lemay à Las Vegas." *La Presse* (Montreal, Canada), August 27, 1966. numerique.banq.qc.ca/patrimoine/details/52327/2698129.

———. "Interrogés par des agents spéciaux les Lemay Sont muets comme carpes." *La Presse* (Montreal, Canada), August 29, 1966. numerique.banq .qc.ca/patrimoine/details/52327/2698133.

———. "Georges Lemay tente l'impossible pour obtenir la libération de sa femme." *La Presse* (Montreal, Canada), August 30, 1966. numerique.banq .qc.ca/patrimoine/details/52327/2698135.

———. "Les 11 mois de liberté de Georges Lemay." *La Presse* (Montreal, Canada), September 12, 1966. numerique.banq.qc.ca/patrimoine/details /52327/2698156.

———. "Loin de se cacher, Lemay s'amusait au grand jour." *La Presse* (Montreal, Canada), September 13, 1966. numerique.banq.qc.ca/patrimoine /details/52327/2698159.

———. "Lemay se laisse déporter à condition que Miami ne porte pas d'accusations." *La Presse* (Montreal, Canada), October 7, 1966. numerique.banq .qc.ca/patrimoine/details/52327/2698203.

Puckett, Allen. "Comsat History Project Interview with Allen Puckett." By Nina Gilden Seavey. Comsat Legacy Project. September 20, 1985. www .comsatlegacy.com/COMSATOralHistory/ComsatHistory-Allen_Puckett .pdf.

Ramo, Simon. "Memoirs Of an ICBM Pioneer." *Fortune Magazine*, April 25, 1988.

money.cnn.com/magazines/fortune/fortune_archive/1988/04/25/70453
/index.htm.

Raymond, Jessica. "In Memoriam: Allen E. Puckett, 94." *USC News*, April 14, 2014. news.usc.edu/61187/in-memoriam-allen-e-puckett-94/.

Reid, Malcolm (Canadian Press). "Lucien Rivard: A Chapter Has Closed on an Outstanding Case." *Ottawa Citizen*, July 24, 1965. www.newspapers.com/image/458340015/.

———. "The Incredible Story of Canada's Lucien Rivard." *Star-Phoenix* (Saskatoon, Canada), July 27, 1965. www.newspapers.com/image/508607798/.

Reiter, Ed. "New Phone Link to Europe Nearly Finished." *Asbury Park Press*, August 1, 1965. www.newspapers.com/image/143662339.

"Report of the Royal Canadian Mounted Police: Fiscal Year Ended March 31, 1965." Ottawa: Roger Duhamel, Queen's Printer and Controller of Stationery, 1967, 24–30. www.publicsafety.gc.ca/lbrr/archives/rcmp-rrcmp -1965-eng.pdf.

Reynolds, Ruth. "Missing Man Holds Key to Secrets of Wrecking Crew Bank Robbers." *Knoxville Journal*, March 6, 1959. www.newspapers.com/image/587668589/.

Riley, Arthur A. "Switchboard in the Sky." *Boston Globe*, October 29, 1967. www.newspapers.com/image/434128628.

Rosen, Harold. "Oral-History: Harold Rosen." By John Vardalas. IEEE History Center, February 2003. ethw.org/Oral-History:Harold_Rosen.

———. Interview by Clay Whitehead, October 30, 2007. Whitehead Archive. claytwhitehead.com/ctwlibrary/documentlib/20130207_Harold RosenandClayWhiteheadFinaleditRedacted.pdf.

———. "Oral History Interview with Harold Rosen." By Volker Janssen. Aerospace Oral History Project, The Huntington Library, San Marino, California. November 2, 2009. hdl.huntington.org/digital/collection/ p15150coll7/id/45066/.

———. "The SYNCOM Story." *Our Space Heritage 1960–2000*, May 19, 2012. www.hughesscgheritage.com/sycom-harold-rosen/.

Rosen, Harold A., and Donald D. Williams. "Commercial Communications Satellite, Report RDL/B-1, Engineering Division, Hughes Aircraft Company, January 1960." In *Using Space*. Vol. 3 of *Exploring the Unknown: Selected Documents in the History of the U.S. Civil Space Program*, edited by James M. Logsdon. NASA SP-4407 (1995): 35–39.

Rosenthal, Alfred. *Venture into Space: Early Years of Goddard Space Flight Center*.

Washington, D.C.: National Aeronautics and Space Administration, 1968; 47, 115–124, 132. history.nasa.gov/SP-4301.pdf.

Roy, Mario. "Une lutte de 'poids lourds' s'engage autour de Georges Lemay." *La Presse* (Montreal, Canada), November 7, 1984. numerique.banq.qc.ca /patrimoine/details/52327/2288061.

———. "Lavoie raconte encore une fois ses 27 meurtres." *La Presse* (Montreal, Canada), November 8, 1984. numerique.banq.qc.ca/patrimoine /details/52327/2288075.

Rybaczewski, Dave. "'All You Need Is Love' History." *Beatles Music History.* www.beatlesebooks.com/all-you-need-is-love.

"Satellite Communications." Montreal: Office of the United States Commissioner General, 1967. WorldsFairPhotos.com. www.worldsfairphotos.com /expo67/documents/press-releases/united-states-67/satellite-communications .pdf.

Schwoch, James. *Global TV: New Media and the Cold War, 1946–69.* Champaign: University of Illinois Press, 2009, 145–48.

Scott, Austin (Associated Press). "2-Way TV Signal Spans Ocean." *Morning Call* (Allentown, Pennsylvania), May 3, 1965. www.newspapers.com /image/275296439/.

Shreveport Journal. "CBS Announces Staff Promotions." April 30, 1965. www .newspapers.com/image/601090095/.

Sierrer, W. H., and W. A. Snyder. "Attitude Determination and Control of Syncom, Early Bird, and Applications Technology Satellites." *Journal of Spacecraft and Rockets* 6, no. 2 (1969): 162–66. arc.aiaa.org/doi /abs/10.2514/3.29555?journalCode=jsr&.

Silberman, Charles E. "Early Bird Heralds New Era—And Problems." *Fortune* reprinted in *Kansas City Times,* March 4, 1967. www.newspapers.com/image /675024769/.

Society of Former Special Agents of the FBI. Paducah: Turner Publishing, 1998, 120–21.

Sosin, Milt. "Fugitive Visited Lemay." *Miami News,* May 10, 1965. www.news papers.com/image/301310145/.

South Bend Tribune. "Early Bird to Give Stake in Space Age." April 30, 1965. www.newspapers.com/image/515560193.

———. "Early Bird Has Other Names." May 22, 1965. www.newspapers.com /image/515560983/.

Space Communications Group Journal. "SCG's Tom Hudspeth Celebrates the

Common Sense of Inventing." June 1984. HughesSCGHeritage.com. www
.hughesscgheritage.com/scgs-tom-hudspeth-celebrates-the-common-sense
-of-inventing-scg-journal-june-1984-transcribed-by-faith-macpherson/.

Space News. "Obituary: Satellite Industry Pioneer Tom Hudspeth Dies."
June 19, 2008. spacenews.com/obituary-satellite-industry-pioneer-tom
-hudspeth-dies/.

Space.com. "May 25, 1961: JFK's Moon Shot Speech to Congress." May 25, 2019.
www.space.com/11772-president-kennedy-historic-speech-moon-space
.html.

Sterba, James P. "Howard Hughes Dies at 70 on Flight to Texas Hospital." *New
York Times,* April 6, 1976. www.nytimes.com/1976/04/06/archives/howard
-hughes-dies-at-70-on-flight-to-texas-hospital-stroke-given.html.

Stolley, Richard B. "The Indispensable Camera." *Life,* December 23, 1966,
90–96.

Straubel, JB. "Who Is JB?" 216.92.244.97/.

A Survey of Space Applications. Washington, D.C.: National Aeronautics and Space Administration, 1967, 14. www.scribd.com/document
/53075244/A-Survey-of-Space-Applications.

Syncom Engineering Report, vol. 1. Washington, D.C.: National Aeronautics and
Space Administration, 1966. ntrs.nasa.gov/api/citations/19660012402
/downloads/19660012402.pdf.

Tampa Tribune. "Betsy Hits Most of West Coast Lightly." September 9, 1965.
www.newspapers.com/image/329967185/.

Tedeschi, Michael A. *Live Via Satellite: The Story of COMSAT and the Technology
that Changed World Communication.* Washington, D.C.: Acropolis Books,
1989, 32–44. www.comsatlegacy.com/ViaSatellite%20published%20
book/ViaSatellite,%20published%20book,%20pp%200-93%20.PDF.

Time. "For Gold, Silver & Bronze." October 16, 1964. web.archive.org
/web/20080421134503/www.time.com/time/magazine/article/0,9171,
876272,00.html.

———. "The Room-Size World." May 14, 1965. web.archive.org/
web/20080102141826/www.time.com/time/magazine/article/0,9171,
898835-6,00.html.

"Tokyo 1964 Welcomes the World to the Olympic Stadium." Olympics.com,
October 10, 2019. www.olympic.org/news/tokyo-1964-welcomes-the
-world-to-the-olympic-stadium.

"The Tortuous History of the Williams Patent." HughesSCGHeritage,

April 2, 2020. www.hughesscgheritage.com/the-tortuous-history-of-the
-williams-patent-jack-fisher/.

Troan, John. "'Early Bird' Joins Comsat in Flying High." *Albuquerque Tribune*,
April 7, 1965. www.newspapers.com/image/783110377/.

Tucker, William. "Way Opens to FBI in Lemay Case." *Miami News*, September
24, 1965. www.newspapers.com/image/302084469/.

———. "T.A. Buchanan Killed by Auto in South Dade." *Miami News*, November 27, 1976. www.newspapers.com/clip/40430553/talmadge-buchanan
-killed/.

Tucson Daily Citizen. "Falcon Seen by Millions in Paris." June 3, 1961. www
.newspapers.com/image/23325101/.

United Press International. "Canadian Thieves Net $1 Million." *Wisconsin State
Journal*, July 4, 1961. www.newspapers.com/image/400527343/.

———. "Lemay, Girl Reported Bound for Montreal." *Gazette* (Montreal, Canada), January 13, 1962. www.newspapers.com/newspage/421030005/.

———. "Reward Posted for Fugitive." *Miami Herald*, February 22, 1962. www
.newspapers.com/newspage/620093212/.

———. "Montreal—April 26." *Bridgeport Post*, April 26, 1962. www.news
papers.com/newspage/60138449/.

———. "Senate Rejects 2 Amendments to Satellite Bill." *Albuquerque Journal*,
August 14, 1962. www.newspapers.com/image/157775315/.

———. "Kefauver Still Fighting Satellite Bill." *Detroit Free Press*, August 27,
1962. www.newspapers.com/newspage/98631151/.

———. "Kefauver Raps Claim By AT&T." *Lawton Constitution*, July 11, 1963.
www.newspapers.com/newspage/22486326/.

———. "U.S. Satellite Launching Set for Next Spring." *Longview News-Journal*,
October 22, 1964. www.newspapers.com/newspage/243184469/.

———. "Top Scientist, 34, Dies." *Tampa Bay Times*, February 23, 1966. www
.newspapers.com/newspage/316220792/.

———. "Dade Sheriff Indicted, Ousted For $25,000 'Lie.'" *Tampa Tribune*,
April 21, 1966. www.newspapers.com/newspage/330135662/.

———. "Lemay 'Fingered' By Trial Witness." *Fort Lauderdale News*, November
11, 1967. www.newspapers.com/image/272418956/.

U.S. Army Engineer District, New Orleans. Louisiana State University. "Report on Hurricane Betsy, 8–11 September 1965 in the U. S. Army Engineer District, New Orleans. November 1965. biotech.law.lsu.edu/katrina
/hpdc/docs/19651100_Hurricane_Betsy.pdf

Vance, Ashlee. *Elon Musk: Tesla, SpaceX, and the Quest for a Fantastic Future.* New York: Ecco, 2015, 93–95.

Vartabedian, Ralph. "Satellite Reshaped World." *Los Angeles Times,* February 1, 2017. www.newspapers.com/newspage/278152294/.

Veillette, Eric. "Me Raymond Daoust." *Historiquement Logique,* August 4, 2012. historiquementlogique.com/2012/08/05/me-raymond-daoust/.

Vinciguerra, Tom. "Lemay in Florida—The Big Spender on a Luxury Boat." *Gazette* (Montreal, Canada), May 24, 1965. www.newspapers.com/newspage /423794682/.

Washington Post. "Journalist Matt Gordon Dies." September 16, 1994. www .washingtonpost.com/archive/local/1994/09/16/journalist-matt-gordon -dies/6c992e2a-2266-4d6a-b0f5-0f8323facaf9/.

———. "Harry N. Stafford Obituary." June 20, 2005. www.legacy.com /obituaries/washingtonpost/obituary.aspx?n=harry-n-stafford&pid= 14324619.

Wedge, Pip. "Thomas Benson (1915–2002)." History of Canadian Broadcasting, October 2002. www.broadcasting-history.ca/personalities/benson -thomas.

Wende Museum of the Cold War. "Hughes Aircraft Company." Accessed January 4, 2020. www.coldwarculvercity.org/hughes-aircraft.html.

Whalen, David J. "Billion Dollar Technology: A Short Historical Overview of the Origins of Communications Satellite Technology, 1945–1965." In *Beyond the Ionosphere: Fifty Years of Satellite Communication,* edited by Andrew J. Butrica, 95–130. Washington, D.C.: National Aeronautics and Space Administration, 1997. history.nasa.gov/SP-4217/ch9.htm.

———. *The Rise and Fall of COMSAT: Technology, Business, and Government in Satellite Communications.* New York: Palgrave Macmillan, 2014, 6–67.

Wheatley, W. R. "Montreal Mobsters Thin Own Ranks." *Windsor Daily Star,* July 27, 1957. www.newspapers.com/newspage/501524566/.

Wheeler, Fred. "Early Bird and After." *New Scientist,* March 18, 1965.

Whitehead, Harold. "People Make News." *Gazette* (Montreal, Canada), June 26, 1965. www.newspapers.com/newspage/421200066/.

Wichter, Zach. "Harold Rosen, Who Ushered in the Era of Communication Satellites, Dies at 90." *New York Times,* February 2, 2017. www.nytimes .com/2017/02/02/business/harold-rosen-dead-engineer-satellite.html.

Wickstrom, Karl. "Grand Jury Indicts Buchanan on Bribe Conspiracy Charges." *Miami Herald,* November 5, 1966. www.newspapers.com/image /621078029.

Williams, Donald D. "Control of the Syncom Communication Satellite." *IFAC Proceedings Volumes* 2, no. 1 (1965): 132–39.

Williams, Verne O. "Wheels of Justice Creaked on the Lemay Case." *Miami News*, October 3, 1965. www.newspapers.com/image/301320834.

Wilson, Jean S. "Nine Doors to Freedom!" *Miami News*, July 25, 1960. www.newspapers.com/newspage/301005057/.

Wu, W. W. "Satellite communications." *Proceedings of the IEEE* 85, no. 6 (June 1997): 998–1010.

© Beth Schneck

ANDREW AMELINCKX is a freelance journalist who has previously written three historical true crime books. He held down a variety of jobs, from bartending in New Orleans to burlesque dancing in New York City, before spending a decade as an award-winning investigative crime reporter for several news organizations, including the Pulitzer Prize–winning *Berkshire Eagle*. His work has appeared in *Business Insider, Smithsonian, Men's Journal, Modern Farmer,* and elsewhere. He lives in New York's Hudson Valley. Find out more at andrewamelinckx.com.